STUDYING BRITISH CINEMA
1999—2009
BY
JOHN FITZGERALD

auteur

First published in 2010 by
Auteur
The Old Surgery, 9 Pulford Road, Leighton Buzzard LU7 1AB
www.auteur.co.uk

Copyright © Auteur Publishing 2010

A version of the chapter 'Dystopian Britain' first appeared in *Splice* Volume 2: 2 (spring 2008).

Designed and set by Nikki Hamlett at AMP Ltd, Dunstable, Bedfordshire

Printed and bound in Poland; produced by Polskabook

Cover: *Children of Men* © Universal / image.net

British Library Cataloguing-in-Publication Data
A catalogue record for this book is available from the British Library

ISBN 978-1-906733-11-7 (paperback)
ISBN 978-1-906733-12-4 (hardback)

791.430941

Luton Sixth Form College
Bradgers Hill Road, Luton
Beds. LU2 7EW

Return on or before the last date stamped below

1 WEEK LOAN

2 8 FEB 2012

10072394

ALSO IN THIS SERIES

CONTENTS

ACKNOWLEDGEMENTS

Many thanks to all on the WJEC Film Studies examination team, especially Jeremy Points. The support from the Media Department at Wyggeston and Queen Elizabeth College in Leicester has been fantastic. And last but not least, special thanks to my great wife Heidi, and fantastic sons Daniel and Liam for their endless patience and encouragement. I couldn't have done it without you.

DEDICATION

For Delia and Billy.

INTRODUCTION : TONY AND GORDON'S BRITAIN – FILM-MAKING IN THE NOUGHTIES

SAME OLD, SAME OLD

Trying to name the opening years of the new millennium in a useful way has been problematic, with the most common handle being the pretty awful 'Noughties'. In assessing the period as a whole, there have been tremendous global shifts, tremors and surprises.

The terrible events of 9/11 leading to the wars in Iraq and Afghanistan, the rise of China, Russia and India as economic powers of the first order and the financial debacle that gave us the term 'credit crunch' provide the backcloth to the roller-coaster ride that was British Cinema at the time. Of course, anyone with even the most casual interest in the subject will be familiar with the issues: the systematic problems of financing, lack of access to distribution outlets, lack of investment and training at all levels but particularly with regard to scriptwriting and directing, the haemorrhaging of talent to Hollywood and, crucially, establishing that distinctiveness that might reflect the complex socio-cultural nexus that is the United Kingdom. Factor in the pressure of trying to get a British movie into American multiplexes and the age-old problems are as fresh as today's newspaper.

This book aims to look at the diverse range of films produced in Britain during this period and outline the major economic and social pressures that led to their creation, by analysing groupings of films in relation to theme, style, directors and production contexts. A useful starting point in this introductory chapter is to survey the ever-changing landscape that has underpinned the production of many of the films mentioned in the next nine chapters, and also to offer an overview of the industry and how British film has attempted to reflect (or not, in many respects) the social changes that have occurred in British society in the 'Noughties'.

Politically, this period saw two more election wins for New Labour under Tony Blair, and the complex relationship between the government and the film industry shaped a great deal of debate so this is a good place to start. Certainly Chris Smith, the Culture Secretary in 1999, was enthusiastic about the potential of the industry, stating:

> 'The UK film industry has been going from strength to strength in recent years thanks to our wonderful array of acting and technical talent. We want to make it even more attractive to film in Britain, and our economy will benefit as a result.' [1]

The debates about the government's involvement with film mostly centred on two issues: firstly, the amalgamation of the previous sources of public bodies concerned with film funding – the British Film Institute, British Film Commission, British Screen Finance and the Arts Council Lottery Film Department – under one umbrella organisation, the UK Film Council, in April 2000; and secondly, the ongoing debates between the film industry and the Treasury on the tax breaks available for producers of films which might be defined as British. Crucially, these discussions raised fundamental questions regarding the sustainability of film production, which centred primarily on the profitability of a film, rather than on any notions of artistic merit and cultural distinctiveness.

Shakespeare in Love, released in 1999, encapsulates many of these contradictions. Although not publicly funded, but financed by the US mini-major Miramax, the film's subject was clearly British, most of the cast and crew, including director John Madden, were also British, but the film's leads, Gwyneth Paltrow and Ben Affleck, were American, playing their parts with English accents. The film's critical and commercial success was seen as a British triumph – although there was still a degree of doubt questioning whether this was truly a British achievement. The touchstone British films that had defined the success of the 1990s also bear examination in this regard. *Four Weddings and a Funeral* (Newell, 1994) and *The Full Monty* (Cattaneo, 1997), although not so much like *Shakespeare in Love* in terms of their cultural content, had significant similarities in their financing and in particular the deals with big Hollywood distributors Universal and 20th Century Fox, which facilitated their strong box office in the United States. The key question to be asked here relates to whether audiences, British or overseas, are really that concerned with where the money has come from for a film which is, in terms of its content, British. The answer is usually 'no'. The fact that any British film found its way onto a cinema screen or a DVD disc was often seen as an accomplishment in itself.

LOTTERY HANGOVERS

The introduction of the National Lottery in the UK in the mid-1990s should have been a huge fillip for the industry with the creation of the National Lottery Film Funding Programme. Cinema attendances were steadily rising due to further investment in multiplexes and a number of British success stories such as the aforementioned *The Full Monty*, Working Title's *Bean* (Smith, 1998) and the cash-in film *Spiceworld* (Spiers, 1997), featuring the global pop sensation of the time the Spice Girls. The industry was buoyant and it seemed to make perfect sense that Lottery money should be used to fund or part-fund film projects. However, the reality was not so clear-cut, with cash from the Lottery being seemingly dispersed with little or no logic to a number of poorly conceived film projects. In the early part of the decade, the apparent spendthrift awarding of grants to films that either struggled onto cinema screens to poor returns or languished on the margins without a distribution deal was of great concern. The Arts Council was in charge of handing out the grants and the people who made the key decisions for the awards were often connected to the films that were receiving the funding.

Films such as *The Secret Laughter of Women* (Schwabach, 1999), a Colin Firth star vehicle, received a grant of just under £1 million but only took £2,832 at cinemas; *The Lost Son* (Menges, 2002) was awarded £2.3 million but its box-office takings were a lamentable £49,302; and *Amy Foster* (Kidron, 1998), with a grant of £2 million, made only £48,711. These films were the tip of the iceberg, and by 2000 Lottery funding had a woeful strike-rate of nine hits but 121 misses. These included films that had been made but had not received any form of distribution. Many – such as *Fanny and Elvis* (Mellor, 1999), *Downtime* (Nalluri, 1998) and *Beautiful People* (Dizdar, 1998) – were panned by the critics and shunned by audiences. Vanessa Thorpe and Antony Barnett, in an extended piece on the debacle in The Observer, pointed out that it had got so bad that a Lottery grant was starting to look more like a blight on a film's chances of audience popularity than a boost, and that in many cases the committing of money to projects was done on little more than the recommendation of a friend (12/03/2000)[2]. Certainly, the halcyon days of the 1990s appeared far away, as these films were often little more than a joke and crucially added neither profit nor credibility to the industry. The nadir was possibly reached when the film *Honest*, directed by Dave Stewart and starring the R'n'B/pop act All Saints, was pulled just three days after its initial release in May 2000. If a film with a high-profile campaign and a clear potential fanbase for a leading girl group had suffered the indignity of being shelved after only 72 hours, what hope was there for a smaller project with less publicity?

Prior to this and flushed with Lottery money the announcement in the spring of 1997 that three film franchises worth a total of £92 million should have been a cause for celebration. These would be awarded over six years to three different companies who would get their hands dirty producing British movies. However this decision stirred up a certain amount of acrimony within the industry. Mike Southworth, ex-head of FilmFour Distribution, angrily remarked, 'You might just as well take £100 million and set fire to the fucking lot'[3]. The successful companies – Pathé, DNA and The Film Consortium – all promised to make films over the six years with help from Lottery funding, but by the autumn of 2002 all the companies were well behind their production targets. There were reasons for the poor release rate, including problems with associate producers and distributors, and coupled with the indiscriminate doling out of scratch-card cash this situation was attracting the ire of various disgusted parties, none more so than Alexander Walker, the acerbic veteran film critic of the *London Evening Standard*. His central argument focused on the fact that films receiving money from the public purse needed to be more commercial in order to ensure some form of return on the original investment.

The three companies, all with mixed results up to this point, had made some money. Pathé, the UK offshoot of the French major, had achieved some success with the screen adaptation of the Oscar Wilde play *An Ideal Husband* (Parker, 1999), and collected considerable plaudits with Lynne Ramsay's outstanding debut film *Ratcatcher* (1999). In fact *Ratcatcher*, which had a limited art-house release, would not have fitted Walker's template for success, but was a deserved addition to the canon of great British films, a piece of art cinema that enriched an audience's cultural experience. Although it was not commercially successful, the aesthetic value of a film such as *Ratcatcher* does not depend on the size of the audience. The Film Consortium, headed by veterans of the successful Palace Pictures, including Nik Powell and Stephen Woolley, had done quite well by utilising Kate Winslet's increasing star profile with *Hideous Kinky* (MacKinnon, 1998) and Michael Winterbottom's *24 Hour Party People* (2002) was well received critically, but distribution issues dogged its overall progress. Perhaps the slowest starting but most high profile and successful of the three franchise holders was DNA Films. Set up by Andrew Macdonald in 1998, early productions – *Beautiful Creatures* (Eagles, 1999) and *Strictly Sinatra* (Capaldi, 2001) – were none too promising. These films smacked of the sort of problems associated with the early beneficiaries of the Lottery windfall. *The Parole Officer* (Duigan, 2001), starring television actor and comedian Steve Coogan, was a step in the right direction, using Coogan's wider persona to sell a low-key comedy. However, the breakthrough film for DNA was Danny Boyle's *28 Days Later* (2002), a dystopian sci-fi thriller which effectively hooked into the general post-9/11 feeling and fears about bio-terrorism that chimed well with both British and, significantly, American audiences. At last it seemed that a relatively low-budget film, made with some public money and with the support of an anointed franchise holder, had fulfilled the hopes of politicians such as Chris Smith. He had adjusted the criteria for funding and tax breaks in 1999 by stressing that 70% of the film's budget must be spent in the UK and 70% of the labour costs must involve EU and Commonwealth citizens. It was hoped that this would free up the UK market and make film production more attractive to overseas investors.

DNA Films went from strength to strength, producing a series of high-profile releases, many of which are discussed in this book. Working with the new UK Film Council and in tandem with 20th Century Fox's massive distribution wing meant a number of interesting and quite successful films made it to the marketplace. The ambitious but flawed *Sunshine* (2007) was another film made with Danny Boyle at the helm and saw a high-budget (by British standards) sci-fi film of £23 million produced in the UK with all the financing coming from DNA itself. What is interesting about *Sunshine* is that the film squarely concentrates on predominantly American characters and in no way feels culturally British, despite the huge amount of British money. Other notable DNA productions have been more recognisably culturally specific in this respect and have included the sequel to *28 Days Later*, *28 Weeks Later* (Fresnadillo, 2007), *Notes on a Scandal* (Eyre, 2006) and *The Last King of Scotland* (Macdonald, 2005), which, although set predominantly in Idi Amin's Uganda, has a Scottish doctor as its main protagonist. The latter two films won numerous awards and were in the main pretty well received. The model set out by DNA films is an interesting one: utilising Lottery money and at the same time holding hands with a Hollywood major, which ensures that the films are at the very least guaranteed a release and adequate promotion.

The arguments about where any potential profits end up vary from film to film, depending on how much finance DNA put in at the outset. For example, with *Notes on a Scandal* DNA put in all the finance but none of the creative input and took 40 per cent of the total box office of $50 million. After taking out Fox's distribution fee any profit is ploughed back into future productions[4]. Despite the welter of deserved bad publicity for the early Lottery awards, DNA Films has proved to be a success story of sorts. Although it isn't really challenging Working Title's success, it has slowly but surely built up an interesting and diverse backlist. Perhaps some of that change in the perception of part-publicly funded films can be attributed to the move away from the supposed clique in the Arts Council of England to the newly established UK Film Council, which in early 2000 took responsibility for government money.

UK FILM COUNCIL – A NEW BEGINNING?

The film establishment in Britain did need a degree of shaking up and Alan Parker's appointment as the Chairman of the UK Film Council (UKFC) in the summer of 1999 was always going to be a contentious decision, although he had, prior to this, been the chairman at the BFI. Most of Parker's work had been in Hollywood where he had won acclaim and Oscars. He was by and large a populist director, who had previously been less than complimentary about government subsidies for art films. On his appointment he stated: 'We have to change the culture if we want to see British films up there with American ones. There is no point complaining. You have got to get in there and do something so that young film-makers coming through now don't have to put up with the same nonsense'[5].

The initial annual budget for the Film Council was £22 million, substantial by UK standards but miniscule in the high octane world of Hollywood. But as the appointment of Parker, coupled with the input of *Four Weddings and a Funeral* producer Duncan Kenworthy, suggested, the emphasis was going to be on the more commercial end of the market. As Xan Brooks noted at the time, 'The aim is to steer clear of the sort of oddball, no-name, small-scale projects that traditionally go belly up at the box-office. Big budgets, big returns – this is what the council is angling for'[6]. That said, the UKFC's remit was wide-ranging and went far beyond streamlining government and National Lottery funding. Over the years the Council has campaigned for more Lottery money, been involved in the training of young film-makers, aided the Regional Screen Agencies in order to loosen the southern/London bias, directed financial help to a range of films often in conjunction with other producers, attempted to offer more diverse options in terms of distribution and exhibition and finally got behind the regeneration of the National Film Theatre on the South Bank in London and the funding of the BFI.

Alan Parker's bullish but realistic address to the UK film industry in November 2002 laid out his vision of an industry that would need to undergo a radical reinvention in order to survive, an industry that would have to accept financial realities and lose the

'Little Englander' stance that it had so often taken in the past. He was also critical of the huge amount of production that had taken place with the influx of Lottery money, for films that were largely unqualified failures. He saw distribution, skills and improved infrastructure focusing on better post-production facilities as the way forward in order for Britain to become a 'creative hub', not only producing 'British' films, but also attracting inward investment. The Section 48 tax break was essential. As a mission statement it was a rousing call to the troops:

> 'How can the Film Council, working with the Government, help the industry achieve that transformation? We must make our crucial financial incentives more flexible. We need to revise the definition of a British film, finding ways to recast it to reflect the fact that actual production increasingly will take place in countries with a lower cost base than ours. We must begin to view the world beyond the UK … We need to strengthen our traditional links with the American industry at every level; encouraging them to continue to invest in production here in order to develop our infrastructure to the benefit of jobs and skills…'[7]

John Woodward, who took over from Parker as the CEO of the UK Film Council, continued this message a couple of years later, again stressing a distribution-led approach and calling for television broadcasters to make a much more substantial contribution than they had done in the past. The commercial imperative stressed by Parker was again in evidence as Woodward explained what he saw as the main issues around government support for the industry outside the obvious financial benefits to the economy: 'that we make films which audiences find enjoyable, fulfilling, challenging even. And if the films financially supported don't consistently reach the public — well, the rationale and political will for the support will very rapidly start to wither' (from keynote address to Screen International conference[8]. He was, however, positive about the state of the industry on the back of *Harry Potter* and *Bond* productions and also the £1.16 billion invested from films such as *Troy* (2004), *Alexander* (2004) and *King Arthur* (2004). Although he was speaking in a climate where inward investment had soared and Parker's vision of Britain becoming a 'creative hub', with a growing excellence in the provision of skills and world-class studios, was becoming a reality, the nagging doubt remained. Were these films actually 'British', even if they were included in the Film Council's highly detailed yearbooks of the most successful UK films?

The UKFC has attempted to realise a sense of commercial nous when funding films, yet has still managed to invest money and time into films that at first glance don't fit the Saturday night, multiplex formula. Jonathan Romney was worried at the Council's inception that 'without a commitment to risk, or a willingness to nurture artistic talents, you can't have a real cutting edge'[9] and cited the increasing willingness of major Hollywood studios to get involved in funding more esoteric projects such as David Fincher's *Fight Club* (1999) and *Being John Malkovich* (Jonze, 1999) and their encouragement of directorial talents like Alexander Payne, Paul Thomas Anderson and

Wes Anderson. The more self-consciously 'authored' cinema of these directors were found on independent arms of major companies like Fox Searchlight with *Fight Club* and Warner's New Line Cinema with PT Anderson's *Magnolia* (1999) and Payne's *About Schmidt* (2002). These edgier companies seemed more in tune with the sort of audience they were trying to tap into and had an appropriate marketing and print-run policy to match. There was also the growing DVD market to exploit. With these types of film the ability of the majors to absorb any losses on their smaller projects is positioned against the potential huge profitability of a film such as *The Dark Knight* (Nolan, 2008) or *The Pirates of the Caribbean* trilogy (Verbinski, 2003–07). This situation just doesn't exist in the British film industry.

Film Council support of *28 Days Later* can be cited as a fine example of a movie that did appeal to a mainstream constituency in Britain and the United States, but it could be argued that this was more by luck than default. More interesting perhaps is its support, through the Regional Screen Agencies, EM Media and Screen Yorkshire, of Shane Meadows' films for Warp. *Dead Man's Shoes* (2004) and *This is England* (2007) were both released in small print runs, tiny in the case of the former, but did fantastically well non-theatrically on DVD. The same could be said for Paul Andrew Williams' harrowing *London to Brighton* (2006), which had a grant to support its marketing and print run. It was also picked up by a DVD and television audience, which had missed its predominantly art-house run. The obsession with box-office returns, films that are supposedly seen by 'everyone', leaves out the vast number who will choose to watch a film at home. This has led to challenging work like Meadows' and Williams' films finding their way onto British screens, albeit smaller than the ones that Parker and Woodward might have envisaged. The demise of FilmFour in 2002 can be linked to the expansionist feeling that took hold of the industry in the early part of the decade, which encouraged a realignment that has led to a world view that transcends the narrowness of purely financial returns from cinema admissions.

THE RISE AND FALL AND RISE AGAIN OF FILMFOUR

The downfall of FilmFour in the summer of 2002 was greeted with equal amounts of consternation at a company perceived to have grown too big for its boots, and sadness that the optimism of the mini-boom of the late 1990s in film production, of which FilmFour had been an important part, had been blown asunder so brutally. The FilmFour model of looking beyond Britain for film projects and a combination of genre films with more art-house fare, predates Parker and Woodward's vision of a sustainable and successful film industry. What went wrong has haunted British film-making ever since.

Between 1983 and 1998, Channel Four, the British television broadcaster, had a long association with successful projects, working with production companies such as Working Title and Palace Pictures. With successes like *Four Weddings and a Funeral* and *The Crying*

Game (Jordan, 1992) to boast of, Channel Four also fostered auteur directors such as Mike Leigh, Stephen Frears and Ken Loach. Leigh's *High Hopes* (1988) and *Life is Sweet* (1990), Frears' *My Beautiful Laundrette* (1986) and Loach's *Riff Raff* (1991) spring readily to mind. With the upsurge in production in the late 1990s, the creation of a separate production and distribution wing called FilmFour Ltd, led by Paul Webster, former head of Miramax's UK production, made perfect business sense. The phenomenal success of FilmFour's iconic *Trainspotting* (Boyle, 1996), the media buzz surrounding 'Cool Britannia' and the election of a young Prime Minister with a seemingly radical agenda suggested that we needed a hip, astute and above all profitable British film company to chime with the positivity of the time. FilmFour Ltd, like New Labour, was sold as a better, brighter model and mirrored the government's brashness and energetic confidence. The publication of *A Bigger Picture* by the Film Policy Review Group clarified this new mood of optimism. FilmFour Ltd would be a key player here.

The model that FilmFour wanted to emulate was that of Miramax, an American mini-major that operated with a varied production slate and distributed both in the US and internationally. FilmFour's huge involvement in over fifty projects during the four years as a mini-major produced mixed results, but never finding a massive hit seemed to be the major reason for its downfall. The high-profile success of *East is East* (O'Donnell, 1999) proved that a well-directed, cleverly shot British comedy could attract a mainstream UK audience, although the film failed to grab American viewers with its tale of the tribulations of a Salford Anglo-Asian family in the 1970s. The fact that it did well domestically was down to a clever marketing campaign with distinctive advertising and extensive television trailers. There were other high points, in particular two of the best gangster films to emerge in the wake of Guy Ritchie's highly successful, but vapid *Lock, Stock and Two Smoking Barrels* (1998), Paul McGuigan's *Gangster No 1* (2000) and *Sexy Beast* (Glazer, 2000), which beat Lottery-funded horror shows like *Rancid Aluminium* (2000) and *Love, Honour and Obey* (2000) into submission, by being smart, tight narratives for whom the Ritchie-led influence of style over substance was avoided. Notably it also made Terence Davies' sumptuous *House of Mirth* (2000), the criminally underrated *The Low Down* (Thraves, 2001) and continued its support of Ken Loach's work with his redemptive *My Name is Joe* (1998).

But by Hollywood's standards these films were low-budget efforts and although they were critically well received there was no real sense that any of them could have the zeitgeist appeal of a *Trainspotting* or the crossover potential of *The Full Monty*. On paper, Peter Cattaneo's follow-up *Lucky Break*, which FilmFour decided to invest in on the back of a seven picture deal with Warner Brothers, should have been a sure-fire hit especially with British audiences. It failed to ignite at the box office. The originality and above all the warmth of Cattaneo's earlier effort was absent from this bland, formulaic prison comedy. However, the film that finally broke FilmFour as dramatically as *Absolute Beginners* (Temple, 1986) had destroyed Goldcrest in the mid-1980s, seemed to have all the right ingredients to make that substantial breakthrough. *Charlotte Gray* (Armstrong, 2001) was an adaptation of Sebastian Faulkes' best-selling Second World War novel and had the highly regarded actress Cate Blanchett as the lead. Faulkes had a strong reputation as a novelist and a readership which straddled both the literary and more mainstream markets. Opening to poor notices, the £15 million film bombed despite a decent advertising campaign, and compounded a £5 million loss experienced by FilmFour that year that led in turn to its eventual submergence back into the auspices of Channel Four. Geoffrey Macnab drew parallels with PolyGram's absorption into Seagram-Universal in the late 1990s, and raised a question that has perennially haunted British film-makers: 'The dilemma facing both companies was the same: do you make big-budget international films with the studios and risk falling on your face or do you make smaller films basically for domestic consumption? Both chose the former'[10]. The drive for the bankable genre-based films, based on a perceived sense of audience 'taste' was not where FilmFour was coming from. Its best received films from that period, for example *Sexy Beast*, *East is East* and *My Name is Joe*, all demonstrated the sense of diversity and originality that had provided Channel Four's films with a unique signature. It was when FilmFour strayed from this template, especially in its dealings with Warners, that things started to go badly wrong. Success at the box office is not an exact science, as many Hollywood producers have discovered to their cost, and cannot be measured by the perceived tastes of the general public. David Aukin, former Head of Film at Channel Four, was quick to make this point: 'Films are not a commodity like a computer game or a car. On the whole, audiences do not know what they want. Probably they want to be surprised. So we [Channel Four] relied on "capricious audience tastes" to discover the films. Each success, if you like, was a fluke, but we were playing for flukes, offering a diet of independent, idiosyncratic films, most of which disappeared but some took off. There was no pretence that we understood the "market", could somehow tailor films to satisfy the appetite of what future audiences might want to see'.[11]

A reliance on flukes and luck was never going to convince understandably risk-averse onlookers of the sustainability of film-making in this country. With time and a more realistic view of what sort of films it could be involved in, FilmFour slowly but surely started to haul itself back into the frame, largely by working with companies like DNA and Warp and utilising Film Council money on films such as *The Last King of Scotland*, *28 Days Later* and *This is England*. It has also had its own notable success story, which could not have been predicted with the analysis of audience demographics. This was *Touching the Void* (Macdonald, 2004), an epic documentary which dramatically retold the story of Joe Simpson and Simon Yates' ill-fated climb up one of the Peruvian Andes' most difficult summits. The film, based on Simpson's memoir of the same name, did wonderful business, especially for a documentary about a niche interest, and received a number of awards including a BAFTA. A combination of Simpson and Yates' heroics, their obvious unease at recounting the controversial business of nearly twenty years before and Macdonald's brilliant switching between cinematic re-enactment of the events with face to camera interviews, offered audiences an exciting, emotionally charged experience. It also showed what limited resources could do provided there was a good enough story to tell in the first place. Nick Roddick, in an article on Channel Four and the BBC's contribution to British film, pointed out that the boom and bust climate that had bedevilled it was one that we had to learn to accept: 'Whenever you think that things are going well for the British film industry, they go pear-shaped. Each time it seems dead, it bounces back'[12].

In many respects the phenomenal, totally unexpected success of FilmFour's *Slumdog Millionaire* (Boyle, 2008) certainly supports Roddick's view, a film that very nearly didn't get a theatrical release. Danny Boyle's Mumbai-based, high-kinetic tale of a poor boy who wins a general knowledge television quiz and gets the girl took the world by storm taking over $377 million at the box office and sweeping the board at the Oscars. Although the film was sold as a feel-good movie, many elements of the narrative challenged this; the murder of a young woman by religious fundamentalists, the blinding of a beggar-child and the over-riding sense of abject poverty seemed rooted in the more characteristic social-realist cinema that had defined Channel Four's early film output. However combined with a huge chunk of melodrama and a rather, far-fetched narrative conceit, the film struck a chord with global audiences. Perhaps it was the perfect film for a world grappling with the consequences of recession and near economic meltdown, a pure sense of escapism where the underdog triumphs.

FilmFour then, after a tumultuous period, ended the decade on a high, but what of its great rival, the BBC, much criticised for its lack of interest in the wider film market?

FILM-MAKING AT THE BEEB – FROM BALLET TO BOLEYN AND BEYOND

The release and subsequent box-office triumph of BBC Films' *Billy Elliot* (Daldry, 2000) has overshadowed all of its output ever since. This tale of a young boy with a talent for ballet, set against the backdrop of the 1984 miners' strike, was an unabashed slice of northern sentimentality. It echoed both *The Full Monty* and *Brassed Off* (Herman, 1998), primarily in its sensitive exploration of masculinity allied to the decline of traditional heavy industry during the Thatcher years. The film struck a chord with audiences both here and stateside. *Billy Elliot* did not lead to a rush of similar storylines by the production company, but instead saw work that might well have been associated with Channel Four in its late-1980s heyday. Its relationship with the Polish director Pawel Pawlikowski led to his remarkable *Last Resort* (2001) and his interesting, if inconsistent, follow-up *My Summer of Love* in 2004. Both films refused to play to the gallery by dealing with uncomfortable issues – asylum and lesbianism – in a forthright and self-consciously artistic way. But equally the BBC showed that it was prepared to make more commercial fare such as the story of the Windmill's dancing girls, *Mrs Henderson Presents* (Frears, 2005), a rather lacklustre, stagey adaptation of Alan Bennett's play *The History Boys* (Hytner, 2006) and the refreshing, undervalued rites of passage comedy *Starter For Ten* (Vaughan, 2006).

David Thompson, the head of BBC Films, was keen to point out in 2004 that his company was more interested in using a slow-burn, small-scale strategy: 'We can only make about seven films a year and a lot of it is high-risk material ... Sometimes we just make popular entertainment, but more often than not we are unashamedly making films that are out on the edge. We take huge risks, because if we don't take risks we are doing nothing' (Thorpe, The Observer, 19/09/2004). Its support of Michael Winterbottom with the angry political film In This World (2002) and his difficult Code 46 (2003) are good examples of this, but a better example is its involvement in Red Road (2006), Andrea Arnold's gripping feature debut, which tackles difficult emotional terrain around grief and is unflinching in its graphic portrayal of the sexual act.

Indeed, the BBC's more self-conscious efforts to reach a mainstream cinema audience often disappoint. The high-profile BBC co-production The Other Boleyn Girl (Chadwick, 2008), made in conjunction with Focus Features and starring American A-Listers Natalie Portman and Scarlett Johansson, cost $35 million and fared poorly at the box office, despite the attractions of the leads. On the other hand, the BBC has been criticised by the Film Council and producers for being neglectful of the industry and unsupportive financially by only spending 0.4% of its licence fee income in 2003/2004 on buying British films to show on its channels. John McVay, the chief executive of PACT, a body representing independent producers, saw the issue as a self-fulfilling prophecy, stating, 'The BBC says it would love to show a great British film at 9pm, but can't find the talent to make it. But we are not going to find the talent if we are not investing in it'[13]. The fact remains that if money from the public purse is funnelled into costly and, by definition, risky products, it is obviously more difficult to justify. The spectre of FilmFour's failure in 2002 loomed large in BBC Films' thinking. However, pledges given in early 2006 to invest between £250 and £300 million, albeit over a ten-year period, gave producers a reason to feel happier about the future.

Certainly by the end of the decade the BBC's position as a major producer of British film was cemented by a diverse range of range of films. By working in conjunction with the UK Film Council, Regional Screen Agencies and overseas producers, the BBC was involved in supporting films such as the brilliant, biting satire of In The Loop (Iannucci, 2009); Jane Campion's moving story of John Keats relationship with Fanny Brawne, Bright Star (2009); Andrea Arnold's coming of age, social-realist drama Fish Tank (2009); Glorious 39 (Poliakoff, 2009), a wartime psychological thriller and the critically acclaimed and commercially successful An Education (Scherfig, 2009) a 1960s set, rites of passage, based on the journalist Lynn Barber's teenage years. While some of these films are rooted in traditional costume/heritage drama (Bright Star, Glorious 39 and even An Education) and in downbeat depictions of working-class life (Fish Tank) which have been the mainstay of British films for decades, BBC Films also branched out into more overtly audience-led cinema with two examples Streetdance 3-D (Giwa and Pasquini, 2010) and Tormented (Wright, 2009). The former was the first British film to be shot in 3-D and concentrated on two diverse groups of young people, a street dance crew and ballet dancers from the Royal Dance School who join forces to compete in a dance competition. The latter, *Tormented* was a story of bullying, zombies and peer pressure in a provincial grammar school and it is readily apparent that both films were clearly trying to tap into the teenage cinema audience. Although BBC Films weren't vast by the end of the decade, with an annual budget of $18 million for production, development and overheads, their importance in the credit crunch hit UK production sector was massive. The aim of producing eight features a year was certainly a laudable one, showing vision and real commitment. As Christine Langan, the creative director of BBC Films stressed diversity was key to the company's production slate and this seems to be borne out by BBC films prolific output at the end of the decade:

> 'Within those eight films, there will always be a place for an auteur-type, authored film where the pure values of cinema are absolutely supported. Ultimately, those eight are an eclectic mix.'[14]

More of an issue throughout the period regarding the expenditure of public money on film, were the tax breaks given out to encourage investment in British film-making. The uncertainty surrounding the renewal of these by the then-Chancellor Gordon Brown and the dubious practices of their implementation did the industry no favours at all.

TAXING TIMES — SECTION 48

> 'Between 1997 and 2005, the government plied the plate of the British film industry with billions of pounds of public funds. It was money that came from working- and middle-class taxpayers who didn't hire accountants but paid as they earned. It was money which might have been spent on schools, hospitals, the army or other fripperies. Instead a part did indeed go up the noses of Soho. More went down the drain. More still went up the wall … The Treasury and the Inland Revenue are furious and have every right to be, although you would never guess it from the obsequious coverage the film industry has received from the broadsheets and Radio 4.' (Cohen, The Observer, 15/05/05)[15]

Certainly Nick Cohen was out of step with his colleagues on the subject of tax breaks for producers, which had quite legitimately been introduced by the Labour government to aid domestic film production, but which had also been exploited as a lucrative tax loophole for rich investors. Initially called Section 48 it provided film-makers with tax relief on 15% of their production budget. This in turn increased the number of movies made in Britain and its benefits were in part responsible for successful features such as *Gosford Park* (Altman, 2001) and *Bend it Like Beckham* (Chadra, 2002). But for all those who were using the tax break in the right way, the Treasury was alerted to the increasing variety of scams abusing the system, so in 2004 it decided to re-examine the arrangement, much to the consternation of the industry.

Early in 2004, production of a film called *Tulip Fever*, with Jude Law and the upcoming new star of British cinema, Keira Knightley, collapsed because of the proposed removal of tax loopholes by Gordon Brown. The portents of gloom surfaced with one film financier behind *Tulip Fever* remarking, 'The Chancellor has lumped us in with the bad guys. He's seen how others are abusing these loopholes, and thrown the baby out with the bathwater. It will destroy the British film industry if it is allowed to go ahead'[16]. After much debate with members of the industry and the then-Films Minister Estelle Morris, the relief was rebranded as a tax credit and with a subsequent tightening up on the abuses. The new scheme enabled producers to claim up to 20% of their costs up to a total budget of £20 million regardless of where the film was shot or completed, as long as it qualified as a British film under the government's definitions. The credit was activated on the completion of the film, which would detract unscrupulous investors. Previously, billions of pounds of income were sheltered in film partnership schemes and these had become a way of deferring tax payments rather than making money through British film. The tax relief was targeted by investors who routinely pulled out before a film could even hope to go into profit (Thorpe, The Guardian, 15/08/2004)[17]. This was as detrimental to the profile of the industry as the Lottery awards debacle had been previously: it left a bitter taste and raised pertinent questions about the use of public money. In 2006 the scheme was extended, but issues with the EU banning state aid for film productions meant that the tax break system might not be eligible for British products filmed abroad. Section 48, the setting up of the UK Film Council and Lottery funding made it clear that the government was committed to supporting British film, but for those within the industry it has never been enough. Add the contribution of terrestrial broadcasters FilmFour and BBC Films and it is hard to imagine what films, if any, would have been produced in this country during the past ten years aside from Hollywood financed money-spinning co-productions.

OVERVIEW 1999–2009

This period saw the re-election of Tony Blair as Prime Minister twice, earlier against the backdrop of huge economic growth and latterly in 2005 after the invasion of Iraq. British film by and large failed to capture the spirit of the times. The best example is the war in Iraq itself. There was a slow Hollywood response to Vietnam, but British cinema has so far made absolutely no response to the conflict in Iraq. It seems that British film has been caught between commercial obligations, which might mean that any films about this unpopular war fail dismally at the box office, and its cultural responsibility to reflect the wider context of the time. Hollywood has responded with films and documentaries largely offering a critical appraisal of the war and its effects on both Iraqis and Americans, for example, *Rendition* (Hood, 2007), *In the Valley of Elah* (Haggis, 2007), *Redacted* (De Palma, 2008) and *Standard Operating Procedure* (Morris, 2008). Many of these have had a mixed response, but they have raised important questions about the West's involvement in the Middle East and the long-term repercussions. The British response has been taken up by television and in particular Channel Four with *The Government Inspector* (Kosminsky, 2005), which tells the story of Dr David Kelly (Mark Rylance), a weapons inspector who, after a grilling by a Foreign Affairs Committee, committed suicide; *The Mark of Cain* (Munden, 2007) focusing on British troops in Basra; and *The Battle for Haditha* (2007), directed by Nick Broomfield, which concentrated on an American retaliatory massacre on a small Iraqi town. Broomfield's acclaimed docudrama did receive a limited run at some cinemas; but by and large British involvement in Iraq and Afghanistan has to-date been virtually ignored by indigenous screenwriters and directors.

The continuing rise of the cult of celebrity has also been largely ignored by film-makers, although it is the fodder of populist television programmes and the tabloid press. Reality television, in particular Channel Four's *Big Brother* (2000–2010), has not given rise to any real serious analysis on the big screen. BBC Films' *Confetti* (Isitt, 2006), with its mockumentary feel, concentrating on three couples involved in a reality television-style competition to find the zaniest way in which to get married, is the one notable entry here. Even though *Confetti* was a light comedy it did attempt to raise questions about intrusion and the downside of sudden fame. During this period British comedy suffered from an over-reliance on television stars and existing properties, which in turn owed a great deal to the tradition (and poor quality) of 1970s British cinema. In terms of international exposure Sacha Baron Cohen's creations have had the most notable success. First aired on Channel Four, his characters Ali G and Borat both turned up in successful films, and in the case of *Borat* (Charles, 2006) made a huge impact in the United States. One of the best examples of a film that felt very much like a throwback to the coarse comedies of yesteryear, but without the wit of the *Carry On* franchise, was *The Sex Lives of the Potato Men* (Humphries, 2004). It received damning reviews and did not enhance the careers of its two leads, Johnny Vegas and Mackenzie Crook, but it did respectable business. Working Title's *Mr Bean's Holiday* (Bendelack, 2007) did considerably better, but comedy spin-offs had mixed responses. One of the better examples was another Steve Bendelack effort, *The League of Gentlemen's Apocalypse* (2005), a surreal black spin-off of the BBC2 sitcom with the three main actors playing most of the roles. Although the narrative was inconsistent, it was visually very funny and inventive.

Many British comedies failed to make any mark at all at the box office. A case in point is *Three and Out* (Gershfield, 2008), yet another Mackenzie Crook vehicle, which, despite having a strong marketing campaign and a decent UK print run, failed to attract a worthwhile audience. Crook, who had found fame in the BBC TV sitcom *The Office* (2001–03), had, however, done better than other cast members: Lucy Davis's little-seen *Rag Tale* (McGuckien, 2005) garnered only £7,000 at the box office and Martin Freeman's *The All Together* (Claxton, 2007) struggled to make over £10,000. The comedy template set down by *The Full Monty* seemed to be the formula most adapted during the decade, concentrating on the obstacles – usually social class, ethnic background, gender, age or sexual orientation – that a protagonist must overcome. The two most successful examples were *Billy Elliot* and *Bend it Like Beckham*, but others failed to make an impact and felt designed solely for a domestic audience: *There's Only One Jimmy Grimble* (Hay, 2000), *Purely Belter* (Herman, 2000), *Calendar Girls* (Cole, 2003), *Millions* (Danny Boyle, 2004) and *Kinky Boots* (Jarrold, 2005).

Two of the best-received and most successful comedy films came from a team that had worked previously on the cult Channel Four show *Spaced* (1999–2001) – director Edgar Wright and writer/star Simon Pegg. *Shaun of The Dead* (2004) and *Hot Fuzz* (2007) were interesting in the way that they subverted and played about with generic conventions. *Shaun of the Dead* was sold as a rom-com-zombie film which does sum up the narrative, as a shop manager played by Pegg takes on an invasion of flesh-eating zombies while attempting to win back his girlfriend. *Hot Fuzz*, on the other hand, was an overblown pastiche of the British police procedural combined with nods to *The Wicker Man* (Hardy, 1973), by placing an over-ambitious police officer (Pegg again) in the wilds of Gloucestershire. Both films did very well at the domestic box office and *Shaun of the Dead* – rather like the more conventional *28 Days Later* – was quite successful in America.

The British crime film, with some honourable exceptions mentioned earlier, did not attempt to play on contemporary concerns about crime, or if it did it did so in a highly stylised fashion, taking the Guy Ritchie approach rather than Paul McGuigan's gritty realism. Ritchie continued to weigh in with his tales of loveable rough diamonds, action-packed plots and mockney platitudes. *Snatch* (2000), *Revolver* (2005) and *Rocknrolla* (2008) were high octane affairs aimed at a teenage boy audience. Ritchie's unofficial crown as the populist 'king of British crime film' seemed to be under threat by Nick Love. His films at first glance appeared to be more expansive than Ritchie's. Love took a number of different views of British crime by focusing on the 1980s in *The Business* (2005), vigilantism in *Outlaw* (2007) and football hooliganism in *The Football Factory* (2004). This subject was also tackled in *Green Street* (Alexander, 2005), which had American actor Elijah Wood inexplicably joining a crew of football thugs. Mentioned earlier was *London to Brighton*, a micro-budget film by a first-time director that reflects some of the best British crime films and in particular *Mona Lisa* (Jordan, 1986). The hellish vision of an amoral London, violent and exploitative, has none of the gloss associated with the films of Ritchie and Love.

London to Brighton felt much more a part of the social-realist tradition that had been upheld by British directors like Mike Leigh and Ken Loach during the 1980s and1990s. Both auteurs continued to produce interesting films and both were honoured by Cannes in the process: Leigh for his thoughtful tale of a working-class woman performing abortions during the austere Britain of the early 1950s in *Vera Drake* (2004), and Loach for *The Wind That Shakes the Barley* (2006). This film focused on a young Irishman who enlists in the IRA during the War of Independence: it pulled no punches in its depiction of post-treaty Ireland and in particular the bitter Irish civil war. Loach's preoccupations with class politics took in religion and gender in his rather ineffectual *Ae Fond Kiss* (2004), which has as its central tension the relationship between a young Muslim man and an Irish Catholic teacher in present-day Scotland. Also set north of the border was the moving *Sweet Sixteen* (2002), where the central protagonist is a boy on the cusp of adulthood heavily involved in various criminal activities, but trying to keep his family together against a backdrop of drug abuse. Loach also made a contribution to the debate on economic migration with his made-for-television film *It's a Free World* (2007). This took the perspective of a working-class woman who sets up an employment agency and is slowly corrupted by her newfound wealth, becoming increasingly exploitative. Leigh's other films showed a slightly wider perspective – prior to *Vera Drake* there was his lavish period piece on Gilbert and Sullivan, *Topsy Turvy* (1999). Leigh did return to bleaker fare with *All or Nothing* (2002), centring on a dysfunctional South London family, featuring a powerful performance by Timothy Spall as Phil, the disillusioned, depressed patriarch. The film did have a relatively optimistic ending, however, celebrating the strength of family. *Happy Go Lucky* (2008) was, by Leigh's standards, extremely light-hearted with its central character, a primary school teacher called Poppy (Sally Hawkins), dispensing good cheer to all and sundry with only hints of darker themes underneath. It is an uplifting film enlivened by Hawkins' wide-eyed, trustful protagonist.

Taking up the mantle from Leigh and Loach were two films that also had council estate life as the centre of the action. Gillies MacKinnon followed up his film *Hideous Kinky* with *Pure* (2002), a disturbing and realistic portrayal of heroin addiction. The ultra low-budget film *The Plague* (Hall, 2004) took a slightly less downbeat approach to life on the margins with a digicam-shot black comedy looking at four friends meeting up for a drug-fuelled weekend. Duane Hopkins' extraordinary *Better Things* (2009) took a more pastoral approach to drug use, by focusing on a group of addicts in the Cotswolds. With its minimalist plot and long takes of the rolling countryside it echoed European art-house cinema at its best; as did *Hunger* (McQueen, 2008). This slow-burning narrative centring on the IRA's 'dirty protest' and subsequent hunger strikes in the late 1970s and early 1980s was a remarkable piece of work. In a completely different vein, Joanna Hogg's *Unrelated* (2008) with its careful exploration of middle-class mores at a Tuscan villa was also a compelling debut. Although these films weren't hugely successful (much like a great deal of Loach and Leigh's output) they are unsparing in their authenticity and they greatly add to the canon. What is important is that in Hopkins, McQueen and Hogg's cases, these are fine debut films and directors to be watched.

A number of films emerged that harked back to the recent past, which reflected a sense of disenchantment with the present. The 1980s were mined for cultural references that perhaps said more about the personal preoccupations of the film-makers than the decade itself. *Son of Rambow* (Jennings, 2008) was a good example of this. It was a film about two quite different boys, one a disaffected abandoned rich kid and the other a member of the Plymouth Brethren, who become friends and decide to make a short film, a sequel to Rambo, to enter in a competition for a BBC children's television programme. The film presents a view of the 1980s that is as highly stylised and remote from the era as *The Business* or the BBC's crime show *Ashes to Ashes* (2008–9). This is nowhere more apparent than in a scene in the sixth-form common room where the gelled-up teenagers dance in unison to an old Depeche Mode track. Much better was Anton Corbijn's *Control* (2007), which looked at the late 1970s and early 1980s by telling the story of Ian Curtis, tragic lead singer of Joy Division. The film, shot in stark black-and-white, feels like a classic northern kitchen-sink drama transposed 15 years later, complete with a post-punk soundtrack. Corbijn sees the film as a struggle between Curtis's commitment to his young wife and child, his burgeoning career and his relationship with a European fan. This, of course, culminated in Curtis's suicide on the eve of a major American tour. The film, unlike Jennings' effort, captures the era wonderfully and realistically. Corbijn's previous work as a photographer with the NME, and his own iconic shots of the band, made him the perfect choice to direct. He balanced the tragedy of the original story with a clear artistic sensibility, but this was all too rare in films about the recent past. Other honourable mentions are *This is England* and the strange and underrated *Brothers of the Head* (Fulton and Pepe, 2005).

This very brief overview of the opening years of the new century only touches on some of the range of British films made during this period. The upsurge in production has led to a wide variation in the quality and diversity of films made and as a result any book endeavouring to cover all bases in any detail is bound to fail. What this book attempts to do is to give a flavour of the times, by looking at a range of films in some degree of depth. So what is this book going to cover?

THIS BOOK

As has been shown, this period of British film-making has been incredibly fragmented and it is hoped that this book will give the period some sense of clarity by grouping together a number of significant texts under a range of perspectives. Chapter 2, entitled Wallace, Gromit and Harry, is a million miles away from debates on public money and British film, and will investigate British cinema from an economic perspective by focusing on the thorny issue of co-productions and their impact on the industry in this country. We will look at two case studies: firstly, a British production company, Aardman, and its difficult relationship with DreamWorks, through its major success *Chicken Run* (Lord and Park, 2000), its masterpiece *Wallace and Gromit in the Curse of the Were-Rabbit* (Box and Park, 2005) and its dismal failure *Flushed Away* (Bowers and Fell, 2006). The chapter will also look at the massively successful *Harry Potter* franchise made possible by Warner Bros.' deep pockets. The key objective here will be to establish if Britain can produce a distinctive and profitable film industry with largely American financial investment.

Chapter 3, Red Buses in the Rain, will focus on what I have termed the 'new heritage film' and will look at a whole range of movies, initially by taking on institutional factors around Working Title, but then focusing on the representation of the middle classes by looking at *About a Boy* (Weitz Brothers 2002), *Love Actually* (Curtis, 2004), *Closer* (Nichols, 2004), *Notes on a Scandal* and *Breaking and Entering* (Minghella, 2007), and, in *The Queen* (Frears, 2006) and *Atonement* (Wright, 2007), the upper classes. Chapter 4, on the other hand, takes an entirely different viewpoint. The New Realism: Girls on Top will analyse British social realism from a slightly different angle by looking at a number of films by female directors that have added greatly to a distinctly British style of film-making. The chapter will look in some depth at Andrea Arnold's *Red Road*, Lynne Ramsay's *Ratcatcher* and *Morvern Callar* (2002), Amma Asante's *A Way of Life* (2005) and Pam Dunn's *Gypo* (2005).

Chapter 5, Welcome to Britain, deals with issues around asylum and migration. This chapter takes as its cue a thematic grouping for a number of films dealing with new arrivals in the UK. It will compare and contrast three films, *Last Resort*, *Dirty Pretty Things* (Frears, 2002) and *Ghosts* (Broomfield, 2007), primarily dealing with aspects of representation, not just of the migrants themselves but how Britain itself is viewed in these films. Chapter 6 takes an auteur-led approach by concentrating on two fascinating, but very different directors working in British film today – Michael Winterbottom and Shane Meadows. This will examine both men's work, firstly by looking at Winterbottom's *Wonderland* (1999), *24 Hour Party People* and *9 Songs* (2005), and then Meadows' *A Room for Romeo Brass* (1999), *Dead Man's Shoes* and *This is England*. The chapter will focus on issues around funding, style and techniques and will reach some conclusions about whether the auteur director has a role in contemporary British cinema.

The primary focus of Chapter 7, Existing Identities, examines how ethnic groups are represented in recent British film. These works take on the black experience in the United Kingdom with *Kidulthood* (Huda, 2006) and *Bullet Boy* (Dibb, 2005) and then Asian Britain in *Bend it like Beckham*, *Yasmin* (Glennan, 2005) and Sarah Gavron's *Brick Lane* (2007). This chapter offers readings which both veer away from and support simplistic notions reflecting the issues surrounding multiculturalism in modern-day Britain.

Chapter 8, The Neo-Colonial Film, explores the recent upsurge in films set in and around Africa, looking at three examples: *The Constant Gardener* (Meirelles, 2005), *The Last King of Scotland* and *Shooting Dogs* (Caton-Jones, 2006).

The final two chapters discuss science fiction and horror. Chapter 9, Dystopian Britain, focuses on a group of films set in the near future that echo concerns about current events. The films investigated here are *Children of Men* (Cuaron, 2005), *V for Vendetta* (McTeigue, 2005), *28 Days Later* and *28 Weeks Later*. Lastly, we examine the mini revival in the Noughties of horror by firstly discussing the films of Neil Marshall: *Dog Soldiers* (2001), *The Descent* (2005) and *Doomsday* (2008). We will also look at two other films that take different angles on the genre: the horror comedy *Shaun of the Dead* and the genuinely unsettling *Eden Lake* (Watkins, 2008).

REFERENCES

1. Smith, C. quoted in 'Government reforms to boost British film industry' in The Guardian, 09/07/1999

2. Thorpe, V. and Barnett, A., 'Lottery movies: 9 hits, 121 misses' in The Observer, 12/03/2000

3. Macnab, G., 'Five years of flack' in The Guardian, 25/10/2002

4. Martinson, J., 'Bringing a ray of sunshine to British films' in The Guardian, 06/04/2007

5. Parker, A. quoted in Gibbons, F., 'Parker to head Film Council' in The Guardian, 05/08/1999

6. Brooks, X., 'Film Council aims for the reel thing' in The Guardian, 02/05/2000

7. Parker, A., 'Building a sustainable UK Film Industry' – Film Council keynote speech, 05/11/2002

8. Woodward, J., Keynote address to Screen International conference, 21/10/2004

9. Romney, J., 'Box office isn't everything' in The Guardian, 05/05/2000

10. Macnab, G., 'That shrinking feeling' in Sight and Sound, October 2002

11. Aukin, D., 'It was logical to create FilmFour. But what is logical isn't necessarily the answer' in The Guardian, 12/07/2002

12. Roddick, N., 'Almost Rosy' in Sight and Sound, January 2007

13. Plunkett, J., 'BBC urged to buy British' in The Guardian, 14/09/2004

14. Macnab, G., 'In the loop' in Screen International, 13/11/2009

15. Cohen, N., ' Lights, cameras, turkeys' in The Observer, 15/05/2005

16. Kane, F. and Smith, D., 'British films wiped out by tax bomb' in The Observer, 22/02/2004

17. Thorpe, V., 'Brown lifts filmmaker's gloom' in The Guardian, 15/08/2004

WALLACE, GROMIT AND HARRY
– BRITISH ECCENTRICS AND
HOLLYWOOD CO-PRODUCTION

'We have to stop worrying about the nationality of money. We want to encourage investment into our film industry from anywhere in the world – without tearing up the roots of cultural film production.' (Alan Parker, 05/11/2002)[1]

In his keynote speech to the newly formed UK Film Council, Alan Parker typically took no prisoners in stressing what his vision of a sustainable and successful British film industry would look like. Although there was a certain slant to his presentation which was hopeful for the future of the UK industry, it was candid in its central idea that films would have to be open to taking on investment from sources which were not British. Parker was critical of public subsidies which he stressed had by and large failed to address the structural problems in the industry. Certainly his central mantra concerned selling the UK as a 'film hub', a place where good distribution, skills and a good production infrastructure would reinvent the British film industry as something that could be successful on a global scale:

'We need to abandon forever the "little England" vision of a UK industry comprised of small British film companies delivering parochial British films. That, I suspect, is what people think of when they talk of a "sustainable" British film industry. Well it's time for a reality check. That "British" film industry never existed, and in the brutal age of global capitalism, it never will.' [Parker, ibid.]

This meant taking money from whatever sources were available, and in order to guarantee the sort of global reach and access to distribution networks that Parker is implicitly suggesting, that meant finance from Hollywood, drawing on the 'film hub' that the UK would provide. Of course co-production with American majors was nothing new. After all, Carol Reed's *The Third Man* (1948), voted the number one British film in a poll commissioned by the BFI, was 'British' but in a highly conflicted way. The director Reed, screenwriter Graham Greene and one of the leads, Trevor Howard, all had impeccable credentials as archetypal Englishmen, but the main producers were London Film's Hungarian Alexander Korda and Universal's David Selznick, from the United States. Like Selznick, the main stars of the picture, Orson Welles and Joseph Cotton, were American, the film was shot beautifully by the Australian Director of Photography Robert Krasker and it was set in Vienna. What is interesting about *The Third Man* is what a wonderful film it is, while retaining its unique sense of Englishness stemming from Greene's deeply pessimistic world view. Reed managed just about to do this despite Selznick's 'input', and was able to create a film that is unquestionably British. This, of course, may provide a problem for any British producer, director or screenwriter working today by raising a key question: is it possible to maintain a sense of cultural distinctiveness in the face of extensive fiscal backing from a major Hollywood production company?

'The UK Film Council and the DCMS [Department for Culture, Media and Sport] defined a British film as one which met certain criteria in relation to the proportion of a film's budget spent in the UK and the proportion of labour costs paid to qualifying individuals. This definition made no mention of culture. Indeed the most successful films of recent years, all of which were co-productions, presented a particular kind of British cultural identity. These included the *James Bond*, *Harry Potter* and *Tomb Raider* franchises, the central characters of which carried with them the British public school ethos.' (Seminar on the Cultural Value of UK Film at the University of London run by the UK Film Council, 03/05/2005)[2]

The examples given in the last quote suggest how that level of distinctiveness has survived even with substantial American financial backing. All of those examples trade off a particular archetypal notion of Britishness, easily recognisable to an American audience. A better example is probably exemplified in the discussion of Working Title covered in much more depth in Chapter 3 of this book. This is a good example of a production company working alongside a Hollywood major, which utilised its writing talent in Richard Curtis and played off those notions of Britishness, albeit in a highly constructed, rather simplified version of this in films like *Notting Hill* (Michell, 1999) and *Love Actually*. The 'film hub' idea here feeds off not just the production team and crew behind these films, but also the sense of what a Working Title romantic comedy amounts to. The largely Hugh Grant-led successes of the 1990s and early 2000s were a branded property in themselves, where audiences could see different versions of the same story from the thoughtful *About A Boy* to the turgid *Wimbledon* (Loncraine, 2004). However, if Parker's 'film hub' idea was to have any real worth, this should include existing material and talent also, which could transcend national boundaries and be successful worldwide:

'Globalization inscribes itself into film-making most effectively at the moment of financing. The global-local logic of big budget blockbusters tends not to involve a globally equal spread of employment possibilities but films shot globally, across the world, often at some cost to local environments, but with the crucial, better paid decision-making and post production industries localized in California.' (Branston, p.67, 2000)[3]

Branston's point is apt certainly in the case of two of the decade's big successes in the British film industry, but fundamentally two very different stories emerge. Aardman's profile in the United States had been enhanced by the success of Nick Park's short films at the Academy Awards, and the Bristol-based production company had the sort of talent, creativity and drive that Parker felt was essential to break out of the implied limited world view that British cinema was deemed to have. It would be the parochial, incredibly culturally specific agenda that its films had that would be both conversely lauded and criticised when the films failed to make the financial impact that the backers, DreamWorks, required. On the other hand, the *Harry Potter* series of novels by JK Rowling had been a much desired property by many Hollywood companies before a deal was struck with Warner Brothers in 2000. These books were just as rooted in a perceived sense of Britishness as the Aardman product, but there was a sense of universality in terms of themes that had made them a colossal success and had gained millions of readers around the world, tapping into a number of literary references such as CS Lewis and JRR Tolkien. Getting Rowling's vision to screen was always going to be a tall order, as the novels had extensive set-piece situations that would require a great deal of costly CGI technology. There was also the writer's legendary control of the *Harry Potter* brand and there would be no attempts to 'Americanise' the boy wizard. Ultimately, it was the combination of AOL-Time-Warner's big pockets, a host of British acting talent and a strict adherence to the ideas from Rowling's original material that was to lead to the biggest British film phenomenon of all time. And, like *The Third Man*, nobody questioned where the money came from.

DREAMWORKS IN BRISTOL

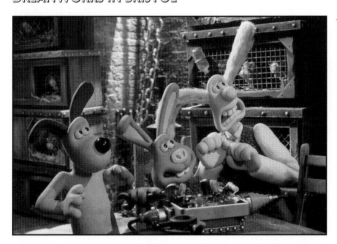

Wallace and Gromit: Curse of the Were-Rabbit

The £150 million deal between Aardman and DreamWorks was, on the surface, perfect for both parties. The animation company had been formed in the 1970s by Peter Lord and David Sproxton and based its success around the use of Plasticine models and stop-animation techniques. All of its work was centred on television shorts and advertising. The *Creature Comforts* shorts of the late 1980s were particularly popular and the idea was subsequently used in adverts for British Gas. Plasticine models of animals were voiced by ordinary members of the British public, talking about everyday aspects of their lives. This was a simple but ingenious idea. DreamWorks, on the other hand, was keen to exploit the potential of Aardman's premier film-maker, Nick Park, who had been behind the success of *Creature Comforts* but who had also come to the company's attention by winning two Oscars for best animated short films, *The Wrong Trousers* (1993) and *A Close Shave* (1995), featuring his most famous creations Wallace and Gromit. The co-production agreement with the Hollywood studio meant access to multi-million pound global distribution, marketing and merchandising, as well as financing for five feature-length theatrical releases. At the time Jeffrey Katzenberg, co-founder of DreamWorks, had said, 'I could not be more thrilled about this new creative partnership and I am very excited about exploring the many story-telling possibilities of this unique art form'[4].

It seemed a perfect arrangement with DreamWorks initially taking a hands-off approach regarding the use of English accents and themes in Aardman's output.

What was clear in Nick Park's short films was a particular slant of English eccentricity in the central characters and also in the highly detailed *mise-en-scène* used. The Wallace and Gromit films are set in the north of England and are clearly informed by Park's upbringing in 1960s Preston. Wallace is a wide-mouthed, softly spoken inventor obsessed by cheese, and his faithful companion is Gromit, a silent dog who is clearly the brains of the operation and whose often-incredulous expressions at Wallace's mishaps provide much of the humour. There was a surreal feel to the shorts: Park's first film, *A Grand Day Out* (1989), much of which was produced while Park was a student at the National Film and Television School in Beaconsfield, involved Wallace and Gromit building a rocket to go to the Moon in search of cheese. What was important to Park was getting the right voice for Wallace. In the early 1980s, the young student approached Peter Sallis, a character actor famous for playing another northern eccentric, Clegg, in the long-running BBC sitcom *The Last of the Summer Wine* (1973–to-date). He agreed to take the part, recorded some dialogue and was surprised six years later when Park made contact to inform him that the film was now finished. Sallis's warm Lancastrian vowels impeccably fitted Wallace's character and he has remained in the part ever since.

The second short, *The Wrong Trousers*, was much more ambitious in scope and by this stage the BBC was funding Park's work. Stop-animation is a time-consuming and laborious process with two seconds of film often taking a day to get in the can. *The Wrong Trousers* was a considerable step-up from Park's debut and involved one of Wallace's inventions, 'techno trousers', being commandeered by an evil penguin called Feathers McGraw for a jewellery heist. Of course ultimately Gromit saves the day in a wonderful finale involving a chase on a model train-set. What was apparent was the sheer attention to detail in terms of set design and the obvious nods to other film-makers, most notably Alfred Hitchcock, but *The Wrong Trousers* was also extremely funny and like other great animation lent itself to repeated viewings. This was followed pretty quickly by Park's standards by *A Close Shave*, in which Gromit is framed by an evil robot-dog, Preston, for killing sheep. It also developed a *Brief Encounter*-style romance between the hapless Wallace and Preston's owner Wendolene (Anne Reid), which ends when it transpires that she hasn't got the same affection for cheese as Wallace. Once again the film was inventive and well observed, but it was clear that Aardman would need more outside investment in order to break into the highly lucrative market for feature-length animation that had emerged in the mid-1990s with Pixar and, subsequently, DreamWorks. Films such as *Toy Story* (Lasseter, 1995) and *Shrek* (Adamson and Jenson, 2001) had been intelligent, funny pictures that utilised the expensive CGI to create movies that appealed to both adults and children alike. They also provided massive merchandising opportunities which added hugely to the overall take of the films. This was something that Aardman was keen to make the most of and although some *Wallace and Gromit* merchandise had been produced on the back of the shorts, the deal with DreamWorks would further develop this trend. The key was to try to avoid compromising Aardman's idiosyncratic sense of Englishness that had been such a feature of Park's films.

Chicken Run, co-directed by Park and Peter Lord, was the first feature produced under the new deal and was a parody of the prisoner of war genre, specifically referencing *The Great Escape* (Sturges, 1963). The film had all the usual elements of the Aardman brand, typically English characters and humour, although in one major concession to DreamWorks the main character, Rocky, was American and voiced by Mel Gibson. The film is set in the 1950s and echoes the nostalgic outlook which is very much in evidence in Park's previous work. He has been greatly influenced by the comics he read as a child, *The Beano* and *Dandy*, and also growing up in 1960s Lancashire where 'everything looked like it was still from the 1950s'[5]. His work seems stuck in an immediate post-war bubble with its old resolutely archaic feel. Peter Lord was very clear about how this particular sense of Britishness was at the heart of Aardman's success:

> 'I think that in the States, we're exotic aliens – we're a different culture. When we spoke to DreamWorks, right from the start, one of the first conversations was us saying to them, "We want to do an Aardman film", and them saying back to us, "Well of course we want you to do an Aardman film. We don't want you to do a film you could do here in Burbank – that would be absolutely ludicrous."' (In Interview with Jeffrey Wachs, www.reel.com)[6]

The film was also greatly informed by Park and Lord's cinephile tendencies: 'research for *Chicken Run* involved studying old war movies. "We watched loads of British war films together, *Captive Heart*, *Colditz*, *Stalag 17*…" '[7] (Buss, The Independent, 11/06/2000). Locating the action on a chicken farm, the film focuses on the attempts to escape by the heroine Ginger (Julia Sawalha), a feisty young hen. The farm is run by a greedy, sinister couple, Mr and Mrs Tweedy (Tony Haygarth and Miranda Richardson), who decide to change from low profit egg-farming to the more lucrative production of chicken pies. The arrival of Rocky, who seemingly flies into the farm, inspires Ginger to enlist him in training the chickens to flap their wings to escape the Tweedy's proposed slaughter. Of course this doesn't work, and after a series of near scrapes, the sabotage of the pie-making machine and the escape of Rocky, the film reaches its conclusion. The chickens build a flying machine with parts scavenged by two crafty and cynical rats, Fetcher (Phil Daniels) and Nick (Timothy Spall). Rocky returns to the farm to help with the escape and the chickens successfully negotiate this, despatching Mrs Tweedy from the machine in the process. The resolution of the film sees the chickens settled happily on a bird sanctuary.

The *mise-en-scène* of small huts and barbed wire clearly references post-war escape dramas and directly echoes *The Great Escape* with Ginger confined to a coal bunker, bouncing a sprout off the wall instead of a baseball as Steve McQueen did in the 1963 film. Similarly, Rocky's tricycling trick near the end of the film is a reference to McQueen's thwarted motorcycle ride. This demonstrates the intertextual nature of *Chicken Run*, enabling another level of meaning for a more adult audience. The film also has its darker moments, with a hen executed by Mrs Tweedy for failing to fulfil her egg production quota, and in this there are clear nods to George Miller's highly successful film *Babe* (1998). That film also dealt with the everyday aspects of life on a farm, especially in the opening sequence where the hero, the pig Babe, is separated from the rest of the family as they head towards the slaughterhouse. *Chicken Run*'s twists and turns, however, largely avoid the spectre of the Tweedy's farm as an extermination camp and instead the primary narrative strand focuses on the tensions between Ginger and Rocky as they plan to get away. Any connections to the horrors of modern factory farming are also avoided, with much of the humour coming from the overwhelming arrogance of Rocky's American rooster placed against the practicality and sheer English single-mindedness of Ginger's character.

The spiv-like cockney rats and the daft, holiday obsessed Babs, voiced by Jane Horrocks, are wonderfully observed British archetypes, and although it is the American Rocky who pulls the final escape together at the film's finale, the movie avoids becoming a caricature or simply an American version of what an Aardman film should be. Although DreamWorks was relatively content with the use of colloquial language and the dominance of English characters, voiced by stars largely unfamiliar to stateside audiences, tensions did emerge over the music used in the film. DreamWorks wanted a 'mainstream composer' to score the film, while Park and Lord were adamant on using English composers. The directors felt that offering a brief summary of what they wanted to British writers would make it much easier to communicate what effect was required on-screen. 'You can say to an English composer, "this sounds like Trumpton" or "reminds me of the Hovis music", and they'll know what you are talking about' said Peter Lord (Buss, ibid.).

Chicken Run's production budget of $42 million was astronomical by British standards, but still nowhere near the vast amounts needed to make CGI movies. Kim Newman saw the film as being pitched as the UK answer to *Toy Story*, although playing off its old-fashioned and handcrafted animation techniques as opposed to *Toy Story*'s CGI high-tech and virtual imagery[8]. The film received a high-profile US marketing campaign and was given a huge print run on 4000-plus screens; it took $17 million on its first weekend, going on to gross an impressive $106 million in the US alone. The film was also highly successful in the UK, taking £29 million, and its worldwide take was an extremely profitable $228 million. It was the ideal start for the new partnership.

There were, however, dissenting voices in some parts of the press. Andrew Pulver was critical of the decision to release the film in the US before the UK. He also questioned the validity of the film's Britishness, focusing on the financial backing and implying that the earlier release on the other side of the Atlantic is a contributory factor in certain films' success in Britain. 'There's no doubt that, for all these films [*The Full Monty*, *Four Weddings and a Funeral*, *Shakespeare in Love* and *The English Patient*], their success at the US box office had a significant impact on their reception in the UK'[9]. The film is unquestionably British in its cultural approach and given Aardman's previous successes it is unlikely that UK audiences would have been swayed too greatly by the fine opening box office in the US. What was highly noticeable was the huge promotional campaign, which felt very different to previous British pictures. The film was used to promote a number of products, Thorntons (chocolate eggs, naturally), Fabulous Bakin' Boys (cookies), Wheetos (cereal) and gift-wrapping paper and cards. This in many respects aped the publicity and promotional campaigns of many previous Pixar, Disney and DreamWorks films, albeit on a slightly smaller scale. The film also spawned a computer game for PlayStation, which was released alongside the video and DVD in January 2001. This seemed like a strange decision for Aardman, which had been seen as quite Luddite in its approach up until this point, by sticking to stop-frame animation and Plasticine. Nick Park wanted 'the humour and originality of the film' to be retained and saw this as 'a way of expanding and developing the world of the characters. Yes, it is a kind of spin-off, but it's an interesting and entertaining one which adds to the fun of the film.' It is clear, however, that it is almost a prerequisite for any Hollywood film with a young audience to tie-in a computer game with its release (Chatterton, The Independent, 08/01/2001). The former cottage industry feel of Aardman was being quickly transformed by the utilisation of every possible method to make money from its products.

Nick Park returned to his first and best-known creations for the second Aardman/DreamWorks feature, *Wallace and Gromit: Curse of the Were-Rabbit* (2005), which he co-directed with Steve Box. The film also had a substantial budget for a British film, an estimated $80 million, and again had a relatively large advertising campaign. What is apparent about the film is how much more at ease it is with itself than *Chicken Run*, which it seemed was much more tailored to the American market. *Curse of the Were-Rabbit* took the strengths of the Wallace and Gromit shorts to new heights in terms of set design and characterisation, and in total took five years to complete. It is even more stubbornly English than *Chicken Run* with, as Simon de Bruxelles saw, a unique vision of 'terraced houses, stately houses, flat caps, silver-haired vicars and fruit-and-veg competitions'[10].

Wallace and Gromit have set themselves up as pest controllers called Anti-Pesto and have been employed by their neighbours to protect their vegetables in the run-up to a local contest. This in itself would be an unusual premise for an American audience, but what Park and his team do really well is show how *normal* this all seems, from the obsessive growers like Mrs Mulch (Liz Smith) to the elaborate *Thunderbirds*-like response techniques of Anti-Pesto, but also their humane approach to dealing with the pests, who all seem to be rabbits. To do this Wallace has devised a gigantic vacuum in the style of one of Heath Robinson's inventions. Anti-Pesto's services are requested by Lady

Tottington (Helena Bonham-Carter) to rid her estate of rabbits. She is a fantastic creation, part Princess Anne, part Joanna Lumley, and Wallace is smitten. He also incurs the wrath of Tottington's uppity suitor Victor Quartermaine (Ralph Fiennes). Park saw echoes of Quartermaine's character in other films that he had seen: 'Victor the hunter – *King Kong, Solomon's Mine* … But also for his pomposity and stuff, Charles Laughton in *Mutiny on the Bounty,* that kind of thing. Laurence Olivier in *Wuthering Heights* I think it was, that kind of dashing aristocrat'[11]. The central conflict in the narrative, however, rests on one of Wallace's inventions back-firing and in a *Fly*-style transformation he is turned into a monster, 'a were-rabbit', who goes on to terrorise the town by destroying vast amounts of their prized carrots and marrows.

The film at this point makes clear reference to old horror films, specifically the Universal cycle of movies from the 1930s and 1940s. Park commented, 'They're all filled with blood and guts and we thought that they would really suit Wallace and Gromit's world because it's absurd. It's about people locking up their vegetables rather than their children'[12]. The initial change from Wallace to the were-rabbit is fantastically lit by Andy Mack and his team, and manages to be pretty frightening as well as very funny. According to Andrew Osmond in Sight and Sound the film also offered even more intertextual readings than *Chicken Run*, as it 'evokes *The Incredible Hulk*, a burrowing *Jaws* and *King Kong*'[13]. In a similar vein to *Chicken Run*, this lends itself to a multilayered reading for older audiences, a key feature of animation in DreamWorks' other films and in particular the fairy-tale pastiche *Shrek*.

Quartermaine discovers by chance that Wallace is the veg-chomping creature and figures out that the only way to kill the beast is with 24-carat gold bullets. The film's finale is on the night of the contest, with Quartermaine pursing the beast while Gromit tries desperately to protect his master. The chase climaxes at Tottington Hall where, in a clear reference to *King Kong*, the were-rabbit climbs onto the roof. Gromit manages to stop Quartermaine's final bullet, but the monster falls; however, revived by cheese Wallace comes back. The film ends with Lady Tottington turning her stately home into a rabbit sanctuary.

The film is also clearly informed, like a great deal of Park's previous work, by the influence of 1940s and 1950s Ealing comedy. The triumph of the underdog is a common feature and in an interesting turn the film also tentatively explores issues of class. Anthony Quinn was one of the few reviewers to pick up on this point, and highlighted the quaint atmosphere of 'cosy front-rooms, string vests [and] bobbies on the beat, not to mention those distinct tremors of class difference, here prompted by Wallace's flirtation with the local aristocracy'[14]. Certainly Fiennes plays Quartermaine as a pompous, boorish snob, whose dislike of Wallace is as much driven by condescension as it is by jealously. The country estate of Lady Tottington is quite at odds with the drab Victorian terraces of Anti-Pesto's customers, whose sole concern seems to be growing the largest vegetables for the annual competition run by Tottington herself. 'A flat-vowelled, suet-eating universe populated by denture-sporting battle-axes and V-neck sweater old men who spend their lives tending to their gnome-decorated allotments' was how Sukhdev Sandhu saw this world and he argued that it is a 'rooted, but surreal northern landscape' that gives the films a specificity which compares extremely favourably with the bland universalism of most films aimed at children[15]. This is a good point: this film's cultural location, which Parks revealed was based on 1950s Wigan, is fundamental to the film's success and its crucial sense of difference. That it harks back to older British film-making traditions such as Ealing and Hammer is important in constructing a much wider sense of context. Equally, however, *Curse of the Were-Rabbit* makes very few concessions to the global marketplace and in particular the all-important US audience, although this was where Aardman found itself in a battle with its Hollywood financers on a number of points. The perfect marriage, it seems, was starting to fracture.

Katzenberg kept a close eye on the slow rate of production, flying into Bristol every few weeks to make 'suggestions'. At the time, Nick Park was quick to diffuse any hints of serious problems between the companies: 'We did have tensions, but they turned out to be quite creative. When Jeffrey came up with a suggestion, we'd go away and come up with a better one of our own.' Other members of the DreamWorks team were less subtle at hinting that some of the main characters needed to be younger or even have American accents. 'One of the complaints was that all the characters were "old". But I knew instinctively that to compromise the vision I had could ruin the whole thing' (de Bruxelles, ibid.). Another one of these battles concerned the use of the word 'marrows' which would have been incomprehensible to US audiences who call this vegetable a squash. To change the word would have meant restructuring Wallace's mouth and taken a number of days in terms of production time, so the word was changed to melon, as Park stated, 'If there is a culture clash, it mainly comes from the fact that DreamWorks are looking out for the American audience. It's not so much the east and west coasts, but that big majority in the middle. They're always reminding us of the difficulty they have in understanding British accents or terminology or labels for things. So we had a big thing with marrows' (Jeffries, ibid.).

The film was well received and well reviewed, with many British critics focusing on the film's lack of compromise in attempting to woo American audiences, with Dominic Wells going so far as to say that the film was 'as English as apple-scrumping, walking widdershins and losing on penalties'[16]. James Christopher enjoyed the film but was worried by 'the shelf-life of this precious franchise', observing that the film's tone was less innocent than previous Wallace and Gromit outings and that 'their feature films are doomed (I hope) to parody the perishable traditions of British film', which he saw as no bad thing[17]. What was of more concern to DreamWorks was the box-office gross, and after a good start in the US the film only took $56 million, although it did much better in the UK with £31 million. In a strange quirk of fate, in the same week as the British release of *Curse of the Were-Rabbit*, a massive fire destroyed the entire archive of Aardman Animations. Perhaps this was an ominous sign of things to come.

The third and, as it transpired, last film made by Aardman and their American backers was the disappointing *Flushed Away* (David Bowers and Sam Fell, 2006). Despite the poor box-office showing of *Curse of the Were-Rabbit*, it did triumph at the Oscars, making it a hat trick for Park, and there was immense pressure on *Flushed Away* to perform, especially stateside. It was also Aardman's first foray into CGI and most of the narrative took place in London's sewers where posh, spoilt mouse Roddy (Hugh Jackman) is trying to survive amongst the effluent of the city, and is pitted against an evil toad who wants to destroy the underworld rodent kingdom. The film, despite having the characters voiced by A-listers such as Kate Winslet, who plays the streetwise love interest Rita, and Sir Ian McKellen, who voices the villainous amphibian, feels flat and certainly lacks the distinctive signature of Aardman's other work. The specificity of place in the *Curse of the Were-Rabbit* feels rather shoe-horned in *Flushed Away*, which lacks the subtlety of Park's work, as Wendy Ide pointed out in her review: 'While Wallace and Gromit had an effortless and unforced Englishness, *Flushed Away* is heavy-handed. It flies the flag for brand Britain, but the tone is more Piccadilly Circus tourist trap than the quirky English-centric approach of the previous features'[18]. From the lazy allusion of McKellen's toad likened to a Bond villain, to Rita's Union Jack trousers, *Flushed Away* presents a simplistic, very stereotyped view of London life which feels tailored to attract audiences across the Atlantic. One of the more grating elements is the fact that the football World Cup final depicted in the film is between Britain and Germany, and this shows a real lack of research. The film had the largest budget of all those that DreamWorks and Aardman worked on, a reported whopping $143 million, but didn't perform blockbuster business, taking a creditable but not outstanding $64 million in its US theatrical run.

The writing seemed to be on the wall with reports of poor DVD sales for *Curse of the Were-Rabbit*, which meant that DreamWorks was forced to make a write-off on its 2005 results. Kim Leslie, chief financial officer of DreamWorks, said, 'We don't expect any significant earnings from this film in the future … It didn't achieve the consumer awareness that we'd hoped for'[19]. The main reason for this would appear to be the uniquely British style of humour and subject matter which failed to make the desired impact in the US in terms of both theatrical and non-theatrical sales, although the film did much better in the UK. It was no real shock then when DreamWorks decided to sever its ties with the Bristol-based studio in the winter of 2007, the spilt being attributed to different business goals, with the Hollywood studio deciding to invest in computer-generated features rather than the stop-motion techniques favoured by Aardman. Tim Robey's opinion that 'the match of Aardman's hand-made sensibility with [DreamWorks'] fiscal nous and canny marketing might have worked out, but in the long run they proved culturally incompatible' is an astute one[20].

The gap between the profit-driven DreamWorks with its high expectations for global reach and merchandising possibilities, and Aardman with its idiosyncratic, quirky world view, made strange bedfellows from the off and only made money on their first feature. That said, a couple of months after the announcement of the split from DreamWorks, Aardman made public details of a new deal with Sony-Columbia. The contract with the new partners was quite different, said David Sproxton, in that 'there is no deadline pressure. They [Sony] are less precious and we can discuss release dates when appropriate' (O'Connor, *The Times*, 03/04/2007)[21]. Although both Sproxton and Stephen Moore, the company's chief operating officers, were unwavering in their vision of Aardman's key strength – the unique sense of Britishness – they also saw the value of being in another arrangement with a Hollywood studio, 'making movies for a global market' as Sony-Columbia CEO Moore put it (O'Connor, ibid.). Only time will tell if the huge investment in the warm, strange world of a talented film-maker like Nick Park will pay financial dividends for its conglomerate backer, while retaining the distinctive nature of his work.

A WIZARD IDEA – THE OTHER-WORLDLY SUCCESS OF THE *HARRY POTTER* FRANCHISE

The story around the creation of the orphaned Harry Potter is almost worthy of a film itself. The book's author, Joanne Rowling, was a struggling single mother who hit on the idea of a novel about a young boy who slowly discovers that he has magical powers and is transported to Hogwarts, a school for aspiring wizards. The initial idea was hatched on a train journey from Manchester to London in 1990, complete with a four-hour delay, and by the time Rowling arrived at King's Cross station the genesis of the idea had been formulated. That said, it was not until her marriage broke up and she was relying on state benefits that the notion of this alternative world really started to take shape. The eventual book, entitled *Harry Potter and the Philosopher's Stone*, took a number of years to get to a final draft stage, and in 1996 it was finally accepted by Bloomsbury after being rejected by nine publishers. Joanne Rowling became the non-gender specific JK Rowling in a homage,

Daniel Radcliffe, *Harry Potter and the Chamber of Secrets*

perhaps, to those other titans of the British fantasy genre, CS Lewis and JRR Tolkien, and the first in a series of Harry-related titles was published. Little did anyone suspect at the time what a colossal success the novel would be: it sold an estimated 120 million copies in 200 countries, was translated into 47 languages and ultimately became one of the biggest-selling works of fiction of all time

The novel seemed to tap into an old-fashioned and typically British form of fantasy and, initially by word of mouth, it became very popular amongst children and adults alike. This was quickly followed by a number of sequels and Bloomsbury used varied marketing strategies to ensure the *Harry Potter* series' continued success: they published adult editions, complete with less conspicuous covers, organised extensive worldwide tours for the author to promote the books and steadfastly refused to release any preview copies until publication, thus building on high levels of reader anticipation. As the novels were published, bigger print runs and higher levels of security and hype were employed. Harry Potter had become a literary phenomenon, and it was inevitable that Hollywood would come calling.

Certainly the *Harry Potter* books had the perfect ingredients for the typical Hollywood family-orientated fare, beside, perhaps, the location for the main action. This was a ready-made franchise with an existing fan-base that would 'grow' with the films as they did with the novels. It had universal themes based on the conflict between good and evil, which were easily transferable to a global cinema audience. It also had tremendous merchandising and tie-in possibilities that would have strained even a large publisher like Bloomsbury. The special effects-led nature of many of the key scenes would have been well beyond the fiscal reality that many British film-makers were familiar with. Quite simply, the filmic Harry Potter could only be realised by a large American conglomerate, but the key fear around this, not least expressed by Rowling herself, was whether her creation would retain the essential sense of Britishness that is part of the Potter charm.

It was AOL-Time-Warner that was to provide the best deal for preserving the cultural distinctiveness for Rowling, and the film wing, Warner Bros, was willing to stay true to the spirit of the books. Rowling's initial deal for the rights was for the relatively small sum of £1 million, but she was entitled to a substantial cut of the film's profits, which was to prove a very good piece of business acumen. Warners did indeed stay very close to the structure and tone of the first novel and employed a slow-burning marketing campaign, in many respects creating the same sort of huge expectancy levels that greeted the publication of each new *Harry Potter* title. Of course, with this came the sort of enormous pressures that face any film version of an existing property that has established a very fixed notion of itself in the minds of the audience. Pottermania had already been rife for a number of years and the buzz around the build-up to the film's release was going to take full advantage of this, although there was still doubt as to whether a much-loved book could ever be fully realised by a Hollywood film company.

Colin Kennedy, deputy editor of Empire magazine, reflected the sense of unease and secrecy around the *Harry Potter and the Philosopher's Stone* production when he was quoted as saying: 'There is a lot riding on Harry Potter for Warner Bros. It was already a huge phenomenon – it's almost a matter of controlling the fan power already there. But there has been an awkwardness. It was filmed very much behind closed doors. Nobody has been allowed to review it and even when we do, each reviewer will have to have photo ID to see it' (Milmo, The Independent, 03/11/2001)[22]. Warners had put up well over $100 million in production costs to create the elaborate Hogwarts set and to adequately reflect the novel's main set-piece scenes, in particular where the eponymous hero is embroiled in a vicious game of Quidditch, and the film's climactic battle with the villain of the piece, Lord Voldemort. The *Harry Potter* film franchise looked on paper to be a certain success but it still had the potential to go horribly wrong if the book's massive fan-base were to reject it as not being what they expected. Warners attempted to offset this with an expensive print and advertising campaign, including a trailer that appeared six months before the film's release to give a taste of the film to a young audience who in many cases pestered their parents to go to the cinema just to see the 90-second taster. Hype came from all quarters: Jess Cagle from Time magazine, closely affiliated to AOL-Time-Warner, said that the film was one which had 'eye-popping grandeur' and 'dazzling special effects and sumptuous production' and there were huge advance bookings in Britain and America. In the UK alone, the Odeon cinema chain sold 200,000 seats in advance and Warner Village and UCI had 100,000 bookings each, which would bring the film's takings to over £3 million two weeks before it even opened (Milmo, ibid., 03/11/01). The film's use of a November theatrical window was also interesting. The book's narrative and setting fit this perfectly making it a clever move. The film was very much a winter's tale structured around the school year at Hogwarts, with much of the main action happening in the autumn term. The film worked as pure escape for cinema-going audiences, given its timing in the wake of the 9/11 attacks in the United States. This was something that no amount of Warners hype could have hoped for.

The film opened in mid-November 2001 and predictably did extremely well. So well, in fact, that it ultimately ended up as fourth on a list of all-time global box-office takings, with $968,657,891 (imdb. com) and at the time of writing it is still the highest grossing film in the UK with a gross of £66 million. What was interesting about Warner Brothers' approach was despite employing an American director, Chris Columbus, who had had a great deal of success with family films such as *Home Alone* (1990) and *Mrs Doubtfire* (1993), and an American screenwriter, Steve Kloves, the film, with its impressive cast of British acting talent, felt resolutely rooted in the mythical fantasyland of Rowling's imagination. The main roles of Harry (Daniel Radcliffe), Ron (Rupert Grint) and Hermione (Emma Watson) were all filled by young British actors and the cast-list included Richard Harris as Dumbledore, the Headmaster of Hogwarts, Dame Maggie Smith reprising her Jean Brodie role as the largely sympathetic Professor McGonagall, Alan Rickman as the sinister Professor Snape and Robbie Coltrane as the good-natured, hirsute Hagrid. With the addition of John Cleese wafting in and out as a friendly ghost and Ian Hart as the initially slight Professor Quirrel, who is revealed to be in league with Harry's nemesis Voldemort, the film uses the British cast to very good effect – with few real concessions here to an American audience by using Hollywood stars to plug the movie.

The film certainly promotes the slightly archaic view of Britain also evident in the Aardman movies, in particular *The Curse of the Were-Rabbit*. Although set in the 1990s, the film feels oddly like something from the 1950s, not so much in the carefully constructed *mise-en-scène*, but more in the way that it represents Harry and Hogwarts. The exposition of *The Philosopher's Stone* is interesting in the way that it depicts Harry as a neglected and unloved orphan looked after by his vile, Muggle (non-wizard) relatives the Dursleys (Richard Griffith and Fiona Shaw), forced to live under the stairs in petit bourgeois suburbia. Certainly the influence of Roald Dahl can be detected here, in particular Nicolas Roeg's adaptation of *The Witches* (1990), with its cloying repressive feel, appalling adults and abhorrence of any semblance of difference.

The steam-train journey across the beautiful English countryside transports the film back by about sixty years. Hogwarts itself is dressed in an overpowering Gothic grandeur that manages to combine the sublime – a typical British public school – and the surreal – moving staircases, talking hats, beheaded ghosts. Perhaps in the hands of a more visually astute director than Columbus, the stifling atmosphere of the place may well have echoed Lindsay Anderson's *If...* (1968), which managed to encapsulate the horrors of the boarding school in a dream-like and perceptive way. The early establishment of the house system certainly reinforces the old-fashioned feel of the text and quickly distinguishes the good – Gryffindor – against the bad – Slytherin. The uncertainty about the historical setting of the film is further enhanced by the students' school uniforms, complete with old-fashioned gowns. The film stays true to the novel, but the visual impact of costume and attitudes seems firmly fixed in the recent past. In many respects there are also hints at issues surrounding social class, namely the bullying of Ron Weasley because of his family background and, in particular, his rather shabby attire. Everything is played out espousing time-honoured British virtues of fair-play and decency. The archetypes are all present from the swotty, precocious Hermione and the upper-class elitist bully Draco to the cold-hearted, but strangely conflicted figure of Snape.

That said, the film itself isn't in the business of raising important social issues or even burying them in a standard high-concept film like this. On the surface, the first and many of the subsequent *Harry Potter* films bear little real relationship to life as it is lived in Britain today. They exist in a misty, nostalgic past and this film and its sequel, *Harry Potter and the Chamber of Secrets*, which was released the following year, do little to alter this view. The choice of Columbus as the director for both films may have a great deal to do with the mass-produced feel that permeates these movies and it is fair to say that they are safe, very worthy adaptations of the novels. They are also, as Jonathan Romney noted, 'critic-proof', and operate on a level for adults which is not at all as knowing as the Pixar or DreamWorks output: 'the Potter books are the only massively popular cultural product in Britain that its adult fans consume without any ironic distance whatsoever'[23].

David Thomson was less than complimentary about Columbus's ability to put 'magic' on the screen: 'There are people in history (Michael Powell or Jacques Demy) who might have made art here. There are some people alive (like Vincent Ward or Terry Gilliam) who might have produced something beautiful and startling. But AOL-Time-Warner is not in the business of being startled'[24]. There are nods to Ray Harryhausen-style monsters and Disney's *Snow White and the Seven Dwarfs* (1937) with magical mirrors, but the overarching feeling regarding *The Philosopher's Stone* was that it was no more than competent. Despite this, critic Philip French was quick to point out that it could certainly be compared to another great fantasy film from an earlier era: '*The Wizard of Oz* offered comfort to American children during the late years of the Depression and to their English counterparts in the early war years. *Harry Potter* affords hope of magical powers available to the brave, the decent and the resourceful in our own anxious times'[25]. Whatever remarks critics made, however, it was quickly apparent that Warner Brothers had found a cash-cow and this was to be fully exploited, with multi-million dollar deals with Coca-Cola and the production of merchandise designed to further enhance the brand and, by default, the subsequent films.

The second Potter film, *Harry Potter and the Chamber of Secrets* (2002) reprises the formula of the first and was also highly successful at the box office. It is a slightly more complex affair where hints of darker territory surrounding Harry's past, his relationship with Hogwarts and his battles with evil are dealt with efficiently. The film is still steeped in echoes of a recent half-imagined past with its preoccupations with class snobbery and its few ethnic children. It clocks in at a whopping three hours that is bound to test the endurance of even the biggest Potter fan. There are indications of teenage crushes here, but these are not acted upon at all, merely mentioned in dispatches. Sex does not encroach from the real world beyond a few knowing glances and embarrassed reactions. New characters such as Gilderoy Lockhart (Kenneth Branagh), a charlatan writer who is employed at Hogwarts as a teacher, are played strictly for laughs, and the inclusion of Dobbie, a strange, mischievous elf, is a clear nod to any number of *Star Wars* characters.

One of the most interesting comparisions was one that Charlotte O'Sullivan made between this film and Neil Jordan's adaptation of Patrick McCabe's *The Butcher Boy* (1997), which sees a virtual orphan, Francie Brady, become locked in a battle with an aspirational housewife who spoils her only son, then gets sent off to an institution in the country, where it becomes obvious that he can see and hear things that others can't. This place, run by a religious order, is dangerous, and Francie becomes more and more aggressive. Voices in his head tell him to kill and as the narrative progresses, the audience realise that he has tipped into madness[26]. The plot of The Butcher Boy resonates here and, as O'Sullivan notes, shares the same unsympathetic matriarch in Fiona Shaw. Chamber of Secrets invests a great deal of time in establishing a sense of paranoia and fear around Hogwarts, including a sense of self-doubt about Harry's own sanity. That said, this is a far less ambitious film than Jordan's, in which the slow psychological decline of Francie is both visually stunning and shocking. This is, after all, a big-budget film which seeks to appeal to a global mass audience, but regarding Thomson's earlier point about the lack of artistry in Columbus's direction, it would be interesting to see the film in the hands of somebody like Jordan. Although Chamber of Secrets does touch on the racism aimed at half-Muggle students like Hermione, it falls short of any real debate. The film's rather simplistic and self-congratulatory resolution omits any sense of threat or movement from the first instalment of the series. Although Warner Brothers kept the highly successful modus operandi from the first instalment intact by employing a cast of strong British character actors and by staying close to the original source material, it was generally felt that some elements should change in order to keep the franchise fresh.

The very nature of the co-production often suggests that a global combination of talents come together, and by and large the first two Harry Potter films were seen as matching a capable, crowd-pleasing American director with a hugely successful novel set in the United Kingdom and a talented ensemble British cast. By the third film, Harry Potter and the Prisoner of Azkaban (2004), Columbus was moved upstairs to oversee producer duties and the surprise choice for the director's chair was the Mexican, Alfonso Cuaron. Cuaron had some profile in Britain, mainly amongst cinephiles, and had done pretty well with his art-house film Y tu mamá también (2001). Certainly, Cuaron's appointment was intended to shake up the franchise and in terms of its visual impact it certainly did that.

Cuaron's approach was one that concentrated more on the central character's journey, building on themes of encroaching adolescence which Rowling herself was starting to highlight in the novel: 'For me everything came down to the theme … the story of one kid trying to find his identity as a teenager. And together with that is a journey of discovery – he's accessing his male energy, his father energy inside. And what I mean is that he gets an identification of an energy' (interview on uk.movies.gn.com[27]).

The film was a great deal darker than the first two, both visually and thematically, with Harry coming to terms with the demise of his parents and focusing on the burgeoning friendships with his sidekicks Ron and Hermione. As David Edelstein is keen to highlight, 'the palette of this film is scarier: The contrasts are higher, the blacks deeper, and Cuaron irises in and out of many scenes like a silent Expressionist master. The colours reflect a new uncertainty'[28]. Cuaron is also unafraid to confront the audience with sweeping camera movements and zooms giving the film a highly kinetic atmosphere. If anything, the beauty and invention of Michael Seresin's cinematography and Steven Craig's elaborate, thoughtful set design seems to be stifled by some of the predictability of the plot. This is something that James Christopher points out: 'Cuaron favours wide-angle lenses, and you could spend weeks drooling over the artwork in a single scene. If there is a weakness in the film, it lies in a fiendishly ornate plot and the director's blind faith in our ability to follow it'[29]. The narrative does certainly twist and turn and at times it can be somewhat impenetrable, perhaps relying a little too much on the audience having read the novel, but it is clear that with its summer release and the change of director (although retaining the same screenwriter, Steve Kloves), Warner Brothers was hoping for a shift in emphasis for the series. An example of this is the way that linearity is fragmented when we see Ron dragged into a frightening underground warren. This is then shown from different perspectives, and by reversing the time-flow the three heroes attempt to alter the events. It is a brave move in a film mainly targeted at children.

The tension of the third instalment of the franchise was augmented by the inclusion of an escaped prisoner, Sirius Black, played by a hardly recognisable Gary Oldman, who is apparently out to kill Harry after being involved in the death of his parents. The relationship of Black and Harry is what carries the narrative and there is a palpable sense of expectation as Black doesn't appear until well into the story. There are nods to Charles Dickens in the way that this relationship is formulated and in particular *Great Expectations*, which had also been previously adapted rather unsuccessfully by Cuaron, who placed the story in a modern, American setting. The spirit of Edgar Allan Poe is reinforced in the gothic horror show with the Dementors, mysterious skeletal creatures who are in pursuit of Black and whose main ability is to suck the souls out of bodies.

Cuaron's direction is assured and supported by yet more British character actors, such as David Thewlis as the intelligent but creepy Professor Lupin and Emma Thompson as the overly enthusiastic, dotty Professor Sybil Trelawney. Interestingly, Michael Atkinson in his piece on the film picks up on the fact that with the casting of Oldman, Thewlis, Pam Ferris and Timothy Spall, 'the producers have this time consulted Mike Leigh's Rolodex'[30]. The film is some distance from a piece of intense social realism set on a grim council estate in south London, but these actors do add a sense of vigour to the proceedings, in particular Thewlis as the knowing, enigmatic Lupin.

Even with its darker tone and less crowd-pleasing aspects, *Prisoner of Azkaban* once again did very good business without matching the huge take of the first two films. In the fourth film, *Harry Potter and the Goblet of Fire* (2005), director Mike Newell was hired to take the helm and seemingly it was his flexibility in a variety of genres that appeared attractive to the producers. His best known film, *Four Weddings and a Funeral* (1994), was a massive worldwide hit, cementing Hugh Grant's status as an A-List star and Working Title's profile as the UK's most successful production company. He had also made the creditable gangster film *Donnie Brasco* (1997) and the acclaimed costume drama *Enchanted April* (1992). Newell's view on his directorial vision of *Goblet of Fire* was, primarily, to think of it in terms of a thriller:

'I was explaining my idea of the story to Dan (Radcliffe), and he said, "What have you been watching?" I told him, paranoid thrillers: *Three Days of the Condor*, *The Parallax View*, *North by Northwest*. They're all about people who don't know what's happening to them. I told him specifically to watch *North by Northwest*, because there you are, it's a sunny afternoon, you're happy with your life, but suddenly stuff starts happening, and then you're up against the bad guy, who had plans for you all along. That's exactly what happens to Harry Potter in this book. I found you could make a movie so driven by Voldemont's agenda that you'd be in a very stressed, creepy world from the beginning, and you'd stalk Harry all the way through.'[31]

Goblet of Fire does retain some of the gloom of Cuaron's film and undoubtedly Newell's conception of it as a paranoid thriller has some validity in terms of the quick nature of the film's plotting, in particular drawing out some of the subtleties around characterisation. The film is structured around an event involving three schools, including Hogwarts, in a Quidditch world cup. The tradition of the suspect new teacher is also played out with the introduction of Mad-Eye Moody, acted with real gusto by Brendan Gleeson.

Newell deals efficiently with Harry and his friends' trials and growing pains, for example the awkwardness of asking a girl out, in this case a fellow student called Cho Chang (Katie Leung). There is a sense in the franchise that the characters are actually appealing directly to the experience of their intended audience with each new instalment. Although *Goblet of Fire* follows key conventions explored in the first two films, it does retain the darkness of Cuaron's vision of Rowling's work. There is a distinct sense of unease that permeates the *mise-en-scène* that has as much to do with the disturbance of adolescence as with the plot. This was something that one of the film's reviewers particularly highlighted: 'The public-school cosiness ebbs away: Hogwarts is no longer a cheerful haven, and its headmaster Dumbledore appears not as an all-wise paterfamilias but an old man scared of the future … Newell's film captures the queasy recognition that accompanies the earliest stirrings of puberty, that parents are flawed, that home is not necessarily safe, that the world at large is unjust'[32]. The film itself does have the large-scale climactic showdown with the revelation of Gleeson's character as loyal to Potter's nemesis Voldemort, but is very much a film in the middle of a franchise setting up narrative strands and developing character relationships that would only be further explored in the later films. The success story did continue, with this film taking nearly $900 million worldwide at the box office and £48 million in Britain alone.

At the time of writing we have reached the sixth instalment of the saga, *Harry Potter and the Half-Blood Prince* (2009). David Yates, a BAFTA-winning television director was hired for both this film and its predecessor, *Harry Potter and the Order of the Phoenix* (2007). In *Phoenix* there was a slight shift away from the darkness and sadness of the third and fourth episodes, with a return to a relatively uncomplicated action-adventure narrative. There is, however, an interesting strand here which places a character called Dolores Umbridge, played by Imelda Staunton (yet another actor to have worked successfully with Mike Leigh on *Vera Drake*), as the by now obligatory new teacher, who has been sent by the Ministry of Magic to spy on events at the school and in effect to undermine Dumbledore's running of Hogwarts. What is interesting about Umbridge's character is the way that it can be seen to act as a thinly-veiled critique of successive British governments' obsession with school results, teaching methods and the climate of change that has left schools in a state of constant flux. She covers the walls of her classroom with a number of meaningless orders, her teaching is through a deathly dull textbook-led approach with little or no variation. She pompously lectures in a pointless argot, but she is also driven by a cruel streak, resorting quite easily to corporal punishment.

The Ministry of Magic itself is seen as a corrupt entity, driven by a desire for secrecy and involved in torture and the distortion of truth. Dumbledore is discredited and Umbridge is appointed headteacher. Potter and his acolytes style themselves as Dumbledore's army and prepare to do battle to reinstate their beleaguered mentor. The psychological battles that Harry encounters are much more pressing, as he seems to be frequently aggressive towards the world, which might be put down to the tribulations of being a teenager, but has more to do with the continuing power of Voldemort to infiltrate the boy's mind with disturbing visions. Most of the film's pre-release coverage centred on Harry's first kiss with Cho Chang, and although this is understated she now drops out of the narrative altogether. As a reviewer pointed out, 'Perhaps Harry is not entirely ready to leave the asexual world of childhood after all'[33].

Once again, the film takes the form of the series of complications to be overcome, moving towards a set-piece confrontation and a clear sense of resolution; in this case a battle with Voldemort in Harry's brain which he repels with memories of love and friendship and the return of Dumbledore to Hogwarts. The film continued the brand's success with a worldwide gross of $938 million. In September 2007 the *Harry Potter* series became the most successful in box-office history, earning a combined $2.2 billion at global cinemas and overtaking both the *James Bond* and *Star Wars* franchises. At the time Warner Brothers' US distribution president, Dan Fellman, remarked, 'It is a thrill to see the Harry Potter franchise reach this unparalleled mark. With two movies yet to come, it is amazing to think what heights the franchise could reach by the end of the decade'[34]. There is no doubting the appeal of the films: the sense of growing up with the actors, the progression of themes and the appeal to a dedicated and wide audience, often fans of the books. The films have been responsible for massive inward investment in terms of the production process, all filmed in the UK. They have also exposed a wealth of acting talent in all the major roles, but do these films reveal anything about Britain itself?

In many respects they are deeply conservative films, with the emphasis on gifted young wizards educated in a public-school environment, but as the series progressed there was more of a multicultural use of extras. There are allusions to class, in particular Ron's persona, but the central motif seems to be the conflict between Muggle and pure-blood characters, and in exploring this the films do offer a commentary on prejudice. The films echo the novels in that they offer a traditional sense of British fair-play in the battle between good and evil. The French philosopher Jean-Claude Milner went so far as to say that the novels (and by extension the films) are diatribes against Thatcherite Britain, with Hogwarts offering a means of resistance against a triumphant middle class represented by the non-magic Muggles, in particular the Dursleys. The Muggles are seen as materialistic whereas Hogwarts offers a refuge for the minority who want to protect civilisation from the dangers of globalisation. He does not view Hogwarts as an elitist institution, instead seeing it as offering real equality where Hermione – a child of Muggles – can outperform the pure-blooded Malfoy. In this, he stressed, *Harry Potter* is a war-machine against Thatchero-Blairism and the 'American way of life'[35]. In terms of retaining its sense of Britishness, Milner's points have some validity. The films are rooted more in one-nation conservatism in the way themes of equality and betterment are explored, and there is a rejection of the suburban values of the Dursleys. Hogwarts as a community is fragmented with its house system, yet comes together in times of crisis and it is the newcomers to the school who by and large upset the natural order. Finally, what the franchise does suggest is that a British intellectual property can have huge global success whilst retaining its initial distinctiveness even though a large Hollywood conglomerate is calling the shots. Unlike Aardman's fitful relationship with DreamWorks, the marriage has been a long, abiding and fruitful one and this has encouraged Hollywood to tackle similar texts such as Phillip Pullman's *The Golden Compass* (2007) and the CS Lewis *Narnia* novels, albeit with mixed results. Only time will tell if the complete series will rank alongside Peter Jackson's *Lord of the Rings* trilogy (2001–03) in terms of gravitas, but what the films do provide is an excellent case-study in how the combination of American money and an existing, highly successful British 'brand' can be a colossal global triumph at the box-office, on DVD and in the shops.

REFERENCES

1. Parker, A., Building a Sustainable UK Film Industry, 05/11/2002

2. Seminar on the Cultural Value of UK Film, UK Film Council document, 03/05/2005

3. Branston, G., Cinema and Cultural Modernity, Oxford: OUP, 2000

4. Lister, D., 'Wallace and Gromit creator in £150m Spielberg deal' in The Independent, 29/10/1999

5. Gibson, O., 'A one-off quirky thing' in The Guardian, 21/07/2008

6. Wachs, J., 'Fire, Water and Gravy: The Secrets of *Chicken Run*' on Reel.com

7. Buss, R., ' It's a clucking good show' in The Independent on Sunday, 11/06/2000

8. Newman, K., Review of *Chicken Run* in Sight and Sound, August 2000

9. Pulver, A., 'Whose film is it anyway?' in The Guardian, 27/06/200

10. De Bruxelles, S., 'British humour and Plasticine puts Hollywood glitz to shame' in The Times, 15/10/2005

11. Otto, J., Interview with Nick Park on ign.com, 04/10/2005

12. Jefferies, S., 'Lock up your vegetables' in The Guardian, 16/09/2005

13. Osmond, A., Review of *Wallace and Gromit: Curse of the Were-Rabbit* in Sight and Sound, December 2005

14. Quinn, A., Review of *Wallace and Gromit: Curse of the Were-Rabbit* in The Independent, 14/10/2005

15. Sandhu, S., Review of *Wallace and Gromit: Curse of the Were-Rabbit* in The Daily Telegraph, 14/10/2005

16. Wells, D., Review of *Wallace and Gromit: Curse of the Were-Rabbit* in The Times, 10/10/2005

17. Christopher, J., 'A rabbit will run and run' in The Sunday Times, 13/10/2005

18. Ide, W., Review of *Flushed Away* in The Times, 30/11/2006

19. Sabbagh, D., 'Wallace and Gromit is a DreamWorks loser' in The Times, 11/03/2006

20. Robey, T., 'The strained marriage between Aardman and DreamWorks' in The Daily Telegraph, 02/02/2007

21. O'Connor, R. 'Aardman refuses to drop British accent to make it in movies' in The Times, 03/04/2007

22. Milmo, C., 'Harry Potter film giant unleashes black arts of spin' in The Independent, 03/11/2001

23. Romney, J., Review of *Harry Potter and the Philosopher's Stone* in The Independent on Sunday, 18/11/2001

24. Thomson, D., 'It might be magic, but is 'Harry' really British?' in The Independent, 26/11/2001

25. French, P., Review of *Harry Potter and the Philosopher's Stone* in The Observer, 19/11/2001

26. O'Sullivan, C., Review of *Harry Potter and the Chamber of Secrets* in The Independent, 15/11/2002

27. Head, S., Interview with Alfonso Cuaron on uk.movies,gn.com, 02/06/2004

28. Edelstein, D., 'The Plot Against Harry' in Slate, 03/04/2004

29. Christopher, J., Review of *Harry Potter and The Prisoner of Azkaban* in The Times, 27/05/2004

30. Atkinson, M., 'Dirty Harry' in Village Voice, 25/05/2004

31. Newell, M. quoted in Gritten, D., 'I was so fearful of breaking the spell' in The Daily Telegraph, 28/10/2005

32. Barnes, J., Review of *Harry Potter and the Goblet of Fire* in Sight and Sound, January 2006

33. Bradshaw, P., Review of *Harry Potter and the Order of the Phoenix*, 25/07/2007

34. Franklin, K., 'Harry Potter films bigger than James Bond' in The Daily Telegraph, 13/09/2007

35. Staff and agencies, 'Harry Potter lives in Thatcher's Britain' in The Daily Telegraph, 29/10/2007

NEW HERITAGE CINEMA — RED BUSES IN THE RAIN

INTRODUCTION

The term heritage film has many connotations and this chapter hopes to position a new type of heritage film that, rather than having an emphasis on the historical, will instead invoke a new type of Britishness, or in this case, Englishness. Sheldon Hall sees heritage cinema as a critical construct; a linked body of films which invoke a common sense of British history, literature and/or an 'approved' cultural tradition. These films had a particular prestige value which was a central feature in their marketing campaigns and their view of Britain made them very desirable to not only domestic but a growing export audience (p191, 2001)[1]. Andrew Higson's work on a cycle of these films was extremely influential; he placed late-1980s films such as *Another Country* (Kanievska, 1984), *A Room with a View* (Ivory, 1986), *Maurice* (Ivory, 1987) and *Howard's End* (Ivory, 1992) within the political context of Thatcherism, seeing the heritage genre/style as symptomatic of middle-class denial of present day social conflicts (Street, 1997, p104)[2].

There has been a slight movement away from the traditional heritage film in this decade with only a few examples that might match the original definition, such as *Pride and Prejudice* (Wright, 2005) and *Elizabeth – The Golden Age* (Kapoor, 2007). The election of New Labour in 1997 with its modernist agenda and the continuing economic upturn of the late 1990s and early Noughties saw a significant shift in these types of heritage film being made at the high end of the industry. I believe that both of these socio-political factors have contributed to a widening of the heritage tag, by primarily locating films in present-day London and tapping into this newfound sense of monetary confidence. Films such as Working Title's *About a Boy* and *Love Actually*; *Closer*, *Breaking and Entering* and *Notes on a Scandal* all examine the city in different ways, exploring elements of the changing metropolis by focusing on class, cultural difference, sexual deceit and reconstituted family structures within a middle- or upper-middle-class framework. *The Queen* and *Atonement* also tackle some of these themes within a different time period: the recent past of 1997 in *The Queen* and *Atonement* concentrating on the years leading up to and during the Second World War. What is also worth highlighting is the use of a leading British star (Hugh Grant, Jude Law, Helen Mirren, Judi Dench and Keira Knightley) for each film and in common with the earlier heritage films, there is as much a concentration on the *mise-en-scène* as the narrative. The typical, highly recognisable shots of London are all present and certainly seek to increase the export value of each film. The role of the screenplay or the original source novel is also given a degree of importance in the wider marketing adding to a sense of the literary, which harks back to the original notion of heritage. The Working Title films do offer a much more generic standpoint and suggest more positive outcomes generally, but there are some indications that these films are at least trying to explore issues around middle-class protagonists in a more European way in the recent tradition of directors like François Ozon and Michael Haneke. Darker themes are dealt with, such as an overarching sense of middle-class angst which is kick-started by an invasive character(s) into seemingly perfect lives as in *About a Boy, Closer, Notes on a Scandal* and *Breaking and Entering*. These films also explore the clash between the progressive and traditional stances on attitudes to social class and bowing to the 'norms' of the day as in *The Queen* and *Atonement*. In their own different ways the films in this chapter offer a popularist, exportable cinema visualising a snapshot of Blair's Britain, as represented perhaps by London as a place where the liberal middle classes are grappling with their own sense of identity in a city/country where the old class and ethnic certainties have become less clear. Whether this is just a crude representation is what the central thrust of the argument aims to provide.

WORKING TITLE — A VERY BRITISH SUCCESS STORY

(l-r) Nicholas Hoult, Toni Collete and Hugh Grant, *About a Boy*

It is interesting that the production company most associated with the new heritage strain of film-making in Britain has a diverse portfolio of projects which question this assumption. These films range from the company's first major venture, the controversial Thatcher-baiting *My Beautiful Laundrette*, to the dark political American satire *Bob Roberts* (Robbins, 1992), cult comedy-noir *The Big Lebowski* (Coen, 1998) and the rom-com zombie hit *Shaun of the Dead*. That said, the association with the screenwriter/director Richard Curtis and the actor Hugh Grant is what has established Working Title's main signature, which at its core presents a middle-class, London-centric view of Britain and utilises romantic-comedy conventions to present a version of life in the United Kingdom that is tremendously popular globally, especially in America. Many of Working Title's films have been enormously profitable and have benefited from a distribution deal with Universal that has seen huge box-office receipts. Both screen adaptations of Helen Fielding's highly successful Bridget Jones novels took well over $260 million each, *Love Actually* made $247 million at the box office, while *Mr Bean's Holiday* took a staggering $229 million (www.thenumbers.com). The director Stephen Frears has said that Working Title has 'learnt to make films for export' and the star most linked with the production company, Hugh Grant, has stated of the films, 'They are energetic, not naïve, not arty-farty, or up their own arse'[3].

The template for some of its most successful films was set by *Four Weddings and a Funeral*, written by Richard Curtis. Hugh Grant plays Charles, a middle-class, professional and romantic failure, who falls in love with Carrie (Andie McDowell), an American beauty who would appear to be out of his league, whom he loses and then wins back. He is surrounded by a group of supportive friends who provide the major subplots and the film ends by reinforcing the belief that love conquers all. The incredibly profitable *Notting Hill*, once again with a screenplay by Curtis, follows a remarkably similar plot-line with Grant playing William, a bookshop owner who falls in love with Anna, a huge Hollywood star, played with a great deal of irony by Julia Roberts; again he loses her and then has to declare his love for her. In their depiction of romantic love between the main British and American protagonists the films implicitly explore the so called 'special relationship' between the two countries, but also were able to attract a large audience Stateside by using a high profile female A list star despite the British setting. It is clear that both films hit upon a highly successful formula: 'Curtis's trick ... has been to make the parochial global. He's a big Englander: someone who, like Richard Branson, gambled that his personal values might be more widely shared' (Lawson, The Guardian, 13/11/2003)[4].

Although Working Title has moved into different genres and styles in this decade, it is clear that the winning recipe has been revisited, but with slight variations, in *About a Boy* and *Love Actually*, which in their own ways provide interesting examinations of life in London and use the star image of Hugh Grant to good effect. *About a Boy*, based on Nick Hornby's novel, and adapted by the American screenwriter Peter Hedges rather than Curtis, offered an interesting change to the Grant archetype established in *Four Weddings* and *Notting Hill*. He plays Will Freeman, a feckless thirty-something bachelor, living very comfortably off the proceeds of his father's estate, who decides to seek out vulnerable single mothers in an attempt to seduce them. He sparks up a friendship with Marcus (Nicholas Hoult), the 12-year-old son of suicidal, depressive Fiona (Toni Collette), but eventually finds romance and responsibility with another single parent, Rachel (Rachel Weitz). In *Love Actually* he plays the new Prime Minister who falls in love with his tea-lady Natalie (Martine McCutcheon). This is set against the backdrop of ten other narratives in a portmanteau structure, all examining different variations of the love story, the stories being loosely connected by the characters' various relationships with each other. *Love Actually*, directed and written by Curtis, posits the view that even in these post- 9/11 times, the simple act and expression of love could overcome all the tragedy in the world.

About a Boy presents a view of London which is rooted in the same sort of rose-tinted view of the capital as perpetuated by the earlier Curtis films. Will lives in a tasteful apartment, surrounded by the accoutrements of the stunted life of the single man: a range of DVDs, books, gadgets, widescreen television. At the start of the film he is at home in the middle of the day watching *Countdown*, deliberately misquoting John Donne to suggest that every man is in fact an island, outlining his 'stand alone' philosophy on life. He is a blank, a man able to make only the very slightest connections with the outside world and only then for his own pleasure. The film follows his slow entry into the wider world and presents Will as searching for redemption for a life which up until now has been without ambition or direction. He is obsessed with his appearance and this shallowness is what defines him initially. In his review, Philip French sees the film adaptation of Hornby's novel as viewing the past as personal nostalgia and the future as a dull threat. The characters, he feels, have abandoned concern for community, politics and idealism, their commitment is to friends, coteries, football teams and pop groups[5]. To an extent this is true of Will. He is cosseted by the royalty cheques and he lives a life that revolves around visits to music megastores, expensive restaurants and exclusive wine-bars. It is only by the chance entry into his life of Marcus that he begins the process of becoming a rounded individual.

Fiona, Marcus's mother, a slightly bohemian hippy, teaches music. She is an extreme example of the vegan liberal archetype and doesn't provide any romantic interest for Will. Her well-meaning inflexibility regarding Marcus in terms of how he dresses creates problems for him at his local comprehensive. It is only with her unsuccessful suicide attempt that darkness enters the narrative and a sense of reality hits home in Will's life.

Marcus's relationship with Will doesn't make him a father figure. He is more of a slightly off-kilter uncle, bestowing time and money on his young charge. However, he does seem to oversimplify the notion of helping Marcus with his problems at school, by purchasing an expensive pair of trainers for him, which Marcus is promptly mugged for. What *About a Boy* does highlight is the disparate nature of living in the capital and although it doesn't quite get the sense of difference experienced by Marcus in the classroom right, there is a sense of middle-class angst in a number of scenes between the boy and Fiona. Although Marcus is clearly not happy, there is little that his mother or the teachers seem able to do about it. Fiona's psychological problems exacerbate this, but her connection with the real world is as flawed as Will's. Will, in his carefree way, provides a more worldly approach to life, while Fiona sticks to her own rigid codes founded on a well-meaning political-correctness and opposition to the mainstream. Although the film does develop a romance for Will with Rachel, this feels like a subplot rather than the main focus of the narrative. It only serves to further draw Will into the real world and an extended family, one that brings complications. London is a place where connections can be made, even with the most diverse range of characters and in this case it does follow the traditional Working Title method. That said, at the end of the film there is a note of slight awkwardness on Will's face as he is surrounded by his newfound community.

The film is scored by Badly Drawn Boy and the slightly melancholic acoustic feel of the music underpins some of the key sequences, especially when Marcus finds Fiona's suicide note and 'A Minor Incident' plays on the soundtrack. It is also interesting how the American directors and writer offer such a well-observed reading of Englishness; this is certainly true in Fiona's Christmas party scene, which has shades of Mike Leigh in its observation of social embarrassment, and in Will's first meeting as the only man at

Spat (Single Parents Alone Together). Grant's wonderfully nuanced performance as Will is appropriately classless and counters his usual on-screen persona, although his wealth in this film does give him access to the trappings of an upper middle-class existence especially in kick-starting his relationship with the successful Rachel whom he meets at a swanky New Year's party. Although *About a Boy* works well because it offers a sense of closure, doubts remain around whether Will is fully convinced by this transformation. The attendant themes of depression, loneliness, fear and deception also counter the apparent sunny disposition of the narrative.

Love Actually's marketing campaign during the winter of 2003 touted the film as a pre-Christmas star fest and was heavily hyped as Richard Curtis's directorial debut. Its multilayered structure, with Grant's strand located near the centre, was a move away from the more linear approaches of *Notting Hill* and *Four Weddings*.

Bill Nighy (centre, obviously) and admirers, *Love Actually*

However, this feels an altogether more mainstream proposition than other portmanteau films like Robert Altman's *Short Cuts* (1994) or Paul Thomas Anderson's *Magnolia* (1999), and rather than developing as a state-of-the-nation address, the film concentrates instead on the personal and only makes occasional nods to address the political. It is a bright, glossy film which plays out nine intertwining love stories in the month leading up to Christmas. *Love Actually* posits the opinion, loud and clear, that love can solve all woe and only in a couple of scenes does the film veer into anything remotely dealing with the complex nature of relationships. As a result, these narrative strands are by far the strongest and, in *Love Actually*'s worldview, the most believable. Liam Neeson plays Daniel, a grieving widower left to cope with a 10-year-old stepson Sam (Thomas Sangster). Although the story implies rather improbably that the boy has fallen in love with a young American classmate, it primarily concentrates on his developing relationship with Daniel, which is slightly reminiscent of *About a Boy*. Karen (Emma Thompson) is being cheated on by her husband Harry (Alan Rickman) and in one of the better scenes, while opening Christmas presents she struggles to hide her realisation that Harry is having an affair. But in Curtis's universe she forgives Harry and a sense of resolution is met.

Hugh Grant plays David, the recently elected Prime Minister. He is a handsome, eligible bachelor, in many respects the polar opposite of the last singleton to occupy Number 10, Edward Heath. He has Blair's charm and some of his media savvy, but where the story falls down is in the romance that he strikes up with the young, attractive working-class

tea-lady Natalie. Even allowing for the conventions of the romantic comedy, this is stretching the boundaries of believability. Lawrence Napper does suggest that the loose affiliation of acquaintances, friends and work colleagues may well be a metaphor for the nation as a whole. He goes on to point out 'that the film dares to fantasise a utopian version of [the] nation in which barriers of class, power and language are permeable in the face of love' (in Nelmes (ed), p328, 2007)[6]. While this may be the case in the central love story, this statement is more problematic when looking at the film as a whole. The major emphasis is on the middle classes, and the tasteful *mise-en-scène* of the homes and the largely office-bound, but unspecified nature of their jobs, totally reinforce this. The real London is never allowed to intrude; the film is bathed in an artificial yuletide glow, the lives of the protagonists are sheltered from the travails of money worries and living in the capital. Catering assistant Colin (Kris Marshall) can't find love in London so he hops on a plane and on arrival in the United States automatically finds himself picked up by three pretty young women. Mark (Andrew Lincoln) arranges a seemingly impromptu rendition of 'All You Need is Love' at his friend's wedding, complete with gospel choir and over-the-top guitar solo. Everything is possible in *Love Actually* as in many of the other Working Title films and especially those films that Curtis has had a hand in. Robert Murphy has suggested that these films show life in Britain as exciting, glamorous and full of romantic possibilities, and are constructed as fairy tales with archetypes. They offer straightforward closure set against the backdrop of London, a 'city of delights'. Crucially he also suggests that these films are

> 'remarkable for [their] evacuation of class conflict and their conservative representation of society, it is less a matter of sympathy switching from the poor and oppressed to the privileged and successful, than of rapprochement, a papering over the rifts that opened up between rich and poor, losers and winners in the 1980s.' (Murphy, 2001, p. 298)[7]

Love Actually's clear avoidance of any sort of class conflict can be compared with, as Ben Walters points out, the film's 'confused transatlanticism' (*Sight and Sound*, December 2003). What is interesting is that although *Love Actually* offers a dreamscape akin to Hollywood with a narrative that could be easily relocated to New York or Los Angeles, it is unsure of the relationship between America and Britain so cleverly exploited by Curtis in the past. Although Chris finds sexual gratification in America and the main American character Sarah (Laura Linney) is written sympathetically, the film's primary representation of 'the special relationship' is played out between Grant's PM and the also newly elected US President (Billy Bob Thornton). Using his status and power, the President makes a pass at Natalie who swiftly rejects him and is witnessed by David, the PM. Previous to this we have seen the President's bullying and arrogant nature regarding foreign policy clearly spelt out, which by and large David has agreed with. In a press conference afterwards

David astounds the President and his own cabinet (who advised him to take a more rigorous stance against the bullying Americans) by standing up for Britain. Invoking Shakespeare, Churchill, The Beatles and even Harry Potter and against the backdrop of patriotic, stirring music, he states that the special relationship will now be on a more even keel. Although, as Napper suggests, this part of the film could well be read within the context of the war in Iraq and liberal anxieties that the Labour government had become a mere pawn in aiding an illegal invasion, it is as much a reaction about David's inability to express his true feelings for Natalie. This is, however, not examined in any depth regarding the obvious gulf in class and status between them. Although Napper quite correctly states that the scene is remarkable given the dependence on the American market, it is clear that David's outburst is as much about a perceived slight by his tea-lady. In many respects he is as ridiculous a character as the oversexed President.

Both *About a Boy* and *Love Actually* continued the success of Working Title in the United States, but the general consensus was that by the second film the game was up. 'Curtis's scenic Thames shots, meanwhile, seem to be his picture-postcard love letters to the US audiences his films have always aspired to impress. That in fact is by far the most convincing courtship *Love Actually* has to offer' was *Sight and Sound*'s perspective (Walters, ibid), while The Guardian felt that 'none of the little plots are all that funny or humanly convincing and none has room to breathe or develop'[8]. But despite slightly underperforming at the US box office, the film still took $60 million. This vapid and overtly superficial film, as Murphy suggested, skirts around showing any form of real conflict, instead opting for a middle-class utopia or as Paul Dave has suggested in writing about *Notting Hill*, a 'metropolitan idyll' which he sees as being 'imbued with an aura in which challenges to the social world it represents become unimaginable' (2006, p46)[9]. However, two films that do offer a somewhat more caustic and cynical view of middle-class London existence are *Closer* and *Breaking and Entering*, which while placed in a similar class-bound milieu as the Working Title films, deal with tensions both within and outside this constraint. Both films also seek to exploit the very different star personas of Jude Law.

SEX, LIES AND LOTS OF WORDS AMONGST THE CHATTERING CLASSES

Although *Closer*, with its big American backing from Sony-Columbia, its experienced American director, Mike Nichols (*The Graduate* [1967] and *Carnal Knowledge* [1971]) and the seemingly obligatory huge stars in Julia Roberts and Natalie Portman, feels like a mid-budget Hollywood project, it is firmly rooted in England. With its London settings, focus on the foibles of the middle classes and the American love interests in Roberts and Portman, *Closer* might, on a superficial level, be said to resemble a Working Title film. But the subject matter surrounding infidelity, lust, failure and secrecy is a million miles away from the work of Richard Curtis. Even Roberts' star-turn is extremely understated and although Nichols' camera does linger on that famous face on occasion, this is kept to a minimum.

Natalie
Portman, *Closer*

Closer was based on the highly successful 1997 stage play by Patrick Marber, who also wrote the script for the film. James Christopher's review of the film placed the play within its context at the cusp of the New Labour era under Tony Blair and the sweeping away of 'the torpor of John Major's Britain. Swinging London hadn't quite re-emerged, but the play caught the mood of the times which coupled the cynicism of the period, with the main players performing 'an indefinite and seemingly interminable dance of relationship swivels'[10].

However, the film is set in the present and centres on interweaving plots between four main characters. Dan (Jude Law) is a disillusioned journalist who writes obituaries and who falls in love with a young American girl, Alice (Portman). It transpires that Alice has had an interesting past and with this she provides the stimulus for him to write his first novel. We see him a year later being photographed for publicity shots by Anna (Roberts). He makes a clumsy pass at her and is rebuffed. Alice is aware of this. Out of spite Dan sets up a false meeting with a doctor, Larry (Clive Owen), while posing as Anna in a sex chatroom. However, this idea backfires when Larry and Anna meet and hit it off. At one of Anna's exhibitions, Dan begs her for a chance, despite her relationship with Larry. One year passes and Dan admits to Alice that he has been having an affair with Anna, despite her marriage to Larry, and Alice disappears. Larry agrees to divorce Anna, but only in exchange for sex. Dan discovers this and it poisons his new relationship with Anna. Larry discovers Alice working in a lap-dancing club, and tells Dan that he slept with her after finding her working there. Larry returns to Anna and Dan momentarily wins Alice back, only to realise that she did sleep with Larry. The relationship ends when Alice returns to New York by herself.

Despite the attractive cast, the sheen of the art gallery openings and sleek warehouse apartments, this is a dark film, reliant on words and the damage that they do. The men in the film are portrayed as weak, vain and cruel, driven by little more than base desires such as revenge and lust. Dan and Larry are by far the main focus here, changing during the narrative due to their relationships with Alice and Anna. Dan starts the film as a flustered, down-at-heel bespectacled writer, frustrated by his work and in search of something that will give him his voice. Larry is a sad dermatologist who surfs message boards which offer cybersex. The film is as much about the relationship between these two men as it is about their dalliances with the American women. The narrative follows the men's highs and lows, but it rarely offers sympathy or even empathy, unlike the depiction of Will in *About a Boy* or even Harry in *Love Actually*. They are thoroughly dislikeable characters, closer in spirit to the main protagonists in the work of Americans like Neil LaBute and David Mamet. Clive Owen, who played Dan in the stage version of *Closer*, offers an interesting angle on Marber's insight into the male gender:

'The two characters together sort of make up a whole person. I think that Larry gets seriously hurt and gets pissed off about it, but he's tough; he comes out fighting. Dan's the sort of artist, and Larry's more practical, so he's also tougher in that way. Dan's in love with the idea of being a writer – in love with the more sensitive side of being a man – and Larry's more of a realist.'[11]

The key sequence is when Dan confronts Larry at his plush surgery, after he realises that Anna is stalling on the divorce. He arrives in a suitably English rainstorm, looking like a drowned rat. Larry in comparison seems physically larger and certainly any power shift that has emerged in the film is in favour of him at this juncture. In his expensive three-piece suit he dominates the proceedings; Dan by contrast seems much smaller and as the truth dawns on him that he has lost Anna for good he starts to cry. It is a well-constructed scene, with the sucker punch kept for the conclusion when Larry reveals that he had sex with Alice. Dan leaves, a crushed man; there are no easy solutions left for him.

Any sort of love in the film feels totally narcissistic for the men; the key battle is between the central male protagonists. Romance in *Closer* can only really be attributed to Alice who is infatuated with Dan until the end of the film when she decides to leave him. What Marber's script does avoid here is the last-minute Working Title dash to the airport. Instead we see Larry and Anna in the marital bed surrounded by reading material and Dan walking around the London square where he first met Alice and realising that she took her name from a memorial stone there. We see her returning to the US, her real moniker is uncovered as Jane Jones and there is a sense of freedom and release epitomised in the last slow-motion shot of her on a busy New York street, walking to the diegetic strains of Damien Rice. In the *Sight and Sound* review, Alice is identified as the moral centre of the film and this is apt[12]. Although she does sleep with Larry it is as a direct reaction to Dan's own misdemeanours. It is suggested that it is possible that she still loves Dan, but when he strikes her at the film's climax, it seems there can be no going back to the relative security of the earlier relationship.

What *Closer* doesn't do is to offer a lengthy exposition mapping out the contours of any of the relationships of the characters; instead we see the start and the end of these brief couplings. The passing of time is not foregrounded by voice-over or captions; the audience must make those connections themselves. The London presented is one that can be identified in the other new heritage films – one of tasteful opulence. The shallow nature of the various occupations all offer a clever reading of the characters' natures; the obiturist eulogising about people he has never met; the lap-dancer offering views but strictly no touching; the fashionable photographer capturing a brief snapshot of her subjects; and the skin doctor pursuing the creation of external beauty only. Even with the secret sexual trysts and the complex entanglement of deceit in the narrative, there is an overarching sense of English repression at its heart. Although *Closer's* male characters seemingly grow due to their association with the exotic American women, both clearly use sex websites. In one of the central and most graphic scenes of the film, we see a drunken Larry in a lap-dancing club confronting Alice in search for some sort of emotional understanding. Dan and Larry are as weak as any of the major male characters in Curtis's films, and although they lack much compassion they do seem by their actions to be much more believable. This may be more difficult for a mainstream audience to accept, however, if they are expecting another Julia Roberts romantic vehicle.

Nichols does try to make the film as visually interesting as possible. The interiors are often low-lit and, as Sam Davies suggests, this creates an 'atmosphere appropriate to the shadiness of the action'; but also the 'muted chiaroscuros of Dan's flat' and the 'tawdry neons of the stripclub' all suggest isolation from which none of the characters can escape (ibid.). This is also echoed in the tight *mise-en-scène* of the exteriors, as the slate grey skies contrast with the dream-like final walk by Alice through Manhattan. America here offers possibilities, England is stuck in the grey gloom and Alice has escaped the wretched aftermath of thwarted love. This view counterpoints wonderfully the Working Title version of romance in the urban fairy-land and here not even Larry's marriage to Anna feels secure or resolved. *Closer* offers no easy solutions and Dan is left bereft wondering what might have been. This conclusive sense of comeuppance is also apparent in Law's next British film, *Breaking and Entering*.

Jude Law and Robin Wright Penn, *Breaking and Entering*

Anthony Minghella's last film before his untimely death in the spring of 2008 was also his first British film since *Truly Madly Deeply* (1991). *Breaking and Entering* focuses its attention on a changing London, one of regeneration and of constant flux in terms of newcomers from Eastern Europe. The central protagonist, Will Francis (Jude Law), is a well-known architect in partnership with Sandy (Martin Freeman) and their company is involved in gentrifying the rough environs around King's Cross. He lives rather unhappily with his half-Swedish girlfriend Liv (Robin Wright Penn) and her autistic daughter Bea (Poppy Rogers). When his offices are repeatedly burgled, he decides to stake them out. Here he makes the acquaintance of a Russian prostitute, Oana (Vera Farmiga), who ends up stealing his car. One night he sees a boy, Miro (Rafi Gavron), on the roof and chases him back to the battered housing estate where he lives and meets his mother, Bosnian refugee Amira (Juliette Binoche). He soon starts a relationship with her. When it emerges that Miro has been involved in the robberies, Amira blackmails Will into standing up for her son at a family tribunal which he initially rejects, but after confessing his affair to Liv he has a change of heart and speaks up for Miro.

It is a film that has been compared to other explorations of well-intentioned neo-liberal guilt such as *Crash* (Haggis, 2006) and Lawrence Kasdan's *Grand Canyon* (1991), where 'a tale of modern miscommunication is clearly meant to soothe rather than to trouble the conscience' (Scott, 25/01/2007)[13]. Importantly, the London setting gives *Breaking and Entering* a very different feel from the troubled browbeating of its sun-dappled American counterparts. It is in many ways as self-absorbed as *Closer,* with the main characters initially trapped in a closed world which insulates them from the reality of life in the metropolis. The London captured here is one of a city in a state of constant instability but also one of inequality, with recent arrivals right at the bottom. It was a London that Minghella was desperate to capture:

> 'I'm intrigued by the issue of migration and how it works in London, and how many languages and cultures and values coexist – all that seemed to be such fertile ground for exploration in the film. And I was fascinated by the fact that there were so many different kinds of life experience in the same corner of London, you could meet people whose language, values, belief systems, and experiences are diametrically opposed to each other.' (In interview, www.femail.com.au)[14]

This notion of cultural clash in a changing Britain is one that has been looked at in more social-realist films such as *Last Resort* and *Gypo* (see Chapter 5). This film is perhaps closer to Stephen Frears' *Dirty Pretty Things* in presenting a slightly more polished depiction of the lives of new migrants, but the critical difference is that, in Will Francis, the main action takes place around this British middle-class character. It is from within his frame of reference that we see a perception of the new London being uncovered. Interestingly, the film feels and looks very European in how it captures a different London, one that has 'an unfamiliar glamour' (Kellaway, 12/11/2007)[15]. The exterior shots by Benoit Delhomme show the changing landscape of King's Cross with real clarity, using a number of telling crane shots, which as Ray Winstone's compassionate police officer Bruno puts it presents an 'area in flux'. Will's vision is of a fluid, modern urban landscape that hopes to transform the area around the Grand Union Canal and the estates patrolled by, as Bruno says, 'Somalians with machetes'.

The film, however, never really investigates this stark juxtaposition of wealth and poverty with purpose or depth, instead more simplistically opting to compare Amira's cramped living and work space with Will's airy, waterside villa. The unseen London that he discovers is remarkably unremarkable. The Serbian gangsters that Miro works for have none of the psychopathic menace or even the organisational skills of the Russian Mafia in *Eastern Promises* (Cronenberg, 2007) for example. His wandering through the tough Camden housing estate in his baggy designer suit and expensive haircut is only met by comments like 'you shouldn't be here mate'. Even his Land Rover, stolen by his erstwhile companion Oana, is returned completely undamaged. Nicholas Barber makes an interesting point about what he perceives to be Minghella's main aim in making the film: 'like a time capsule with "contemporary Britain" embossed on the side. It's packed with immigration, crime, class, identity, step-parenting, depression, autism and urban regeneration'[16]. What it also captures quite unknowingly is the last blast of economic self-confidence before the credit-crunch took hold. Will's landscape dreams of revitalising this deprived part of north London would have struggled to see the light of day a mere couple of years later, even with Olympic money filtering through.

Liese Spencer, in her review of the film, found Will and Liv to be 'over-familiar characters, whose middle-class trials seem designed to be unsympathetic'[17] and this is true to an extent, but Minghella does attempt, however tenuously, to give some motivation for Will's affair with Amira. The relationship between Will and Liv seems in crisis right from the start, as the pressures of dealing with Bea are central here. Although these problems are only glimpsed, through windows and dinnertime tantrums, the film does seek to eschew the total avoidance or smoothing over of real problems that characterises the Working Title new heritage movies. However, in common with those films and also with *Closer* are the representations of exotic, foreign women and the implausibility of some of the romantic matches in terms of social class. Certainly, Will's relationship with the damaged Amira is the main example, but Sandy's schoolboy pining for the company's Nigerian cleaner Erika (Caroline Chikezie) is as equally implausible as PM David falling for Natalie in *Love Actually*. This can be seen as a prime example of Blairite cinema, where the class and racial divide is no barrier to romantic love. Minghella directed a party political broadcast for New Labour in 2005 so it is clear where his loyalties lie. The film's sense of inclusiveness comes to the fore at the end. Bruno, the verbose, philosophical Cockney cop, re-emerges as a paragon of liberalism, firstly taking Miro to Kew Gardens to warn him off a life of crime and then encouraging Will and Sandy to stand up for him at the family hearing at the film's conclusion, after he has been arrested. The Crown Prosecution Service sees the charges against Miro as 'hollow' and the end result is that he escapes a custodial sentence. However, instead of him and his mother trying to resurrect their fortunes in London, they decide to return home to Sarajevo. It feels like Minghella is implying that London has failed them, that the post-conflict peace that they have sought hasn't been found on the mean streets around Camden. In this respect *Breaking and Entering* follows the template set down by more social-realist films like *Last Resort* and *Dirty Pretty Things*, where the characters' only real escape comes by leaving Britain.

Law exudes some of his obvious star quality in this film and, like Dan in *Closer*, his character encapsulates some of the up-to-date attitudes and prickly smarts which David Thomson sees as central to his persona (p502, 2002)[18], but this is not fully exploited in either film. The climactic scene on Primrose Hill where Amira begs him to stand up for

Miro is a good example of this, where she practically offers herself for her son. Although he dismisses her, it feels half-hearted, so that when he changes his mind and decides to testify it comes across as believable. That said, Law's almost cruel good looks lend themselves to another sort of reaction, perhaps a different sort of character. *Breaking and Entering* ultimately does at least try, as Minghella suggests, to deal with London in a 'dialectical, complicated' (Kellaway, ibid.) way, by utilising a small-scale story and setting it against, perhaps, too many well-intentioned issues.

FEMALE PERSPECTIVES IN THE NEW HERITAGE FILM

What we have seen in this chapter is the evocation of male dilemmas played out within resolutely middle-class constraints that concentrate on a range of themes, including reactions to anti-American imperialism, sexual infidelity, deception and dealing with liberal guilt. In the middle of the decade, three films were released which took female protagonists as their main focal point and offered interesting fresh outlooks on the new heritage film, but in markedly different ways. Two were adaptations of heavyweight, highly regarded recent literary works, Zoë Heller's *Notes on a Scandal* and Ian McEwan's *Atonement* (written in 2003 and 2001, respectively) and one a film about the current Queen, but looking in particular at the most difficult event to face the Royal family for a generation. There are parallels between the three films, *The Queen*, *Notes on a Scandal* and *Atonement*, but what is important about all three is the elevation of the female point of view above all else.

Michael Sheen (kneeling) as Tony Blair and Helen Mirren as The Queen

The Queen strove to unpick some of the mythology surrounding the monarchy by focusing on the tumultuous events surrounding the death of Diana, Princess of Wales, in the late summer of 1997. It takes the most exportable icon of Britishness and creates a factional narrative built on the reaction of Queen Elizabeth (Helen Mirren) to her former daughter-in-law's demise and also interestingly develops the relationship between the monarch and her newly elected Prime Minister Tony Blair (Michael Sheen). The film was written by Peter Morgan, who had previously examined the decline of Richard Nixon on stage in his play *Frost/Nixon* and the fraught relationship between Tony Blair and Gordon Brown in his television screenplay *The Deal* (2003), also directed by Stephen Frears. Morgan is a master at adding a fictional twist by directly responding to real events as the centre-point of his narratives. This was also key in his adaptation of *The Last King of Scotland* for Kevin Macdonald in 2005.

Peter Morgan has said of his work: 'You have to ask yourself as a dramatist, "Do you believe there is a relationship between truth and accuracy? It may not be accurate – you don't know – but is it truthful, is it truthful and fair, are you giving the character a fair hearing?"'[19]. In his recreation of the spring and summer of 1997, the film certainly echoes the overt optimism of *Love Actually* where tradition and adherence to class-bound certainties seem to be swept away in a flood of emotion: Hugh Grant's David is like Blair, a master of the soundbite who appears on the surface to be a breath of fresh air in the stuffy corridors of power, dancing around to The Pointer Sisters, ending up with his young tea-lady; but unlike Blair, David refuses to be the American President's lapdog. *The Queen* starts with Blair's triumphant election victory, after eighteen years of Conservative rule, on his way to meet the Queen. The intricacies of Royal protocol are spelt out and it is clear that the film is going to centre on the new Britain as represented by Blair and his reformed Labour Party. It seems from the start that the central conflict of *The Queen* will be the New Labour project positioned against the entrenched traditional values surrounding the House of Windsor. In focusing on the Queen herself, this is the ultimate representation of the reserved and repressed upper classes, and the contrast with Blair's all-encompassing inclusiveness is particularly telling.

The catalytic moment of Diana's death in Paris was met by a mass hysteria and outpouring of grief unknown in this country before. The Queen and the Royal Family were holidaying in Balmoral at the time and what Frears' film clearly captures is the monarchy's indecision in dealing with this unprecedented event. Morgan had researched the subject thoroughly, calling on a wealth of biographical and insider information and Frears intercuts the dramatic reconstructions with television news footage. *The Queen* does avoid a straightforward drama-documentary approach to the material by locating the drama in the personal. The audience is placed directly within the frenzied events of the week leading up to Diana's state funeral. What is fascinating is the way that despite the servants and obvious privilege, Frears reveals the sheer ordinariness of the Royal Family's existence, clustered around the television watching the events unfurl, but completely misjudging 'the mood' of the nation. Phillip Kemp sees them portrayed as a 'pitiable clan, locked into patterns of tight emotional repression'[20] and this is partly true. Certainly Prince Phillip's (James Cromwell) rather brusque reaction to dealing with his grandsons' grief – a hunting expedition on the surrounding Scottish moorland – and his overall indifference to Diana's demise supports this (although he seems fond of the boys). This is also true of the representation of the Queen Mother (Sylvia Syms) and her outraged reaction when the plans for her own funeral are transferred to Diana's, although Frears positions her as the wise matriarch rather than a figure of fun. However, one of the tabloid villains of the piece, Prince Charles (Alex Jennings), is actually represented with a degree of tact and thoughtfulness. His reaction to his ex-wife's death is an audible and believable groan of despair. We also spy him giving the awful news to his sons through a half-open door and it is clear that it is his insistence to do the right thing regarding the removal of the body and the subsequent funeral arrangements, which elevates his character above one who is also simply repressed.

Sheen's and Mirren's portrayals are well-observed. Blair's over enthusiastic schoolboy manner is to the fore and Sheen captures his tetchy nervousness with a variety of visual tics, as Robert Hanks observes in his review: 'the fiddling with the cuffs, the ill-fitting suits, the easily flashing smile'[21]. His main advisor, Alistair Campbell (Martin Bazeley), is by contrast shown as a conniving opportunist, jotting down the key phrase 'the people's princess' within an hour of Diana's death, which Blair would use to great acclaim in his first address to the television cameras following the accident. However, it is interesting to assess how Morgan's script makes the Prime Minister's sympathy grow for the increasingly beleaguered monarch. David Gitten sees this as reflecting 'Blair's growing respect for the Queen's stubborn desire to maintain her privacy [which] smacks initially of political expediency, but comes to look like simple human decency. Her old-fashioned desire to keep the funeral arrangements discreet is seen to stem from personal convictions to duty above self'[22].

It is this notion of duty that is central in Mirren's Oscar-winning, detailed and complex performance, which skilfully avoids simplistic caricature. She always appears controlled and only on occasion is any vulnerability shown. Royalty's belief in the stiff upper lip and the reluctance to join in with the outpouring of national mourning is apparent in all but one scene. After her jeep breaks down in the middle of her estate, she spies a magnificent stag and it is the only time in the film that we see her shed tears at the beauty of the animal. But there is little indication that she is crying for Diana. Frears chooses not to show her in close-up, opting instead to show only the back of her head, so the effect is brief, cursory. Perhaps it is the realisation that this is the moment when things have to change, that perhaps the old barriers of self-restraint have to be questioned.

When she discovers later that the stag has been shot on a neighbouring estate she pauses briefly and continues with the business of the day. 'It is an unsubtle, but ferociously unsentimental piece of symbolism' (Bradshaw, 15/09/2007)[23]. It is entirely true that she is 'wry, dignified, ultimately human, pragmatic, a survivor' (Tweedie, 27/02/2007)[24]. This is for the most part correct, in particular her hesitant agreement to make a televised address to the nation and her difficult meeting of the crowds outside Buckingham Palace, amongst the massed floral tributes to her dead former daughter-in-law. It is clear that the intention of *The Queen* was to present a very human representation of that late summer week in 1997. It was something that Mirren herself was well aware of, in terms of the importance of getting the tone of the performance just right: 'It's delicate material, dangerous material in a way, so you have to be confident that the people you are working with have the intelligence and ability to put a story like this on the screen without a cheap portrayal of the subject' (Gilbert, 18/08/2006)[25].

The film contrasts the stuffiness of the Royal house with the changing times as exemplified by Blair and the footage of the grieving hordes and crying newsreaders, while fundamentally painting a picture of the Queen torn between observing age-old tradition and bending to the will of the people in adjusting her stance on Diana's death. It isn't shown as an easy decision, she reads Blair's praise for her humility as one of humiliation, but the central irony of the film is that the young Prime Minister's crusade for modernity actually saves one of Britain's oldest and most seemingly secure institutions. The scenes at the beginning and the end of the film give *The Queen* a very real sense of this gap between the ambitious, over-eager Blair and the stoic, experienced monarch. This is apparent in Blair's initial meeting with the Queen, where he is clearly overawed by the occasion, and this is shown with a humorous touch, which also permeates the rest of the film. His wife Cherie (Helen McCrory), identified from the outset as a republican, is bemused with the complicated, antiquated protocol and this is shown by her awkward body language. The Queen meets Blair and in a short exchange he is transformed from a victorious party leader who has notched up a massive landslide election win to a dithering schoolboy, sitting, he is told, where Winston Churchill had previously sat. The final scenes take place two months after the funeral: Blair arrives to meet the Queen to spell out his agenda for change. Once again he starts off the exchange on the crest of a wave, the self-appointed saviour of the monarchy, but tellingly the Queen has the upper hand, informing him quite correctly that popularity is always destined to fade. They then turn to the business of the day. Everything is how it was, but not quite.

The film is certainly 'not solemn, earnest or elegiac' as Philip French suggests[26] and in its intelligent deconstruction of that early September week it proved that with a good script, an established director and a stellar cast, a low-budget, Granada-produced British film could punch well above its weight. The film does feel televisual, in taking a large-scale story and placing it within the personal, but what stands out are the performances rather than the cinematography. This makes its box-office success in the United Kingdom, and more importantly North America, all the more remarkable. Its place as a new heritage film is cemented by the fact that it takes that most British of symbols and breathes new life into it, far beyond a crude interpretation or touristic impression. It encapsulates that remarkable week which in many ways set the tone for Blair's first term as Prime Minister, until the travails of 9/11 began to have an impact.

Notes on a Scandal also has at its centre a strong female presence in the shape of another Dame, in this instance Judi Dench, who it could be said at first glance is as emotionally stunted as the Queen. The film was adapted for the screen by Patrick Marber and it shares some similarities with *Closer*: a comfortable middle-class London setting, lives fractured by lies, jealousy and sexual indiscretion. Marber's main problem was to maintain the tone of the original novel: 'I think that I stayed true to the darkly comic tone of the novel, at least I hope I did. The thing that seduced me about the book was the truth of it and the comedy of it and the nastiness of it' (www.Indielondon.co.uk)[27].

The film itself, directed by veteran theatre director Richard Eyre, retains a great deal of the spite of Heller's book, much of this manifested in the on-screen persona of Dench's embittered history teacher Barbara Covett who develops

Judi Dench and Cate Blanchett, *Notes on a Scandal*

an obsession with an attractive and idealistic colleague, Sheba Hart (Cate Blanchett). Barbara's narration is full of envy for Sheba's life and her supposedly liberal ideals. The film is as much a dissection of class mores as it is a predatory tale of a delusional lesbian. Barbara oozes middle-England frustration at the state of her sad, lonely life, at her co-teachers' laissez-faire attitude and at her underclass, comprehensive school students. If Robert Murphy's idea of the urban fairy-tale was to be used in Eyre's film, Barbara would certainly be the wicked witch, a dried out spinster, angry at the world, spilling out her thoughts in her only confidant, the diary that provides the basis for her withering and possibly unreliable voice-over. By contrast, Sheba is the beautiful fairy princess, living in upper-middle-class luxury in a leafy Victorian terrace with her older university lecturer husband, Richard (Bill Nighy), and her two children, teenager Polly (Juno Temple) and Ben (Max Lewis), who has Down's Syndrome. The scandal of the film's title is Sheba's affair with her 15-year-old student Steven Connolly (Andrew Simpson), which Barbara discovers; although she initially feigns sympathy, she later uses this to her advantage to entrap Sheba into a 'friendship' based almost totally on deceit. But it is when Barbara drops hints to another teacher, Brian Bangs (Phil Davies) – who is also in love with Sheba – that Sheba may be more interested in young boys, that the scandal starts to break, with the attendant tabloid interest. Richard throws his wife out and she moves in with Barbara, but only after she finds the older woman's diary does she really understand the level of Barbara's obsessive nature. She leaves and returns to Richard, although later she is sentenced to prison. The final shots of the film show Barbara befriending another young woman.

The film has an uncertain tone and it isn't quite sure what it wants to be, veering wildly from high camp melodrama to stalker-based thriller to a Jacobean restoration comedy. This sense of generic unease is underpinned by Phillip Glass's insistent and, at times, portentous score.

The film manages to create a fascinating dissection of social mores and, in its portrayal of the north London comprehensive where the women work, offers a fine representation of the changing face of education under the Blair government. The well-observed *mise-*

en-scène portrays both Sheba and Barbara absolutely accurately. Sheba's naïve approach to the world is suggested in her faux-hippy sense of chic, all flowing skirts and designer tweed overcoats. She seems to be fulfilling a teacher archetype – probably one half-remembered from her 1970s youth – the liberal, overly idealistic art tutor. It becomes quickly apparent that she doesn't have to work, that this is the act of someone off-loading all that middle-class guilt. She could have turned up alongside Will in *Breaking and Entering* dispensing good works as she progresses through the narrative. Even her illicit relationship with Steven has, as Sukhdev Sandhu points out, 'the thrill of sexual tourism: he's Irish, working-class, and claims to come from a broken home'[28]. It also seems that she is scrabbling about, looking for excuses for her relationship with Steven, perhaps due to dissatisfaction with the older Richard or maybe the pressures of rearing a child with disabilities, but what Marber's script also implies is that she is terrified of getting old. This is made clear with her harking back to her art school days and her tales about being a New Romantic and wanting to be the pop star Siouxise. It could equally be argued that Sheba's role echoes the self-obsession of the characters in *Closer* and *Breaking and Entering* and also the sense those characters have, as Patrick Marber puts it, of 'modern loneliness', which Barbara also suffers from. These films eschew the communal feel of *Love Actually* and *About a Boy* by pulling together disparate, isolated characters, linked purely by desire/lust or their shared occupation, or often a combination of these. They feel like they are in their own individual bubbles and the drama unfurls as a result of a sudden collision, much like the main protagonists in other more realist London dramas like Tony Marchant's excellent BBC television series *Holding On* (1997) and Michael Winterbottom's *Wonderland*.

It seems that Barbara's life has also been one of solitude, and the film seeks to avoid just presenting her as a predatory dangerous stalker in the style of *Single White Female* (Schroeder, 1992) or *Fatal Attraction* (Lynne, 1987). She is a jumbled collection of neuroses, ranging from utter need to vindictive resentment; this is manifested in her measured and darkly comic voice-over, although *Notes on a Scandal* struggles somewhat with the literary conceit of the unreliable narrator, which in film is notoriously difficult to pull off.

Cinematographer Chris Menges does a wonderful job of, as Jonathan Romney notes, 'capturing the nuances of Dench's facial performances'[29], glacial stares and longing looks, her mouth pursed to make some acerbic comment. The antipathy that she has for Sheba's social status is a strange combination with the desire she also feels for her, but the film, unlike the novel, gives the sense that this is one related first and foremost to sexuality and not companionship. As Heller herself has remarked, 'The movie's Barbara is more thorough-goingly villainous than the original, with a much more conscious and explicit mission to entrap her victim. Most audiences seem to perceive her as a closeted lesbian with a clear sexual motive for stalking Sheba – and again that was not the case in the book' (Thorpe, 17/12/2007)[30].

A key scene that represents the class gulf between the two women is a Sunday lunch at Sheba's grand house, which she has inherited. Barbara has bought a new outfit for the occasion and had her hair done, but she misreads the formality of the situation. For Sheba and her family it is a normal lunch; they swan around in jeans and there is an effortless casual feel to the whole event. Dinner ends with them, including a clearly ill at ease Barbara, dancing around their antique filled sitting room to Toots and the Maytals' 'Funky Kingston'. It is, however, in Barbara's diary, a 'gold star' day, as she has entered the personal life of her colleague. It is Sheba's supposed social superiority that takes the place of any overtly sexual imagination, which Barbara seems to avoid at all costs. Her 'abysmal and intensely English sense of being one rung down the social ladder', according to one review of the film, is central here (Bradshaw, 02/02/2007)[31]. Her observations on Sheba and Richard are cutting, but they are biting in their accuracy, especially her points on the upper-class disposition to cut to 'immediate, incautious intimacy', as Sheba gives her a long summary of her life so far. One could never imagine the furtive Barbara revealing anything outside of her detailed journals, which are for her eyes only.

The finer points surrounding Sheba's affair with Steven are shown in flashback, after Barbara has found them together. It paints a picture of the student pressurising the teacher rather than the other way round, with Sheba finally relenting to Steven, buying his stories of a sick mother and abusive father. She enters this transgressive affair, as she calls it, feeling 'entitled' after years of caring for her children and being the dutiful wife to a considerably older husband. Richard Eyre commented on the great wit surrounding Blanchett's performance as someone who isn't very self-knowing (Gritten, 26/01/2007)[32] and this is a fair observation, certainly when she responds to Barbara's point about Steven only being fifteen, to which Sheba replies without a trace of irony, 'but he's mature for his age'. Her rather ingenuous nature regarding the teaching profession, along with her 'trendy politics', as Barbara refers to them, have little place in this large comprehensive, where her reading of extra-curricular activities is completely inappropriate. She is a character who has glided through life on the strength of her beauty rather than any sense of intellect or talent. Her major mistake here is not so much the sexual relationship with Steven, as her misguided confiding in the delusional and dangerous Barbara.

What Eyre and Marber do well are the snapshots of the school, which avoid the shock tactics employed in, say, Huda's *Kidulthood* (see chapter 7) and present a believable, very recognisable reading of staff-room gossip and politics. The school's headteacher, Sandy Pebblem (Michael Maloney), is the well-intentioned, gently hectoring Blairite leader who believes in 'reform through nurture'. The new term's meeting in which he takes each Head of Department's reports is well observed, as is his response to Barbara's waspish assessment of the history department's work. His attention to surface detail and his intentions towards issues like inclusivity certainly draw some comparisons with the New Labour education project. That said, Sheba represents, as stated before, her own dated idea of the uplifting role model who can transform the lives of her charges through learning. Barbara, meanwhile, sees the job as crowd control and one of purely getting the students to read, write and count.

The upper-middle-class cocoon is only shattered when the truth about Sheba's affair with the boy emerges, when Steven's mother attacks her in her own home. All of this is of course witnessed by the omniscient Barbara. This is the chaos that she has caused and the resulting break-up between Sheba and Richard benefits her, when the chastened Sheba moves into her dingy, austere Archway basement. The film ends in a climactic fight between the women, after Barbara's secret chronicles come to light. The depth of Barbara's longing for her finally becomes apparent to Sheba.

It is a film that ultimately may be remembered for two very strong central performances, issues around inappropriate relationships and the thriller aspect centring on Barbara's obsession with Sheba. What is more interesting is that it does subtly show that within the seemingly classless society the nuances of class division are still rife. In Barbara's awkwardness we see a woman that strives for the sense of social superiority that a friendship with Sheba would give her. In Sheba's world, she seems to be (in a bizarre way) alleviating any middle-class guilt by sleeping with, as she sees it, an underprivileged, working-class, Irish boy. Her motives may well be similar to Will in *Breaking and Entering*: have an affair with someone completely outside your social sphere, be found out, learn a bitter lesson, but ultimately be forgiven. It is interesting that the film starts and ends on the top of Primrose Hill, where Amira begged Will to help her son. Eyre and Marber, however, give the real villain of the piece, Barbara, a second chance but little sense of redemption.

James McAvoy and Keira Knightley, *Atonement*

Joe Wright's *Atonement* is different from the other films in this chapter as it locates much of the narrative in the past, namely the mid-1930s and the protracted lead up to the Second World War. Yet it shares many of the characteristics of the new heritage film, despite its older setting. Produced by Working Title, it is one of the films that heralded a move into more substantive and serious film-making towards the end of the decade. The central conflict of the narrative is based on a lie and that mistruth initiates a chain of events that have a direct bearing on the fates of the main protagonists.

Issues around romantic relationships across the class divide are also at the nucleus of the plot here. The film can be identified with more traditional heritage cinema, for example Joe Wright's first film *Pride and Prejudice* (2005) with its picturesque country house settings, but the entanglement of sex, lies, class division and the search for redemption position it nearer to films such as *Closer*, *Breaking and Entering* and *Notes on a Scandal*.

It is a brilliantly wrought tale based on Ian McEwan's lauded and apparently 'unfilmable' novel, which attempts to utilise the star persona of Keira Knightly in the role of Cecilia Tallis, working with Wright again after playing the lead in his Austen adaptation. One review referred to Knightly as 'iconic', and commented on 'the clipped, brittle accent of the period [suiting] her chalky Englishness' (Ide, 06/09/2007)[33]. The central conceit of the story surrounds misconstrued readings of two situations by her younger sister, 13-year-old Briony (Saorise Ronan), involving Robbie Turner (James McAvoy), the housekeeper's son. The major themes are developed in *Atonement* via a number of different perspectives, but the overriding voice is that of Briony and it is her misinterpretation of these events and her subsequent atonement that is at the core of the film. It is structured in three parts: the opening events at the Tallises country house in the high summer of 1935; four years later, in the early days of the war, taking in the Blitz and the evacuation of Dunkirk; concluding in the present with the revelation of the real events by aged and dying Briony, who has since become a successful, prolific novelist. The adaptation of the source material is literal, as Nick Bradshaw has commented of Christopher Hampton's screenplay, "'Adaptation" here means finding pictures for McEwan's words rather than shifting the mirror's gaze onto the movie itself'[34] and this is true, while the languid cinematography by Seamus McGarvey is also extremely impressive.

The fundamental issue of class is exemplified in the character of Robbie. He has been taken under the wing of the rich Tallis family, who have paid for his education, which has facilitated his entry to Oxford and a potential future as a doctor. But he is still very much a servant when we see him at the opening of the film. It is the hottest day in the summer of 1935, and it is clear from his appearance and his gardening work on the Tallises extensive estate where his social position lies. By locating Briony as a writer and teller of tales, what the film and novel allow for is a complex reading of what occurs in the narrative. The early argument between Robbie and Cecilia, seen from afar, has none of the repressed feelings that they hold for each other observed at close quarters. Through Briony's eyes, however, it has the threat of a violent sexuality that is still just outside of her pre-pubescent understanding. *Atonement* also stresses her girlish crush on Robbie, which may well be a catalyst for the chain of cause and effect that eventually ends with Robbie's wrongful arrest for rape. Her second observation, the consummation of Robbie and Cecilia's relationship in the darkened library and the explicit note that Robbie has written for Cecilia, further enlivens Briony's fevered imagination. Her misreading of these situations and her reactions to them could be seen to echo Barbara's in *Notes on a Scandal*, with *Atonement* being a further twist on the problems of an unreliable narrator, although Wright revisits key sequences more than once to broaden the audience's perspective. There are also parallels in Briony's witnessing of Robbie's arrest through the stair-rails much as Barbara observes the disintegration of a marriage from the Hart's landing, the key difference being that it is Briony's innocence rather than Barbara's unscrupulousness that creates the conflict.

Of all the characters that suffer in *Atonement*, it is the mild-mannered, intelligent Robbie who gets the rawest deal. He is wrongly accused of the rape of one of the Tallises cousins, Lola Quincey (Juno Temple), when the assault was by the upper-class friend, Paul Marshall (Benedict Cumberbatch), of the Tallises older brother, Leon (Patrick Kennedy). This is based on the circumstantial evidence amassed by Briony that results in a prison sentence, but Robby's eventual release is only granted if he enters the army. What is interesting is the way that his fellow soldiers treat him as an officer because, despite his working-class origins, he has the obvious social standing and accent that his education has given him. It doesn't save him from his untimely demise from septicaemia while waiting for the evacuation at Dunkirk. Still, Cecilia and Briony's contribution to the war effort is equally revealing in what it expresses about notions of class here. The war is viewed as a time when those pre-war distinctions are cast aside for the greater good. In many ways *Atonement* is as insistent about class unification as some of the other films covered in this chapter. It is also interesting that Paul Marshall is spotted later in the narrative by Briony, marrying the young woman that he assaulted five years previously. He has become a successful industrialist who has switched to producing weaponry and it seems that his class appears to survive the onslaught of war by profiteering from it. However, this could equally be contradicted by the death of Cecilia in the flooding of Balham tube station, acting as an air-raid shelter, side by side with ordinary Londoners seeking refuge from the bombing.

The period detail echoes the films of Merchant-Ivory in not only the *mise-en-scène* but also in the restrained way in which Wright presents the main protagonists, establishing, as David Gritten suggests, the 'establishment of dramatic relationships with a look, gesture or a lowering of the gaze, rather than by dialogue alone'[335]. Certainly the epic sweep of the middle section of *Atonement* has at its core the audacious, Steadicam five-minute tracking shot of the chaos on the beach at Dunkirk, which is reminiscent of the more visually stunning film-making of David Lean or that found in Anthony Minghella's more grandiose work. The scene is remarkable but, as David Jays remarks, the way that audiences may interpret this is through the recognition of the personal against the overpowering, detailed spectacle:

> 'If we cling to Robbie and feel slightly panicked when the camera loses sight of him, it's because we have no other way to make sense of our grief, muddle and anticipation; the weight of other stories, none of which we'll have time for, becomes overwhelming.'[36]

Despite this, Wright also does the simple things correctly, by exposing not only the initial crisis of class boundaries that means that Cecilia and Robbie can't reveal their longing for each other, but also the sense of loss that this creates as seen through the

eyes of the older Briony, played as an 18-year-old by Romola Garai and in old age by Vanessa Redgrave. The 'atonement' of the film's title comes in two ways for Briony: in her younger days by scrubbing hospital floors until her hands bleed and witnessing at first hand the misery of war by comforting the ailing young men in her charge; for the older woman it takes the form of a public revelation of the truth and by the construction of an alternative and perfect ending for the long deceased couple, by imagining them in a mythical future, still in love, overlooking the highly symbolic white cliffs of Dover. It is this optimistic vision that closes the film, which has echoes of the Working Title template. Even though the happy ending is yet another of Briony's contrivances, the message that love can ultimately triumph is very close to both *About a Boy* and *Love Actually* and is highly ironic.

There have been some criticisms that *Atonement* doesn't work at the level of simple romance, that the sheer meta-narrative nature of the film is too close to being just a clever postmodern view of a love story. 'The film's authenticity is smothered by stylistic artifice', was Cosmo Landesman's contention[37]. The film, however, is much closer to more traditional melodrama in its depiction of the impossibility that surrounds some relationships, in which differences in class are often insurmountable. *Atonement* just chooses to delineate the story in a less than traditional way. It takes a novel that certainly has a cinematic feel, and shifts effortlessly between reality and unreality, fact and fiction, and seeks to employ different viewpoints in a revealing fashion. The post-modernity of the film becomes much more vivid at its coda, where the audience realise that they have been watching a version of the older Briony's novel and all that is left for her to provide is the alternative ending, the ending that she would have wished for. Jays' point that its ending 'reshuffles all we thought we knew, while parlaying literary seeing into the cinematic' is particularly pertinent here (ibid., October 2007). In *Atonement* the visual techniques employed and the obvious strength and style of the narrative are given equal billing. The result is an increasingly dark and complex film which deals with the horror of war and, as The Daily Telegraph's review quite correctly asserts, 'manages to condense and magnify the romance and pity of the story, and perhaps more successfully than the novel, to unify its intellectual concerns with its emotional centre'[38].

REFERENCES

1. Hall, S., 'The Wrong Sort of Cinema: Refashioning the Heritage Film Debate' in The British Cinema Book, Murphy R (ed.), London: BFI, 2001

2. Street, S., British National Cinema, London: Routledge, 1997

3. Morris, M., 'Britflicks twin towers of power' in The Guardian, 08/04/2003

4. Lawson, M., 'It's magic' in The Guardian, 13/11/2003

5. French, P., Review of *About a Boy* in The Observer, 28/04/2002

6. Napper, L. in Nelmes, J. (ed.), An Introduction to Film Studies, Abingdon: Routledge, 2007

7. Murphy, R., 'Citylife: Urban fairytales in late 90s British Cinema' in Murphy, R. (ed.), The British Cinema Book, London: BFI, 2001

8. Bradshaw, P., Review of *Love Actually* in The Guardian, 21/11/2003

9. Dave, P., Visions of England, Oxford: Berg, 2006

10. Christopher, J., Review of *Closer* in The Times, 13/01/2005

11. Unaccredited profile of Clive Owen in The Times, 02/01/2005

12. Davies, S., Review of *Closer* in Sight and Sound, February 2005

13. Scott, A.O., '*Breaking and Entering*: A film of apology, forget the remorse' in The International Herald Tribune, 25/01/2007

14. Minghella, A., in interview on femail.com.au

15. Kellaway, K., 'Home is a foreign country' in The Observer, 12/11/2006

16. Barber, N., Review of *Breaking and Entering* in The Independent on Sunday, 12/11/2006

17. Spencer, L., Review of *Breaking and Entering* in Sight and Sound, December 2006

18. Thomson, D., The New Biographical Dictionary of Film, Little Brown: London, 2002

19. Hanks, R., 'Peter Morgan: Drama King' in The Independent, 24/02/2007

20. Kemp, P., 'Royal Blues' in Sight and Sound, October 2006

21. Hanks, R., Review of *The Queen* in The Independent, 15/09/2006

22. Gritten, D., Intriguing, provocative and majestic *Queen* wins warm reception in Venice' in The Daily Telegraph, 04/09/2006

23. Bradshaw, P., Review of *The Queen* in The Guardian, 15/09/2006

24. Tweedie, N., 'How they created a Queen for the screen' in The Daily Telegraph, 27/02/2007

25. Gilbert, G., 'Helen Mirren: Her crowning achievement' in The Independent, 18/09/2006

26. French, P., Review of *The Queen* in The Observer, 17/09/2006

27. Interview with Patrick Marber on indielondon.co.uk

28. Sandhu, S., 'A mad, magnificent monster' in The Daily Telegraph , 02/02/2007

29. Romney, J., Review of *Notes on a Scandal* in The Independent on Sunday, 04/02/2007

30. Thorpe, V., 'Illicit passion and a walk on the red carpet' in The Observer, 17/12/2006

31. Bradshaw, P., Review of *Notes on a Scandal* in The Guardian, 02/02/2007

32. Gritten, D., 'How to make a scandalously good movie' in The Daily Telegraph, 26/01/2007

33. Ide, W., Review of *Atonement* in The Times, 06/09/2007

34. Bradshaw, N., Review of *Atonement* in Sight and Sound, October 2007

35. Gritten, D., 'Joe Wright: A new movie master' in The Daily Telegraph, 24/08/2007

36. Jays, D., 'First love, last rites' in Sight and Sound, October 2007

37. Landesman, C., Review of *Atonement* in The Sunday Times, 09/09/2007

38. Sandhu, S., Review of *Atonement* in The Daily Telegraph, 07/09/2007

THE NEW REALISM — GIRLS ON TOP

INTRODUCTION

British cinema has always been closely associated with realism. One of the most interesting recent aspects of this strain of film-making is the number of so-called 'realist' films that are being directed by women and with central female characters. These films can be loosely labelled as 'realist' in so far as they depict social and economic circumstances, which certain echelons of society, particularly the working classes, find themselves in (Hayward, 1996, p320)[1]. I say loosely labelled, because stylistically these films are all very different and in terms of their representation of women, they offer in the main a complexity which seems sadly absent from mainstream cinema.

The aims of this chapter are to look at a number of films in terms of how they conform to and in some cases subvert some of the key associations with British realist cinema, and to assess how women are represented in a variety of different situations. In the context of their representations, it will be fascinating to note the impact of having largely female directors. Crucially, there will be an investigation into whether these repressed and marginalised stories, as Linda Ruth Williams calls them (2002), concerning female protagonists, remain 'marginalised' in terms of access and interest by a mainstream audience. The films that will come under discussion here are Andrea Arnold's *Red Road*, Pam Dunn's *Gypo*, Lynne Ramsay's *Ratcatcher* and *Morvern Callar* and, finally, Amma Asante's *A Way of Life*.

WOMEN IN THE BRITISH FILM INDUSTRY

According to the Film Council and Skillset, even by 2006 women were a significant minority in terms of participation in making films in this country[2], although this overall figure had risen from 33% to 40% since 2002. Crucially, in terms of their roles as assistant directors this was as little as 38%; the experience offered by being an assistant director can be very important when going on to direct a film by oneself. The poor position of female directors in Britain's film industry is echoed in Hollywood. Commenting on this, Jane Cousins, chief executive of Women in Film and Television, said that 'The studios pigeonhole women directors and think that they can only make a chick-flick about lots of women trying to make a quilt'[3].

Being a film director, whether in the UK or in Hollywood, is still very much a relatively closed shop for many women. Some of the attitudes are still very much rooted in old-fashioned sexism. Lynne Ramsay was told at film school that she would never make it. The problem wasn't her talent, but something more basic: her male tutor didn't think that she would be strong enough to carry a camera (Pendreigh, 14/08/99)[4]. It is troubling that there has been a considerable gap since Ramsay's last film (although she was for a long time associated with the film adaptation of *The Lovely Bones*) and also that Amma Asante has struggled to find a project since *A Way of Life*. For British film-makers, male and female, trying to secure a second or third picture deal can be incredibly difficult. This is also the case in Hollywood particularly if the director is a woman. The film-maker Tara Vaneruso has said, 'Women have to prove themselves over and over, men don't have that issue' (Krum, 24/02/06)[5].

What is apparent, though, is that these directors don't go for easy subject matter. As we shall see, the female voice is very much intact and the central female characters are well drawn and are placed in credible situations. In terms of the directors' backgrounds, Ramsay and Arnold had both made well-received short films. In Arnold's case *Wasp* (2003) had won an Oscar for Best Short Film. Amma Asante had been a child actress starring for a time in *Grange Hill* (1978–2008) and has also worked in television, writing and directing the BBC2 drama series *Brothers and Sisters* (1998). Pam Dunn's background was also in acting and she started her film-making career with shorts and documentaries. What is interesting is how they have avoided making the 'chick flick' films that many American female directors get offered. Instead, their films are rooted in the realist style of British cinema, which as we shall see has been male-dominated in terms of subject matter and production context.

THE OLD NEW WAVE

The British New Wave of the late 1950s and early 1960s led by directors like Tony Richardson, John Schlesinger, Karel Reisz and Lindsay Anderson strove to break away from the studio-produced films that had gone before. Cameras were used in real locations mainly in the north of England and the emphasis was on working-class people, 'tart and passionate' (Brown, 2001, p249)[6]. In films such as *A Kind of Loving* (Schlesinger, 1962), *Saturday Night, Sunday Morning* (Reisz, 1960) and *This Sporting Life* (Anderson, 1963), the male protagonist battled against what was expected of him; he was often angry and frustrated, a rebel railing against what he perceived as the injustices of post-war British society. He was normally young, from the north of England and, fundamentally, working class. Set against industrial landscapes and bleak northern skies (Brown, p252), these films were very much a product of their day, especially in their depiction of women.

Female characters were on the periphery, as wives, prospective wives or married lovers. They were seen in many cases as curtailing the central male characters' ambitions and drive, perhaps most notably in *A Kind of Loving* and *Saturday Night, Sunday Morning*. There were exceptions of course: Jo in *A Taste of Honey* (Richardson, 1961) and Liz in *Billy Liar* (Schlesinger, 1963) showed free-spirited, independently-minded young women trying to live on their own terms. But even in *Billy Liar*, Liz's character was counter-pointed in clear terms by Billy's other 'two' fiancées, the brass-faced, bottle-blonde Rita and the motherly, aspirant Barbara.

With the advent of 'Swinging London' and more experimentation with film form rather than using the camera as a tool for recording a version of 'truth', British realist cinema became sidelined, with some notable exceptions such as Ken Loach's *Kes* (1970). Realist texts became much more the preserve of television, a prime example being *Play for Today*, a series of stand-alone dramas that was broadcast on BBC1 in the 1970s. This was a fertile training ground for a number of key film-makers such as Stephen Frears, Alan Clarke and Mike Leigh. With the advent of Channel Four in 1982, its offshoot FilmFour saw once again theatrical releases for films rooted in realist cinema, often set against the backdrop of Mrs Thatcher's Britain, but in the main these lacked the polemic edge of the first wave of 1960s social-realist films. Films such as *My Beautiful Laundrette*, *Rita, Sue and Bob Too* (Clarke, 1986) and *Life is Sweet* used humour and irony in order to reach audiences. Although not huge mainstream successes, they did at least once again put the focus on ordinary people living everyday lives. Films like these were trying to reflect some sort of reality, but again the female perspective was often neglected. There were very few key female directors during this period and it wasn't until the early 1990s with the breakthrough of women such as Sally Potter and Gurinder Chadha that this changed.

Potter's *Orlando* (1992) is a long way from realism, a playful reflection on gender and sexuality grounded in the heritage film genre. By comparison, Chadha's *Bhaji on the Beach* (1994) feels much more familiar, focusing on a day out taken by a group of Asian and British-Asian women. It captures a sense of time, place and identity in a changing Britain – but it does so by combining humour and melodrama. However, other key productions by female directors during this period, such as *Under the Skin* (Adler, 1996) and *Stella Does Tricks* (Giedroyc, 1996), seem much closer in feel and spirit to the films that I am going to discuss in this chapter.

The diversity of these new realist film-makers is emphasised by Lynne Ramsay, whose films, although situated in realism in part through their subject matter, stylistically are as much concerned with the look of the frame as anything else. There is a surreal strain in her films that can be very much at odds with her subject matter. Asante's *A Way of Life* is much more in the traditional vein of the social-realist text with its main attention being positioned on a single mother living in South Wales. However, Leigh Anne's actions certainly don't conform to any stereotype that we may have come across before.

Charlotte Brunsdon identifies a strain of desperation linked to the female condition in these films, where the heroines are struggling to overcome an impossibility or intolerability in their lives. According to her they are films that address and contest the dominant tradition of British film-making and the look of the provincial (p.168, 2000)[7]. I would certainly say that the first two films that I am going to focus on, *Red Road* and *Gypo*, also take as their cue this notion of desperation. With their stripped down, minimalist approach they also redefine that look of the provincial as Brunsdon puts it.

THE GOOD, THE BAD AND THE MINIMAL — *RED ROAD AND GYPO*

(l-r) Natalie Press, Martin Compston, Kate Dickie, *Red Road*

Red Road's production context didn't bode well for the end product. It was made as part of a Danish project called The Advance Party inspired by the director Lars Von Trier, who challenged Andrea Arnold and two other directors to create three films, all set in Scotland, but all involving the same group of characters played by the same actors (Leigh, 18/10/06)[8]. Von Trier had, with a group of other Danish film-makers, formulated a set of rules and restrictions called The Vow of Chastity, which was seen as a manifesto for their work. Von Trier's movement was known as Dogme 95 and its influence is clearly seen in both this film and in *Gypo*.

The rules were designed to produce a more truthful cinema, with a concentration on the following: all films be shot on location, all sound and music to be diegetic, use of hand-held cameras and colour film with natural lighting and no filters, no superficial action (murders, for example, shouldn't occur), the film should take place in the here and now, no genre films, 35mm film format and no credit for the director (Benyahia, Gaffney and White, 2006, p156)[9]. Although *Red Road* has this connection to the Dogme movement and stuck to most of the rules, it also had other limitations: the location and characters are predetermined, but the main constraint was that it was shot for under £1 million. Arnold's debut low-budget feature had, then, a rather unconventional genesis, even by British film industry standards.

The film is set in contemporary Glasgow and centres on Jackie (Kate Dickie), a CCTV operator, who it transpires has lost her husband and daughter. She lives a solitary life punctuated by soulless sex with a married colleague. She receives an invitation to her sister-in-law's wedding and this leads to a meeting with her dead husband's family, with whom relations are strained as Jackie will not let his ashes be buried.

One night she notices on-camera a man that she recognises having sex with a woman against a wall. He is later revealed as Clyde (Tony Curran), the man responsible for the death of her spouse and child and it transpires that he has just been released from prison. She starts to obsessively track all of Clyde's movements on-camera and finally follows him to the Red Road block of flats where he lives. She overhears him in a café saying that he is having a party; she gatecrashes, drinks too much, dances rather closely with Clyde and then flees in a panic.

On-camera, she spots Clyde and two of his friends, Clyde's ex-cellmate Stevie (Martin Compston) and his runaway English girlfriend April (Natalie Press), enter a pub. She follows them there, takes off her wedding ring and puts a rock into her handbag. She flirts with Clyde. There is an altercation with Stevie and his father and they leave the bar. Jackie and Clyde go back to the flat and have sex. After she leaves, she goes to the bathroom, hits her face with a rock and tears her clothes. Off-camera she tells the police that she has been raped and Clyde is arrested.

Jackie feels bad about what she has done and rings the police to have the charges dropped. She confronts him as he is released and he tells her that the deaths of her husband and daughter were as a result of a car accident rather than a purely intentional act and that he is trying to get clean after years as a crack addict. An uncomfortable reconciliation is reached between the pair. She visits her in-laws and agrees that her dead family now be laid to rest.

On the face of it, it seems like a slow-burning thriller with a rather pat resolution, but *Red Road*, which won the Jury prize at the Cannes Film Festival in 2006, offers the spectator so much more in terms of how it deals with the representation of gender and also in how the narrative twists and turns until the relative conventionality of the final twenty minutes. Placing the film within a broader context, its initial concentration on the use of CCTV very much positions *Red Road* in the thick of surveillance obsessed Britain.

 Many foreign journalists assumed that Arnold had invented the massed cameras observing Glasgow's streets, but of course these all-seeing eyes are a staple of most high streets across the United Kingdom. But rather than spelling out the obvious points about invasion of privacy and the Big Brother connotations, the film sees the watchers as nothing more than underpaid skivvies responding to the daily horrors that occur on Britain's streets. Arnold herself expands on this line of thought:

'When I started this research, I was very worried, and I've certainly heard a lot of unsettling stories about CCTV. But the people I met watching the screens were the kind of people you see in the film. That was the truth of it, so it was important to reflect that.' (Leigh, 18/10/06)

In technical terms it is interesting how Arnold used the CCTV strand to tell her story. All the material that Jackie is watching was recorded beforehand, a process that the director found to be intricate but exhausting:

'The first week we were doing CCTV during the day. We were filming, and I was up at three, finishing up at eight, then going to edit, falling asleep in the director's chair because I had to edit the CCTV stuff to go into the following week's shoot. We had a very complicated system, because I wanted the sequences to run as one. That meant that if she's following somebody who moves from one camera to another and then it moves down here in time, somebody would have to leave that one, come into this one, come into this one and drive down that one.' (comingsoon.net April 2007)

Red Road's stark emotional territory is also mapped out in the bleak *mise-en-scène*. Urban Scotland is presented as highly atomised, where the notion of community seems to have been lost in this post-industrial landscape. Rubbish strewn streets, a perpetual wind blowing, grey, overcast, unforgiving skies all give the film a claustrophobic feel. As mentioned earlier, Clyde is first spotted involved in an unsubtle sexual encounter as Jackie's cameras scan a piece of deserted wasteland. Arnold creates a distinct sense of unease as the narrative unfurls and Jackie appears to get closer to Clyde.

 Jackie is a complex character, a study in grief that echoes films such as Krzysztof Kieślowski's *Three Colours Blue* (1993) and Pedro Almodóvar's *All About My Mother* (1999). Thirtyish, attractive, withdrawn, the reasons for her initial fascination with Clyde seem unclear. This complexity is enhanced by the sense of control that Jackie seems to have at the outset. As she spots Clyde's van (he is working as a locksmith – perhaps not the best career move for an ex-con) she follows his progress through Glasgow's suburban estates. Certainly this sense of the power of surveillance is also found in other film texts, most notably and famously in Alfred Hitchcock's *Rear Window* (1956) and more recently in *Hidden* (Haneke, 2006) and *The Lives of Others* (Von Donnersmarck, 2006). The enigma that Arnold creates regarding Jackie's growing obsession with Clyde unfurls slowly. As Philip French noted in his review:

> 'When it comes to information about the past, Arnold feeds it to us grudgingly, teasingly, on something less than a need to know basis and things become clear only at the very end.'[11]

This of course adds to the uncertain feelings the spectator might have about Jackie and her motives. As the narrative reveals its secrets, it becomes clearer what may be behind Jackie's goals as she begins to fulfil a number of possible archetypes according to Hannah McGill in her excellent Sight and Sound article on the film; 'stalker, spurned lover, vigilante avenger' (November 2006)[12].

The quiet, detached presence of the main protagonist is contrasted with the animalistic Clyde. There is a 'feral and oral' (McGill, ibid.) sense of sexuality surrounding his actions, best exemplified when Jackie gets close to him at his local dirty spoon where he flirts with the waitress while licking his plate. 'You are a fucking animal', she exclaims, but it is this rawness in Clyde's character which makes us further question Jackie's interest in him.

The initial meeting, when Jackie gatecrashes Clyde's party, is interesting. The clear desperation of the party is apparent with the bargain booze, cheap lager-fuelled, singing/

shouting of Oasis's 'What's The Story Morning Glory', perhaps recalling better times. The high-rise hell of Red Road is clearly shown with the poorly furnished flat with its filthy kitchen floor. Dogs seem to be a constant motif, starting with the overweight mutt that Jackie spies on her camera earlier in the film, whose death leaves his owner a broken man. Her sexual liaisons with her colleague double up as a chance for his dog to have a run in the Strathclyde countryside and here at the party she is introduced to April's new charge, a small puppy. Dogs seem to offer a tiny scrap of comfort in this cruel world.

Her dance with Clyde certainly hints at the sexual tension that becomes much clearer later on in the narrative; however, in this case she bolts. Her omnipresent view of proceedings leads her to a second and more decisive meeting with him. She follows him to his local bar – the sort of pub which is a universe away from Glasgow's trendy city centre nightspots. He spots her but it is difficult to discern the back-story between the two characters, other than what we have seen in the film. His shocking line to Jackie, 'I've been wondering what your cunt tastes like', seems to shift the balance of power towards him. This however doesn't prove to be the case.

The subsequent sex scene at Clyde's flat is explicit and it was for this that the British Board of Film Classification decided to give Red Road an 18 certificate. As stated earlier in the chapter, the role of the female director is informative here. Andrea Arnold uses the scene to flesh out Clyde's character with information about his daughter, a young girl that Jackie has seen him with on CCTV that we initially suspect he may be having a relationship with. He also talks about his interest in tree sculpture, again harking back to his branch-dragging activities again caught on camera earlier in the narrative. But where Arnold's role as a female director becomes vividly apparent is in the way that she shoots the sexual encounter between Jackie and Clyde. Here she shows full female nudity, erect nipples and cunnilingus. Clyde brings Jackie to orgasm and it differs greatly from her relationship with her colleague. In a strange way, his sexual gratification is put on hold, which once again, along with the other information in this scene, makes us question what we feel about him. Lit by a cheap lava lamp, Arnold leaves no illusions about what has just happened. It looks and feels incredibly real. After they have full intercourse, Jackie leaves straight away, although there seems to be a sense of enjoyment on her part – she has regained power, leaving Clyde to bemoan his fate: 'Was it just a fuck that you wanted then?' he shouts after her as she leaves.

Vanessa Raison sees this scene as pivotal. 'The foreplay educates men on how to give women pleasure. But they don't kiss and penetrative sex leaves her [Jackie] cold. It is a reversal of the male getting good sex out of his enemy before disposing of her'[13]. Certainly this is true, but the complex nature of Jackie's motives becomes obvious as she cries 'rape', in order to ensure that Clyde returns to prison.

Although much has been made of the realist approach to the sex, the plot device which saw Jackie accusing Clyde of sexual assault didn't quite hold up. It would be soon clear to the police that Clyde had killed Jackie's husband and daughter and that her claims may well be seriously questioned. A much more potent and emotionally disturbing sequence comes soon after her dalliance with Clyde. We see Jackie in her lonely, half-dark house dressing a doll in her dead child's clothes and crying uncontrollably. It is a raw, incredibly moving piece of film-making and Kate Dickie's performance is heartbreaking when for the first time in the film she reveals her true emotions.

Perhaps after such an intense experience, Arnold felt forced to offer some sense of redemption and closure. Jackie drops the charges against Clyde and although we may feel that he has moved on, he offers a rather cold response of 'Shit happens'. His life, it is hinted at here, has been one of neglect and failure. Sympathy can be offered to Clyde, but only begrudgingly. That said, Jackie's agreeing to disperse her loved ones' ashes at Loch Lomond, suggests that she has started the process of letting go. The other stories hinted at in *Red Road* are kept tantalisingly open – the cleaning woman spotted in the office window, John's family and the damaged Stevie and April. It is hoped that we will return to these stories in the remaining two films in the Advance Party project.

While Arnold's film is unremittingly dark, there are moments of beauty. The wind that surrounds the high-rise blocks of *Red Road* creates an updraft that both scares and invigorates the characters. The battered Glasgow streets, the perpetual Scottish half-light and the ultimate final feeling of forgiveness show Jackie's desperation starting to slowly disappear.

Pam Dunn's *Gypo* stylistically tackles similar emotional terrain. The film has the distinction of being the first Dogme feature to be produced in Britain eschewing the use of non-diegetic music and sound, shot on location in natural light and using largely hand-held cameras. Although the director gave the film a scripted structure, this was mainly written in prose. Dunn decided to give a great deal of freedom to the actors to develop largely improvised dialogue. Set on the Kent coast, *Gypo* is structured around three interconnected narratives. The main plot focuses on the disintegration of a 25-year marriage of Asda night-shift worker Helen (Pauline McLynn) and carpet-fitter Paul (Paul McGann). They hardly speak to each other anymore, leading distinctly separate lives. Into their world enters an 18 year-old Romany Czech refugee, Tasha (Chloe Sirene), who acts as a catalyst for their eventual split.

The narrative attempts to shed light on the same events by using the different perspectives of Helen, Paul and Tasha telling their own individual stories, although it is clear that the main sympathies lie with that of the ever-optimistic, downtrodden wife Helen. Helen is certainly taken for granted by her family and especially her husband. Her youngest daughter Kelly (Tamzin Dunstone) is still living at home and has a baby called Jordan, who she seems to be incapable of looking after properly, referring to the child as 'it' on more than one occasion. Helen's life is only enlivened by her night-classes in drawing and sculpture, until the arrival of Tasha, one of Kelly's college friends.

Certainly the feeling of desperation, of entrapment is one that is deeply felt in *Gypo*. Helen's working-class heroine seems to be exhausted by decades of child-rearing (extended now, it seems, with the arrival of Jordan). Her belief that there must be something more becomes the central driving force in Dunn's narrative.

Dunn, true to the central tenets of the Dogme way of working, places a great deal of the exposition in the family home, which looks exactly like the sort of home in which Helen and Paul would find themselves. A newish, suburban semi, complete with its open-plan sense of space, its wallpapered matching borders and cramped, confined, fake cosiness seems to be the height of aspiration in Blair's seemingly classless society. But Helen's appearance is weighted with resignation – cheap clothing and split ends seem to suggest somebody who has given up caring. Constant slanging matches with a perhaps too thinly drawn Kelly, the monotony of stacking shelves and a loveless marriage to a depressed and dour Paul have all taken their toll.

Helen's story certainly hints at the lesbian relationship that is made much more explicit later in the narrative in Tasha's story. Perhaps this is because Helen is in denial of her true feelings – much like Jackie's largely emotionally blank state in *Red Road*. Her life seems to be a series of trials, of running around after her largely ungrateful family and her new friends, Tasha and her mother (Rula Lenska). Certainly her relationship with the xenophobic Paul has broken down. The scene in which Paul has sex with her borders on rape. There is no attraction, least of all love. Sex has become purely functional in this marriage and affection non-existent. There is no support from Paul for Helen's artistic endeavours, just a self-satisfied dismissal.

Helen's attitude towards the refugees marks her out as the liberal conscience of the film, although Kelly's reasoned arguments, in the dinner scene, against Paul's ingrained attitudes also distinguishes her (very much against type). The scene where she leaves the art-class with her friends when she is met by Tasha and her mother after an attack on them by local youths is key here. The yobs are moaning about how things have gotten worse in the town since the arrival of the refugees. Helen defends them, drawing on her own experiences as an Irish immigrant in Britain. They are incredulous and like Paul dismiss her defence of them out of hand as totally irrational. The backdrop to this film and the issue of economic migrants most notably echoes Pawel Pawlikowski's *Last Resort*. This was something that Pam Dunn was well aware of when scouting a setting for *Gypo*:

> 'If you are going to set the story, certainly in this region of Kent, we are very near Dover here. If you want a contentious story, then the most obvious decision is to incorporate asylum seekers in some way or another. For the local community here, it is a huge, huge issue.'[14]

If Helen is the undoubted heroine, Paul is presented as the villain. Even in his own segment, there are only very occasional hints of a more sympathetic side to his character.

In an interview with The Independent this is further expanded on:

> "'I had to be prepared for him to be irredeemable,' says McCann. "He is unremittingly miserable." Fed on a diet of tabloids and Talk Sport, McCann says that his character belongs with the "huge majority of these little Englanders with their easy assumptions. At one point he talks about Africa being a big country – that's about the level of him.'" [15]

Dunn presents some complexity around Paul. He is angry about his lack of sleep, money and sex. He blames asylum seekers for his woes but he is quite prepared to use cheap Iraqi labour to help him fit carpets at a seafront hotel. He calls Tasha a 'gypo', but he is happy to pay an Irish traveller for sex. Although Dunn attempts to give some sense of the frustrations that he feels, as a neglected husband, as someone who is not sure where he fits in anymore, it doesn't wash. This is probably most apparent when in Helen's narrative he forces her to have sex with him, whereas in his story his advances are rejected. However, Helen is the character that we are constantly drawn back to – even the attempts to present her as a shrew-like harridan don't quite work, as Paul's miserable, self-pitying presence lurches from television to work to pub to whore.

Like Tanya in *Last Resort* and even Jackie in *Red Road*, Tasha cuts a striking figure. Flame-haired and pretty, equally confident and bashful, it is clear that she is a survivor from the first encounter with Helen. Paul attempts to make her uncomfortable at the dinner table, which she handles with good grace. When Helen next meets her, she and her mother are fleeing an attack from some local thugs. This seems to be an everyday occurrence for her and there are indications of a difficult past as a runaway wife and teenage prostitute. What might seem rather implausible is the development of a sexual relationship between Tasha and Helen. Perhaps this offers an escape for both women. The film itself won a number of awards at lesbian and gay film festivals but it is worth noting that the relationship isn't the main plot in the film; it just happens that these two women find each other and fall in love. There are hints of the burgeoning relationship in Helen's story and in some of the cutaway shots of Tasha, but it does still come as a surprise. It breaks conventions in that there is an implicit sense that Paul and Tasha may well have been involved – certainly as client/prostitute. It does, however, become clear that the woman he is paying for sex lives very close to Tasha's caravan so this might be why some form of recognition is hinted at.

Helen's relationship with Tasha certainly suggests a new beginning for the character. Tasha and her mother are tracked down by her husband and are forced to return to Europe. Helen's dash to the port (aided ironically by Paul) looks to have been in vain, as the Czech women are spirited through customs. However, Tasha and her mother escape – Tasha ending up evading her pursuers by jumping into the sea. The film ends with Helen and Tasha together and some form of hope is hinted at, in what has been a dark narrative.

Like Jackie's realisation that life is worth living in *Red Road*, it seems that the release from a worn-out marriage and a more fulfilling relationship has the potential to make Helen a more complete and happier person.

In their minimalist and stark style, both films show women in desperate positions: Helen the neglected, hard-working wife and Jackie the grieving mother and widow. But they fight against the feelings of entrapment and revenge and ultimately come out on top, Jackie as a more rounded individual, ready to move on and Helen no longer to be taken for granted, ready to explore a new world, even in the bleak Kent light.

A DREAM-LIKE REALISM: THE PARADOX SURROUNDING LYNNE RAMSAY'S FILMS

William Eadie, *Ratcatcher*

Scottish director Lynne Ramsay announced herself as an important British director with her first feature *Ratcatcher* in 1999. Her background prior to that was in photography and then film school to study cinematography where her short films *Small Deaths* (1996) and *Gasman* (1997) won her great acclaim. These shorts are rooted in her own Glaswegian childhood and this is further explored in her debut feature film. The lovingly crafted framing of each scene and the bleak but beautiful *mise-en-scène* mark Ramsay out as a director with a good eye for detail, and the influence of that other great Scottish *auteur,* Bill Douglas, looms large.

Ratcatcher is set in the late 1970s during a strike by dustmen. The quiet, damaged James (William Eadie) accidentally causes the death of another boy during a fight in a polluted canal. We follow his friendship with an older girl, Margaret Anne (Leanne Mullen), and his ambivalent, rather difficult relationship with his drunken father (Tommy Flanagan). The film centres on James' guilt and the sense of broken promises that confront him at every turn. The backdrop of shabby tenements and piles upon piles of festering black plastic bags reflecting the mood of the film, one that won near universal acclaim. Peter Bradshaw points out the ways in which Ramsay transforms the ordinary and everyday into something other-worldly and odd:

> 'The opening dream-like shot over the credits shows James twirling himself up in the net curtains and losing himself in his own strange dervish snow scene; net curtains, the dullest things conceivable, are made agents of the sublime.'[16]

Although Bradshaw highlights the inherent wonderment in the banal that Ramsay's camera picks out, this seems to go against a number of preconceptions that the film is firmly rooted in the British social realist tradition. Ramsay is quick to dismiss any accusations that *Ratcatcher* is merely a 'realist' text:

'A lot of people have misconstrued this film as social realism and I don't think it is. I try to avoid some of the clichés of that. To be honest, I was trying to go into the psychology of the scenes, going into why we're shooting this way, why we're looking at it that way, trying to get under the skin of it a bit, inside the boy's head. It's a bit of a risky thing to do because essentially we are using non-traditional actors, so you go from this harsh reality into something that's much more hard to pin down. It's more unreal, I guess. It's almost like two opposing styles. Don't ask where that comes from – I think it's something I realize I've developed in my shorts.'[17]

With its dark, pessimistic subject matter, its inner city *mise-en-scène* and its focus on working-class protagonists, it would appear to perhaps contradict this view, but the film does not preach nor is it issue-led like so many other 'realist' texts. Philip French's point that 'we are left to infer almost everything from the way people act'[18] is particularly apt here, with Ramsay leaving it completely up to the audience regarding how to read the actions of the main protagonists. The metaphorical use of the stinking, rodent-ridden rubbish echoes the hopelessness of James' life. Even the occasional bright interlude in the film, for example James' father saving Kenny from drowning, is undercut by him being attacked and beaten by a group of boys and his subsequent attack on his wife. As Charlotte O'Sullivan comments: 'Ramsay seems desperate to push home a grim message: good deeds are rewarded only by punishment'[19].

The film is startlingly beautiful and in its rather tainted splendour shows Glasgow to be a wonderfully cinematic city, as was also shown in *Red Road*. Ramsay is also unafraid to use silence, which she does extremely effectively. There is a scene in which James has his turn with Margaret-Anne, after she has been molested by a number of boys. Rather than doing what they did, he lies, very quietly, on top of her to shield her from their lecherous gaze. He is offering possibly the only sort of protection she is ever likely to receive. *Ratcatcher* is a deeply pessimistic film. James' guilt for Ryan's death permeates the whole narrative. This is enhanced when he admits council inspectors into the family's chaotic flat and in doing so damages the chance to move to a new estate on the edge of Glasgow. Rather surreally, the film hints at two different forms of resolution. Initially we see James in the canal, where he is fully submerged and appears to be drowning. This feels like the rather cyclical ending that had been expected by what had gone before. The second ending shows the family moving their few possessions across a golden field of wheat against a cobalt blue sky. They are heading towards a new house and perhaps a new beginning for their fractured family life. The dream-like possibilities of both endings set the scene for Ramsay's second feature *Morvern Callar*.

Morvern Callar was an adaptation of the 1995 novel by cult Scottish novelist Alan Warner and stylistically and thematically shows a massive progression from *Ratcatcher*. The film focuses on the eponymous heroine, Morvern, played by Samantha Morton. She is a supermarket worker living in a small port town in Oban in the west of Scotland. The film opens with Morvern clutching her dead boyfriend who has committed suicide, leaving a parting note on his PC along with his recently completed novel.

The bleak midwinter setting and the limited exposition initially give the impression that Ramsay's film is going to be a meditation on the grief and pain associated with a partner's death. But the film, like the novel, takes a very different turn. Morvern appears in shock at the outset, but this seems to pass quickly. She opens the Christmas presents that he has left for her. She loads her personal stereo and puts on the tape that he has made for her, which subsequently soundtracks the film. She also takes money from his pocket, while apologising to the corpse.

The body remains on the kitchen floor for a number of days, as Morvern visits the local pub with her best friend Lanna (Kathleen McDermott), and dances and parties her way through her grief. When finally confronting the reality of the situation, she reads his suicide note which entreats her to 'be brave' and tells her that the novel was written - for her. It also gives her details about publishing the book. It is at this point that her grief ends, with Morvern replacing her dead partner's name with her own, taking quite literally the fact that the book is now hers and denying any possible posthumous acclaim for the real author. She dispatches his body with the ease of a trained surgeon by cutting it up in the bath to the strains of the weirdly appropriate 'I'm Sticking with You' by The Velvet Underground, Moe Tucker's little girl vocals contrasting greatly with Morvern's cool dismemberment of the cadaver.

After getting rid of the body and armed with her partner's credit cards, she leaves the Scottish gloom and heads to Spain for a holiday with Lanna. We see the grey dampness of Oban replaced by the warm Technicolor glow of the Mediterranean sun as the film takes another turn. Lanna just wants to take drugs, get drunk and have fun, but as time goes on Morvern grows bored of the 18-30 package nightmare and wants to see the real Spain. Along the way she has drug-fuelled sex with a fellow holiday-maker, who we never return to; the cause and effect seem to be purely functional. The critical view of the young British abroad is never forced; it is impressionistic, but completely recognisable. It is something that Jonathan Romney highlights to good effect in his review of the film:

'The sequence is euphoric, yet completely out of key with the usual depictions of youth-culture hedonism. The shots of Morvern framed against a wall of hotel balconies reveals the merciless factory-farmed fun ethic of such places: another memorable, fleeting shot reveals a girl's agony at being roped into a brutally jolly poolside romp.'[20]

The trip into the real Spain doesn't go well and Lanna and Morvern go their separate ways. Meanwhile, the novel has been optioned by a publishing company, which sends its representatives to court Morvern. They offer her a large advance for the book. Morvern briefly returns to Oban to tie up loose ends and try to reconcile her relationship with Lanna, but in the final shot she is back in a Spanish nightclub, glassy-eyed, walking through the throng listening to her own personal soundtrack of The Mamas and The Papas' 'Dedicated to the One I Love'.

The way that Samantha Morton plays the role is crucial. We are given little indication in the narrative about Morvern's motivations – unlike in the novel, which was written in the first person from Callar's perspective. Her reaction to the suicide is amazingly emotionless, her face blank and difficult to read, her actions refreshingly ambiguous. Morton's complex performance has been linked to her own difficult upbringing, a grim childhood in Nottingham and adolescence spent in foster families. Perhaps in Morvern, the English outsider (Scottish in the novel) in the remote Scottish town, there is something of Morton, the troubled teenager. Lynne Ramsay's views on the casting of her central character are revealing:

'I saw a photograph of her and it just didn't look like a glam actor's picture. It looked like a girl who was really bored, so I thought that she must be quite interesting to put out a picture like this. She looked like a girl who could work in a supermarket; she didn't look super glamorous. She's also beautiful in a child-like way. I thought that there was something otherworldly about her and that she looked like the character in the book.'[21]

The point about how Morton could fit the role of a supermarket worker is important – yet the use of the soundtrack and Alwin Kuchler's sharp and eerie photography intensifies the experience of her otherwise mundane job. When Morvern returns to work it is to the sound of Lee Hazelwood and Nancy Sinatra's 'Some Velvet Morning' on her headphones. The artificial light and the wide aisles, along with the slow panning point-of-view shots, give the store a slightly strange feel. This dream-like atmosphere continues when Morvern notices a maggot making its way out of a mouldy carrot and the camera settles on this. As Linda Ruth Williams comments, 'whether Morvern has an inside is questionable; like the details she notices, she's fascinating but unfathomable'[22] (Sight and Sound, October 2002). This lack of knowledge about what drives her could be explained by suggesting that perhaps there is no complexity to her actions. Her motives may be embedded in her desire to break out of the dull life that she has in Oban and may purely lie in financial gain – although nothing in her past could have prepared her for the enormous advance of £100,000 that she receives from the publishers for 'her' novel.

Morvern is an opportunist anti-hero who deals with her partner's death in a totally unconventional way. Ramsay thankfully neglects to fill out the back-story about how the novelist and the quiet shopgirl got together. Morvern is seen as essentially good-natured, not lying about her partner – 'He's gone,' she tells Lanna – but not telling the whole story either. Near the start of the film, she answers a phone at a railway callbox and has a conversation with someone she doesn't know, spelling out her name – something she does a number of times in the film. The confusion with her name goes as far as having a necklace she has found with the rather simpler 'Jackie'. During this strange phone call she also tells the person that 'I'm not from here.' In many ways this short sequence seems to sum Morvern up – a character who is hard to judge and totally fascinating. But perhaps the main trick is that there isn't much there anyway: as Anthony Quinn remarks, she is 'an unreachable blank'[23] and as a result her actions are possibly more straightforward than at first thought.

Certainly this could be supported by her Spanish meeting with the people who want to publish the novel. In the warm Almeria sunshine and wearing a bright, patterned summer dress, Morvern's opinions on why she writes are taken as ironic by her London suitors. She likes writing because 'you can knock off when you want, have a cup of coffee. Take a shower. Have a cigarette.' Placed against the rigid humdrum of shelf-stacking, the freedom offered by writing seems more appealing. That said, the grind and graft of churning out (what turns out to be) a highly regarded novel, is completely alien to Morvern. Her reactions to the publishers may seem fresh and unpretentious, but actually they are Morvern's true thoughts.

Morvern has a great deal in common with the central female protagonists of both *Red Road* and *Gypo* in the way that she seeks to perhaps escape her past and find some sort of redemption. Jackie in *Red Road* finds a new start at the end of the film, reconciling the past in realising that what she did to Clyde was wrong. *Gypo*'s Helen finds a new start in her separation from Paul and in her burgeoning relationship with Tanya. The climax of *Morvern Callar* is much more open-ended (rather like *Ratcatcher*) with Morvern's slow walk through a Spanish nightclub, complete with close-ups of her soporific smile framed in flashing red and white lights. The use of music and those final images may well reflect that somehow she has come to terms with what she has done and reached some sort of peace. It is something that Linda Ruth Williams is keen to highlight:

'As *Morvern Callar* closes (inconclusively), its heroine once again departs, but it's music that begs the final question of whether she's escaped, and from what. Morvern plugs in her usual soundtrack – "*Music for You*" – her individualised virtual reality. Sound and images are dissonant, the Mamas and the Papas crooning '*Dedicated to the One I Love*' over yet another chaotic rave scene. As a prayer from the dead – don't forget that he chose this one too…' (Sight and Sound, October 2002)

At first Ramsay's film, with its long shots of windswept small-town streets and by boasting a string of downbeat themes (suicide, grief, abandonment, loneliness, disloyalty and plagiarism) feels and looks like a slice of artful social-realism, close in spirit to *Ratcatcher* and the films of Bill Douglas and even Terence Davies. But with its long takes of two very different landscapes, its resonant use of lighting, its use of elliptical editing techniques and spellbinding use of sound and music, *Morvern Callar* is much more like a European art film which just happens to begin in a dour Scottish port. It expands outwards both visually and aurally: Morvern's journey from her drone-like existence is presented by Ramsay as a trance-like experience; the flashing lights of the Christmas tree in Morvern's flat at the beginning of the film are replicated by the club's lighting later on in the narrative; the eclectic soundtrack, ranging from Can's experimental prog-rock to the dreamy dub soundscapes of Lee Perry, provides extra layers of meaning to a range of events, from the dismemberment of the body to arriving at a supermarket for a day's work.

Ramsay's approach in using a mixture of professional and non-professional actors, and by having an emphasis on improvisation, gives the film a particular edge, although this was tied to constraints on time and money. This was clear in the film's one sex scene and the sequence where Morvern cuts up her boyfriend:

> 'Ramsay and her crew decamped to another room, leaving Morton and her male counterpart to 'fuck about' – a choice of words that makes the director bury her head in her hands. Another day, for one of the film's most pivotal sequences, the director took charge of the camera herself as Morton ran riot in a tiny bathroom, knocking back brandy instead of cold tea, "because we'd done that many takes I was going to be sick otherwise. And I'm in the bath with the make-up guy squirting me with blood, me in the nuddy, tits hanging out. Lynne standing there … and part of you thinks, God, this is ridiculous.'"[24]

Morvern Callar is a stunning film to look at, built around very little plot and a central character who is both distant and perhaps totally unknowable. Unlike her friend Lanna who is content to stay in Scotland and who tells Morvern to 'stop dreamin'', she is a restless soul who wants more from life even if she doesn't quite know what that is yet. Ramsay's film shows the possibilities of what British film can do when it reinvents the ordinary and strives for the extraordinary.

INTO THE VALLEY: AMMA ASANTE'S *A WAY OF LIFE*

At first glance '*A Way of Life*' seems the polar opposite of *Morvern Callar*, with its narrative situated in the terraced streets of South Wales and its central protagonist a teenage mother, Leigh Anne (Stephanie James), we are positioned in

Stephanie James (and baby), *A Way of Life*

traditional social-realist territory. Asante's film is defiantly provincial in its setting and deals with racism intelligently and without appearing worthy. It also presents Leigh Anne as a character who is as complex as Morvern, a fiercely protective, but quite clueless young mother who conversely leads and takes part in a vicious attack on her Turkish neighbour, Hassan (Oliver Haden), whom she suspects of reporting her to the authorities for neglect of her daughter Rebecca.

By tackling issues of race hate, set in a place long overlooked by film-makers, Amma Asante was able to show how commonplace casual racism is in predominately white areas of the United Kingdom. But she also wanted to give some sense of a voice to the attackers, rather than just presenting them as easy stereotypes. Perhaps as the victim of racism herself, growing up in a white area of London, she was able to articulate both sides of the argument:

> "'I started writing this during the Bradford-Burnley riots. You'd listen to Asian kids and they'd say one thing, and then you'd listen to the white kids and they'd say exactly the same. 'We have no future, we're frightened.' I wanted to say, "It's all of us."' (Sherwin, S. 28/11/03)[25]

By making Leigh Anne the leader of the gang and the chief instigator of the attack on Hassan, Asante was also tapping into the growth of female perpetrators of violent crime:

> '[Asante] … cites "'the Ladbroke Grove rape in 2001 when an 18-year old woman was found guilty of rape, along with girl muggings and a murder in South Wales led by a girl gang" as a source of inspiration.' (ibid.)

Leigh Anne lives in a damp and often 'electricity-less' house in 'Lakedown', which is actually part of Swansea's inner city, an area called Portend. A limited back-story attempts to give some sense of how she has arrived in this situation. Her mother has committed suicide and reference is made to her abusive father (who has remarried her aunt – her mother's sister). She is close to her brother Gavin (Nathan Jones) and his friends Robbie (Gary Sheppeard) and Stephen (Dean Wong), who have all had difficult and traumatic upbringings. Stephen is in a care home and wants to change his surname, Rajah, to the more Welsh sounding Hughes. He is teased about this by Robbie and by losing his surname hopes to reinvent himself to fit in more with the gang's problematic views on race.

What permeates the narrative is a desire to escape, but Leigh Anne and Robbie in particular blame many of their problems on 'Pakis'. In Robbie's case, there is a constant feeling that he wants to get away from the cycle of petty crime and reinvent himself somewhere away from Lakedown. When he mentions London, he is told by Stephen that it is 'full of Pakis, there'. Ignorance about the multicultural nature of Britain is shockingly apparent in this sequence. But when he makes a concerted effort to find a job at an old people's home, it is clear that the interviewer disregards him because of where he is from. So Robbie appears to be as much an 'outsider' as the people that he blames for his problems.

Hassan lives opposite Leigh Anne and he provides the focus for much of her anger. He is a widower with a teenage daughter, Julie. He is unafraid to stand up to the taunts of Leigh Anne and her cohorts and exposes their stupidity by stressing that he is Turkish and not a 'Paki' and that he has lived in Wales for longer than they have been alive. Julie represents everything that Leigh Anne perhaps wants – a loving and attentive father and the prospect of a bright future. Gavin, however, falls in love with Julie and they begin a secret relationship that results in Julie getting pregnant at the film's end. Julie ends up as lonely and abandoned as Leigh Anne.

Leigh Anne's parenting skills are limited. Although it is apparent that she has tremendous love for Rebecca, she is incapable of properly looking after her.

The child is suffering from eczema and is badly burnt by a candle, which Leigh Anne attempts to treat herself so that the authorities will not discover this and 'take Rebecca away' as she puts it. She is constantly being monitored by her social worker and also by Rebecca's paternal grandmother Annette Lewis (Brenda Blethyn), and Asante's camera captures her paranoia brilliantly with some interesting point-of-view shots, which place us right with Leigh Anne. It is also clear that Annette has had her own problems – Dylan, Rebecca's father, is in prison and her other son tried to kill himself after being abused by his step-father. This world is dark in every respect.

Nowhere is this more apparent than early on when Leigh Anne negotiates a deal in a back street pub where Helen, a young girl from her street, is 'sold' for sex to one of the pub's customers. The sexual act is grim and takes place in wasteland, the money used to buy designer trainers for Rebecca, ironically paid to Helen's mother. It shows what Leigh Anne is capable of, the lengths that she will go to and the power she exerts to get other characters to do her bidding. This is also true at the film's climax.

Hassan, who she wrongly believes has been feeding information to her social worker about her parenting, becomes the target for a ferocious attack. He is found by the gang in the local library, collecting Julie who has been studying there. He is chased from the library to his van and then the gang, hoods up, set about him, kicking and punching. It is the scene that bookends the film, the camera is everywhere, the editing sharp and jagged. It feels real. Leigh Anne eggs on the boys, pushchair at her side. Rebecca and a young boy also watch, the cycle of violence passed on. The final, perhaps fatal, kick is delivered by Leigh Anne. Hassan lies bloodied and dead in the suburban Swansea street, Julie at his side (after being hit by her erstwhile lover Gavin as she tried to protect her father). The gang walk off for chips, still covered in Hassan's blood.

It is a horrific scene, but sadly totally believable. The boys are arrested, as is Leigh Anne, who at the police station is finally separated from her daughter. 'What did you think would happen?', the police officer asks her. For once, Leigh Anne has no answer.

The film is a grim indictment of the effects of poverty and the way that it can fuel racism and violence. Although difficult to watch, Asante's film is also visually and aurally very interesting. The street that Leigh Anne lives on is closed in and totally claustrophobic, the means of escape difficult. (But it is between a high hill at its top and the sea at the bottom, means of escape in either direction.) The narrow streets on which she pushes Rebecca about in her buggy intensify an overall impression of entrapment. Yet the use of wider landscapes and brilliant sunsets give the film a pastoral feel. The largely acoustic soundtrack, featuring David Gray's songs, is thoughtful and on occasion tremendously moving. Even The Stereophonics sound relevant, when Leigh Anne and the boys sing aloud, in one of the few scenes where the characters appear joyous.

Ultimately Leigh Anne is the victim of her own past. Her actions are unforgivable and difficult to understand, but what Amma Asante doesn't do is judge. She, like Andrea Arnold, Pam Dunn and Lynne Ramsay, leaves it up to the audience to decide what feelings we have about this young woman. This is a key factor in all the films that have been looked at. However there is no sense of cathartic release from grief as in *Red Road*, no new relationship as in *Gypo* or the new start as in *Morvern Callar*. Unlike the other characters that we have encountered in this chapter, Leigh Anne, rather than having some sort of escape from the travails of her desperate life, is made instead to confront her mistakes and perhaps that is the most realistic statement of all.

REFERENCES

1. Hayward, S., *Key Concepts in Cinema Studies*, London: Routledge, 1996

2. *UK Film Council Yearbook* 2006/07

3. BBC News, 'Female film-makers face struggle', 05/07/02

4. Pendreigh, B., 'The catcher in the eye' in The Guardian, 14/08/1999

5. Krum, S., 'Beware! Queen Kong is coming' in The Guardian, 24/02/2006

6. Brown, G., 'Paradise Found and Lost: The Course of British Realism' in The British Cinema Book, Murphy, R. (ed.), London: BFI: 2001

7. Brunsdon, C., 'Not Having It All: Woman and Film in the 1990s' in British Cinema of the 90s, Murphy, R. (ed.), London: BFI, 2000

8. Leigh, D., 'I Like Darkness' in The Guardian, 18/10/2006

9. Benyahia, S. C, et al, A2 Film Studies, Abingdon: Routledge, 2006

10. www.comingsoon.net/news/movienews.php?id=19735
    Andrea Arnold on Red Road with Edward Douglas

11. French, P., Review of Red Road in The Observer, 29/10/2006

12. McGill, H., 'Mean Streets' in Sight and Sound, November 2006

13. Raison, V., 'Reading Red Road' in Media Magazine, May 2007

14. http://shootingpeople.org/shooterfilms/interview.php?int_id=s3
    Pam Dunn interviewed by James McGregor 19/10/2005

15. Mottram, J., 'Paul McCann: The latest twist in his tale' in The Independent, 20/10/2006

16. Bradshaw, P., 'Poetry from the rubbish tip' in The Guardian, 12/11/1999

17. www.indiewire.com/people/int_Ramsay_Lynn_001013.html
    'Glitter Jewel – Lynne Ramsay finds beauty in Ratcatcher' by Andy Bailey 13/10/2000

18. French, P., 'He killed a boy and the binmen are on strike. Life really stinks' in The Observer, 14/11/1999

19. O'Sullivan, C., Review of Ratcatcher in Sight and Sound, November 1999

20. Romney, J., Review of Movern Callar in The Independent on Sunday, 04/11/2002

21. Andrew, G., In conversation with Lynne Ramsay in The Guardian, 28/10/2002

22. Williams, L.R., 'Escape Artist', in Sight and Sound, October 2002

23. Quinn, A., Review of Movern Callar in The Independent, 01/11/2002

24. Leigh, D., 'About a girl' in The Guardian, 05/10/2002

25. Sherwin, S., 'How grim is my valley' in The Guardian, 28/11/2003

WELCOME TO BRITAIN – ECONOMIC MIGRANTS AND ASYLUM SEEKERS IN BRITISH FILM

INTRODUCTION

Historically Britain has always been a country that has welcomed economic migrants. With its strong links to the Commonwealth and with Europe, there has been a recognisably fluid migratory pattern into this country since the Second World War. Films have sought to reflect the particular tensions and issues around the new arrivals in a variety of ways. In the late 1950s and early 1960s two key films set the template for two different forms of representation. They were *Sapphire* (Dearden, 1959) and *Flame in the Streets* (Baker, 1961). As Jim Pines has noted, these films highlighted clear anxieties about the relatively new black presence in the UK, as they centred on

> 'white racial prejudice partly in terms of blacks being represented as "victims" (*Flame in the Streets*) or as "social problem" (*Sapphire*). Neither film is particularly concerned with notions of social justice, integration or assimilation, although both can be read as liberal humanist pleas for racial tolerance.' (in Murphy [ed.], 2001, p179)[1]

The initial post-war migrants came largely from the Commonwealth. The peak period of mass immigration was in the early 1960s and was in part due to the Commonwealth Immigrants Act of 1962, which allowed in migrants with employment contracts or specific skills, or the dependents of immigrants who had already settled in Britain to remain in this country. The pinnacle of anti-immigrant sentiment was in the late 1960s (Sandbrook, 2006, p627)[2], some of which was inspired by the leading Conservative MP Enoch Powell's infamous 'Rivers of Blood' speech. Tensions were not eased with the expulsion of Ugandan and Kenyan Asians and their subsequent migration into Britain. There was an absence of films around these significant social and cultural shifts which were happening in many of Britain's major cities. Most of the key discourses were being played out on television, but black representations were largely focused on in terms of the black or Asian relationship with wider white society. As a result, these representations clearly signposted black characters and cultures as the 'other' (Pines in Murphy [ed.], 2001 p180)[3].

In Chapter 7 (Existing Identities), films looking at these more established racial groups will be explored in much more detail, but it is interesting to note here how some of the films made during this decade, based on more recent economic migrants and asylum seekers who have come to Britain, also present this notion of the 'other'. This is often played out in a far more complex fashion than either Dearden or Baker could have imagined, because of the growing opening up of access to this country.

The 2001 census revealed that 4.9 million people, 8.3% of the UK's total population, were born overseas, which was more than double the 1951 figure. The increase in the absolute numbers of the foreign-born population between 1991 and 2001 was greater than in any of the preceding post-war decades. Many of the new foreign nationals were young and were here for a relatively short stay (National Office of Statistics). So the picture of Britain was once again changing and this has been further transformed with the expansion of the European Union in 2004 to include countries from the former communist bloc: Poland, Latvia, Lithuania, Czech Republic, Hungary, Estonia, Slovakia and Slovenia, with Romania and Bulgaria admitted in 2007. This expansion gave migrants from Eastern Europe the right to come to Britain to seek work. Since 1997, according to the Statistics Commission, 1.4 million new workers were born abroad, with 1.1 million being foreign nationals[4].

In terms of people seeking asylum in this country, figures seem to be more uncertain, but as of December 2007 there were between 400,000 and 450,000 files in a huge backlog of applications for asylum to the Home Office. This was reinforced with a National Audit Office estimate of 283,000 unsuccessful asylum seekers still living in Britain[5]. All these figures, both for recent immigrants and asylum seekers, are as close to the 'official' numbers as one can get, but there is likely to be many more people living in the United Kingdom illegally.

The media, especially the tabloid and middle market press, have responded strongly to this issue with a succession of stories stoking up fear and questioning the figures released by the Home Office. A good example of this was the lead story from the Daily Express by Tom Whitehead on 13 February 2008, titled 'Over 860 Migrants Flood in Every Day'[6]. The article raises concerns over the effect on public services due to the change in population, but also develops quite graphic scenarios:

> 'The influx means that an additional 2.3 million immigrants have officially moved to Britain since Labour took power – more than the entire population of West Yorkshire.'

> '…new clusters of settled migrants could be developing in the suburbs and may cause tension with residents.'

> 'Earlier this year, immigration minister Liam Byrne even admitted that mass migration is "deeply unsettling" Britain and piling pressure on communities.'

Against this backdrop film-makers have responded in a variety of different ways to the new arrivals' experience of living in Britain, but all have been largely sympathetic to the challenge of starting to live and fit in to a new country. There have been numerous television dramas that have also followed different paths and issues around this subject. *Sex Traffic* (2004), written by Abi Morgan, looked at the exploitation of young women from Moldova in the British sex industry. Ken Loach's *It's a Free World* (2007) focused on the setting up of a work agency by a young woman from Essex, which uses foreign workers and concentrates on the moral dilemmas that surround what she does. *Exodus* (2007) took a surreal, almost hallucinatory approach to the subject.

The main focus of this chapter will be on three films: Pavel Pawlikowski's *Last Resort*, which favours a dreamlike, romantic approach; *Dirty Pretty Things*, directed by Stephen Frears, which also has a central love story at its core but is much more conventional in its overall mood and feeling; and Nick Broomfield's stark drama-documentary *Ghosts*, based on the deaths in 2004 of a group of Chinese cockle pickers near Morecambe Bay. It is also interesting to note that both *Last Resort* (BBC) and *Ghosts* (Channel Four) had early television screenings, but had limited releases in art-house cinemas.

These films are all effective in attempting to address some of the complex issues around national identity, social justice and representation. They are all, in their own individual ways, angry films seeking to challenge some of the tabloid preconceptions around this area by showing characters that are well-rounded and sympathetic. They also crucially show a different view of Britain, often from the perspective of the migrants themselves – which can be a strange and revealing experience for a British audience. These aren't mainstream, big-budget films and all have their production context solidly linked to television. They all utilise social-realist and documentary techniques in both their narrative and formal style, but they also provide a fascinating view of Britain during the decade, encouraging audiences to perhaps look beyond the scare stories from the media regarding influxes and unwanted social change.

LAST RESORT: 'THE ARMPIT OF THE UNIVERSE'

Paddy Considine, Dina Korzun, *Last Resort*

BBC Films' *Last Resort* was perhaps the first film to deal with this subject and did so in a highly creative and revealing way. The title of the film was from photographer Martin Parr's depiction of working-class life in a dying English seaside resort. Pawel Pawlikowski, who wrote and directed the film, had worked for many years for the BBC on a series of very creative documentaries made for the *Bookmark* series and this background, along with his own personal dimension as a Polish émigré film-maker, greatly inform this, his second feature.

The film wasn't intended originally for theatrical release and was shown on BBC2, but ended up getting a limited print run in London and at some provincial art-house cinemas. This micro budget film is a reminder of the contribution that television has made to the British film industry and adds Pawlikowski to a list of directors who have made a notable transition between the two mediums: Alan Clarke, Mike Leigh and Ken Loach to name but a few.

The plot is deceptively simple. Twenty-something illustrator Tanya (Dina Korzun) arrives from Moscow, 10-year-old son Artiom (Artiom Strelnikov) in tow, to meet her English boyfriend Mark, and to start a new life. When he fails to show she is detained by the immigration officers at the airport, and in desperation lies about her situation, claiming political asylum by saying that her life is under threat back in Russia. She and her son are taken to a holding area called Stonehaven, a bleak seaside resort. She is quickly befriended by Alfie (Paddy Considine), an exile from the Midlands, who works at an amusement arcade and as a bingo-caller. He also acts as an unofficial 'fixer' for the immigrants in Stonehaven, by offering cheap cigarettes and phone-cards. Mark's absence is confirmed and Tanya wishes to return home but soon finds that she is caught up in the backlog for asylum applications and is informed that she will have to wait for at least a year before she can be 'processed'. Her relationship with Alfie develops tentatively and he also forges a strong bond with Artiom. Tanya tries unsuccessfully to raise money to escape Stonehaven and agrees to play a part on an internet porn site run by Les (Lindsey Honey). However, she breaks down on the webcam and flees the scene, disgusted by what she has had to do. Sometime later Les turns up at her flat and tries to coax her back to work for him, stating that the punters loved her tears. She refuses but takes his money, but Alfie and Artiom find out what she has done. Alfie storms off and Artiom refuses to talk to his mother and gets drunk with his new English friends. He is found by Alfie and brought back to Tanya, whereupon Alfie agrees to help them escape. He heads to Les's centre of operations and assaults him. They escape on a boat and Alfie flags down a lorry to take them to London, and they part. The final shots are of Tanya and Artiom on the airport shuttle. We are back where we began.

Tanya's expressive eyes and obvious beauty are strongly indicated right from the start of the film. The doughty customs officer half-interrogates, half-flirts, shyly taken aback by her good looks. He questions her about her intention to 'solicit' work while in the United Kingdom, an interesting choice of word considering the fate of many women that come to this country, exploited in the sex trade. It is also an extremely subtle piece of foreshadowing, given Tanya's later excursion into the shadowy world of internet sex.

The airport sequence, although short, underpins the sense of Tanya's apparent innocence and rashness, driven by pure emotion, and Artiom's apparent maturity, guiding and reassuring his mother, when in reality it should be the other way round. It also gives a sense of the bureaucratic nightmare that faces Tanya and the way in which she is dehumanised through the mug-shots and the questioning. This continues with the trip to the waiting police-cars, shot in jerky Steadicam, with Alsatians barking, Artiom swearing and protesting, having to be coaxed gently into the vehicle by his mother. Pawlikowski maintains that the film is set in the near future, but this sequence feels very much rooted in the here and now. Tanya and Artiom have left a country with a police state history (and possibly present under Putin) and have ended up in a place that initially feels no different. This is further reinforced by their experience in Stonehaven.

Pawlikowski is clear in how he wanted his characters to appear: 'What always interested me in films as in life were people who defied the norm, whose personalities defied their environment, who despite being social underdogs haven't lost their humanity and their ability to yearn' (from Norton-Smith's review of the film on bbc.co.uk)[7]. This sense of yearning and the focus on outsiders is certainly the major focus in this film.

Iain Sinclair's view of Tanya, 'a doll-like, kabuki presence; high thin eyebrows, always arched, astonished. Slavic melancholy … a china-white face and blood-red lips', is particularly apt (Sight and Sound, March 2001)[8]. She stands out. When Alfie meets her he tells her that she doesn't look like an asylum seeker. When she is rounded up for the first time, she is easy to pick out in the crowd. It is of course this striking beauty, this sense of a distinctive 'otherness', which draws the pornographer Les to her.

 Alfie has also been already introduced; lean, dark, shadow-boxing in his small flat, breaking up rows in his hallway, arguments not conducted in English, young children winding him up. He seems to fit in, but also seems a man in transition like many of the occupants in the large holding cell. He calls out the bingo numbers to groups of locals who already look like they have given up on life, holding out for the last big win that might change things for them. As the film progresses we see his life unfurl. He runs a sea-front arcade, where anorak-wearing migrants queue up for cheap fags. Alfie 'establishes himself as a self-appointed authority figure, one of those Englishmen who feels equally comfortable protecting foreigners and pushing them around' (Romney, 18/03/2001)[9].

Tanya and Artiom are brought to a huge tower block, something that seems long abandoned by locals and given over to the newcomers. It resembles the blocks built across Eastern Europe at the height of the Cold War; it is faceless and utterly functional, a home in the sky for the poor and dispossessed. The exteriors, shot by Ryszard Lenczewski's Super 16 photography, are stunning and capture the tarnished mid-winter beauty of England's coastline. His long, static shots of the small-town seascape, the grey sky meeting the grey sea and the empty night-time backstreets make the everyday look somehow poetic. This combines well with the hand-held movement of the camera, which often gets uncomfortably close to the actors, emphasising the intimate relationship that is developed with the characters.

The combination of the poetic and the realistic is also supported by the *mise-en-scène* of the flat itself which is incredibly minimalist – some uncomfortable chairs, an old table and a battered, flea-ridden sofa. There seems to be the constant hum of diegetic noise, more fights and shouting, snatches of music from across the globe – but all seems very indistinct. The bleak *mise-en-scène* is contrasted with the vivid orange wallpaper depicting an imaginary beach bathed in warm hues, complete with palm trees. The characters, foregrounded in front of this, seem out of place against this imaginary idyll:

> 'Stonehaven, a grey pit of a coastal town. A holding bay for asylum seekers. Stonehaven is perhaps more accurately the limbo before the inferno; a concrete townscape…'[10]

The camera catches the view from the window – Dreamland, the ironically named old-fashioned theme park, is in view, along with the misty aspect of the bay, a shot which is returned to many times in this film, offering some indication that there may well be an escape from this place. The horrifically false feel of Lindsey Anderson's *O Dreamland* (1953) is also invoked here. The film was shot in Margate in winter, like Pam Dunn's *Gypo* (see chapter 4). The place itself doesn't look like the most inviting one for anybody to end up in and this is developed in both films to good effect, reminiscent in parts of Dogme 95 in terms of its naturalism and immediacy.

Pawlikowski further emphasises this with his use of other exteriors. Tanya and Artiom decide to make for the train station to reach London only to find it closed and more or less abandoned. They walk through deserted, windswept precincts covered in fast-food related litter, captured by the ubiquitous close-circuit cameras, only to be told that there will be no trains until further notice. The sense of claustrophobia is very much in evidence, the town seems to be surrounded by fences and the police and the authorities appear to be everywhere. In many respects the place seems much like a less frenetic Bexhill-On-Sea as portrayed in Cuaron's *Children of Men*, but the potential for major social disorder seems to be constantly bubbling under the surface.

The music also adds to the despondent, bleak feel of the film with a strange fairground-style score that sounds like an extended instrumental from a Tom Waits album, perhaps *Swordfishtrombones* or *Rain Dogs*. It was a highly deliberate move by the director:

> 'I distorted [the music] to add to the sinister mood of the place but then it is also quite romantic at times too. I like it, some people say you don't need music in this film but you need music in films.'[11]

The queues we see early in the film for the town's one call-box do date the film. For example, mobile phones play a big part in Nick Broomfield's *Ghosts* in creating narrative tension, but their absence in *Last Resort* mean that it is in her first attempt to contact Mark that Tanya first meets Alfie. She is unsure about how to use the phone-cards and Alfie acts as her guide. It is clear from these opening exchanges that he is interested in her, although it is also clear that those feelings may not be reciprocated. Tanya is someone who 'has to be in love' and she tells Alfie that it is this fault that has brought her to

Stonehaven. She sees her exile in what Artiom has named 'the armpit of the universe' as her punishment for past failed relationships. It is apparent that the impulsive nature that was responsible for her past mistakes is been fought against in relation to her feelings for Alfie.

The British characters, apart from Alfie and Les, remain very much on the periphery. They are the authorities – the senior police officer who warns them that any attempts to escape will be met with a withdrawal of privileges; the aggressive café owner where there is no fish in the batter, berating Africans for stealing the cutlery; the faceless benefits officials struggling under the weight of backlogs, giving the party line about procedure; the ambulances standing idly in side-streets procuring cut-price blood from the newcomers. Artiom's friends selling knock-off heaters and portable televisions seem almost feral, there doesn't seem to be any parental control or any attendance at school. They roam around Stonehaven unfettered and largely unchallenged, sharing cigarettes and vodka, shouting at the singing asylum seekers to 'go back to your own country', dancing on desolate evening beaches to the unfamiliar strains of Balkan folk music.

Les, in his own way, is part of this new global market, selling pornographic fantasies worldwide. He sees himself as 'Mr Stonehaven'; with his blazer, stonewashed jeans, dyed blonde hair, denim shirt and flashy jewellery he is almost a caricature of the faded 1970s rock star, beached up far from his glory days. He is charming and is only made to appear threatening by his regulation bodyguard. Artiom, unlike his naïve mother, spots at once that he is a pimp. As Sinclair notes, 'Les offers the only work there is: soliciting. "Always looking for beautiful girls," he yawns, touch-feely. "Gorgeous cheekbones," adds his minder Frank. The red-top aesthete.' (Sight and Sound, March 2001)

This is essentially a love story. Alfie's courtship of Tanya involves a trip to his other place of work, the gaudily lit bingo hall. Tanya steadily gets more and more inebriated on halves of cider as Alfie calls the numbers out; she cries and berates her own lack of control when it comes to giving her heart away. In a lovely touch they initially sway and then dance to a Russian cover version of Petula Clark's lovelorn 'Downtown'. The journey home with the customary bag of chips is through Stonehaven's broken streets as Alfie gives Tanya an insight into his boxing career and ironically we glimpse an assault at the corner of the frame. Alfie warns her not to look. She can't understand why Alfie has chosen to come to Stonehaven, why he isn't a 'prisoner' in the town like her. There are indications of a troubled, violent past, jailed for something serious. Alfie is like Tanya, on the run from the past and looking for some kind of redemption. He lingers outside her block of flats, waiting for the offer of coffee. It doesn't come.

A second date, this time with Artiom, leads them to a boat, a windswept pier straight from a Turner painting and an interrupted pub conversation. In a close-up two-shot, Pawlikowski catches Alfie mid-flow filling in more gaps about his childhood, recounting a beating from his father for throwing eggs. Tanya watches intently, understanding little of what Alfie is saying, but enjoying his north Midlands accent. A seaside hug, a plea from Alfie and he is left outside on Tanya's doorstep once again. It emerges slowly that Tanya is attracted to Alfie, but she fights it all the way, terrified of replicating the same past mistakes.

The film ends with a tense night-time journey by boat along the coastline and away from the prying eyes of the authorities. A final stolen moment between Alfie and Tanya, by a blazing beach bonfire, shot in striking close-up, draws the relationship to a close. Tanya realises that she must return to Moscow without Alfie in order to give Artiom the stability that seems to have been missing in the past.

It is a very subtle and quite moving farewell. Alfie flags down a London-bound juggernaut and says his goodbyes. Artiom, in tears, gives him a bear hug; Tanya gives him a kiss and one of her pictures, of an ark that Alfie had previously said had made him want to cry. Iain Sinclair once again picks up on the natural and perfectly pitched feel of this parting from Tanya's perspective:

'You expect a standard reflex, a last embrace, a brave speech, a sniffle. Korzun offers a miraculous half wave of dismissal. Blink and you could miss it. It's our unfamiliarity with these faces, not knowing how they'll behave, that adds immeasurably to the charm of *Last Resort*.' (Sight and Sound, March 2001)

The film reaches its emotional highpoint here. We see a reprise of the opening scene at the airport, as Tanya and Artiom return home. Alfie is left adrift – bereft of the woman and boy that he loves, destined to return to a lonely life in Stonehaven with retribution and revenge waiting for him in the shape of Les and Frank. It is an uncertain end for him, but *Last Resort* shows that the personal certainly can be political. Points about the plight of asylum seekers are made both implicitly and explicitly, but ultimately this film is about two people searching for love and a sense of belonging and it offers no easy solutions, no pat resolution.

DIRTY PRETTY THINGS – HEARTBREAK HOTEL

Stephen Frears has moved back and forth between making Hollywood and British films with relative ease over the past 25 years. He learnt his profession in the mid-1960s by working on some interesting British films such as *Morgan – A*

Audrey Tautou, *Dirty Pretty Things*

Suitable Case for Treatment (Reisz, 1966) and as an assistant director on Lindsey Anderson's *If....* The bulk of his early career was spent in television drama during the 1970s and early 1980s. He restarted his film career with gangster film *The Hit* (1984) and he returned to prominence with Channel Four's *My Beautiful Laundrette*.

Despite its subject matter centring on a homosexual relationship between a British Pakistani laundrette owner and a racist thug, the film was a relative commercial success and won great critical acclaim. Frears' follow-up, *Prick Up Your Ears* (1987), based on the short life of 1960s playwright Joe Orton, also had a good reaction. Frears started his relationship with Hollywood in 1988 with the costume drama *Dangerous Liaisons* and this has continued with rather mixed results from his neo-noir *The Grifters* (1990) through the expensive failure of the Julia Roberts star vehicle *Mary Reilly* (1996) and his successful adaptation of Nick Hornby's *High Fidelity* (2000).

An interesting project during this time was his take on Roddy Doyle's novels *The Snapper* (1993) and *The Van* (1996), both made for BBC Films. *The Snapper* was by far the more compelling film centring on a working-class Dublin teenager who finds herself pregnant and was by turns hillarous and knowing, signalling a return to the more social-realist approach of his earlier television work and his 1980s films.

After the relative failures of *The Hi-Lo Country* (1998) and *Liam* (1998), Frears was offered *Dirty Pretty Things*, a film based on the immigrant experience in London, with a contemporary feel that harked back to some of his previous movies. The film had a fascinating production context. Miramax, part of the Disney corporation, provided the bulk of the budget, ensuring a decent distribution run. BBC Films renewed its relationship with Frears by providing some money and Celador Films, a new player in the business, also had some financial input. *Dirty Pretty Things* was a first-time script for writer Steve Knight who had strong production and development connections with Celador, best known for its television work on hit programmes like *Who Wants to be a Millionaire* (1998–present).

Knight had started to write *Dirty Pretty Things* in the late 1990s as a novel and it started life as a straightforward thriller set in a hotel. He was particularly drawn to the invisibility of the hotel staff and was interested in how this invisibility could be used within a dramatic context. Although he has denied that there was any explicit political agenda, the central focus was of course going to be on the people that largely work in hotels – those from other countries:

> '…if you want to live outside the law, you have to obey the rules and most menial staff in hotels have, at best, very precarious legal status. The plot of *Dirty Pretty Things* is initiated and sustained by the desperation of people who have no legal protection for the rules of the underworld.'[12]

Knight researched the film by talking to the head of the Russian desk at the National Criminal Intelligence Service who confirmed that many of the maids and kitchen porters were illegal, recruited on street corners and down kitchen alleys. What was interesting to Knight was not only the experience of coming to Britain or the life that they were trying to forge here, but the incredible back-stories that many of these recently arrived workers had. In its approach, *Dirty Pretty Things* certainly attempts to reflect this.

Okwe (Chiwetel Ejiofor), the main protagonist, is an illegal Nigerian immigrant who has two jobs: during the day he drives a mini-cab and at night he is a porter at London's Hotel Baltic, keeping awake by chewing herbal leaves. In his home country he had been a doctor. He had also been a political activist, framed for murder by corrupt officials and is hiding in Britain under an assumed name.

He sleeps on the sofa of his fellow worker at the Baltic, illegal Turkish chambermaid Senay (Audrey Tautou). The first major complication in the film occurs when Okwe discovers a blocked toilet in one of the Baltic's rooms only to find the waste pipe backed up with a human heart. Although this sets up the generic premise of the film as a thriller, Knight's script and Frears' assured direction take the film in a different direction.

The chief concierge, the Spanish Juan (Sergi Lopez), nicknamed 'Sneaky', dismisses the find and reminds the horrified Okwe of his illegal status when the Nigerian stresses that the police should be involved. When Okwe tries to treat a middle-aged Somali man who is in pain after a botched operation to remove one of his kidneys it becomes apparent that Sneaky is running an elaborate scam trading in body organs. Sneaky wants to cut Okwe in, because of his medical background, but he refuses. That is, until he discovers that Senay has been tricked into being a donor in order to get a passport that will enable her to escape to New York. It appears that Okwe will perform the operation on Senay but, aided by a British prostitute, Juliette (Sophie Okonedo), and his Chinese mortician friend Guo Yi (Benedict Wong), he drugs Sneaky and takes his kidney instead. The transaction follows this and Okwe uses the money to return home and Senay to pursue her dreams in the United States.

Clear demarcation is made between Okwe's assured sense of morality, his utter goodness and self-sacrifice and Sneaky's amoral, unfettered greed. Both characters present almost polar opposites and when extended to archetypal representations they are most revealing: the noble African and the untrustworthy European. The Independent's review of the film highlights the central conceit of Ejiofor's performance in that 'Okwe [has] goodness without piety, and nobility without arrogance'[13]. His appearance – dressed down to blend in, his hotel uniform hiding his main identity – and his professional background is in sharp contrast to Sneaky's slicked-back hair, expensive car and the general air of menace that surrounds him.

We first meet Okwe at Heathrow Airport picking up cab fares, and this introduces a sense of circularity to the narrative as this venue acts as a point of departure for him and Senay at the end of the film. His shift ends at a shabby north London cab office, where it becomes apparent that all the drivers there are like him, working in the black market, cash in hand, far away from their place of birth.

Frears uses an interesting device here which gives us an indication of Okwe's medical background, but at first glance suggests another sort of transaction. Okwe's boss at the cab office, a genial West Indian, invites him into the back to do something for him and then in mid-shot pulls down his trousers and underwear. It is at first glance a scene that could go in several directions: Okwe's initial bartering and tracking down rides at Heathrow isn't dissimilar to a street prostitute's actions and this scene could well be an extension of this; it is a distinct possibility that Okwe is being asked to perform fellatio on his boss. After a short but uncomfortable take, framed behind glass, where Okwe studies the man's penis, it becomes apparent that the transaction is not what we might have thought. The boss has a sexually transmitted disease and asks his driver to get something to treat it. This darkly comic scene in the dingy office does set the tone for the film, but it is the shift to the Baltic Hotel that provides the bulk of the action.

What is apparent quite quickly is how the production design really reflects the often uncertain, often surreal nature of the hotel itself. As the main focus is on Okwe the hotel is always shot at night and the neon strip lighting of the interiors adds an unnatural feel to the film, a transitional mood that reflects the nature of the workers' lives. There is a faded grandeur to the Baltic with its red and gold *mise-en-scène*, contrasting well with the quiet desperation of the hotel staff. The use of clocks to suggest the slow drawn-out pace and the quiet nocturnal nature of the business conducted there is very effective. Black-and-white CCTV close-ups of the hotel staff seem to give a sense of anonymity to the faces. Senay's sullen beauty stands out, certainly due to Tautou's star presence and this seems to render the other waitresses and kitchen porters' features as entirely forgettable. In fact, the impact of the central characters' attractive faces was something that Frears really wanted to exploit by making them leap from the screen and attract an audience:

'It seemed to me that the characters deserved to have a glamorous film made about them. If I was a Turkish immigrant I would like to be played by Audrey Tautou. People want to be shown in a nice light. In my experience they don't want to be shown to be boring, miserable or victims.'[14]

The relationship between Senay, the young Muslim woman who has fled an arranged marriage in Turkey, and Okwe is beautifully handled and the racial issue is one that is underplayed, although the romance, like that in *Last Resort*, is extremely chaste with brief glances, quiet dinners and stolen kisses. Senay, the pretty, naïve virgin who disguises her domestic arrangement with Okwe, is a character who appears at first glance to be quite thinly drawn, but is gradually revealed to have hidden depths as the narrative develops.

She is pursued by the stereotypical immigration officers, complete with cheap suits and unshaven faces, and is forced to abandon the Baltic. She ends up at a textiles factory, in reality a backstreet sweatshop run by an overweight middle-aged Asian who forces her to perform oral sex on him in return for his silence to the authorities. She bites back, quite literally, and her dream of escape to America seems in ruins. Sneaky convinces her that giving up one of her organs will guarantee her a passport and cash for a new life. Part of the deal is that she surrenders her virginity to him, in a disturbing scene which clearly outlines her utter sense of despondency. The notion that there is a point to the apparent lack of detail to Senay's character arc outside of reaching New York is one that Nick Roddick sees as deliberate:

'Perhaps this is the point. As Okwe puts it, "For you and I there is only survival" – a desperate pragmatism which effectively buries matters of identity and personal history.' [15]

The sense of 'glamour' as highlighted by the director by the casting of Tautou and the lack of an effective back-story might well level accusations of a lack of realism in *Dirty Pretty Things*. In many respects there is a hyper-reality in the *mise-en-scène*, framed beautifully by veteran cinematographer Chris Menges. London is a key character in the film, 'a weird city' as Guo Yi observes and the film avoids the mainstream, over-clichéd view of the metropolis by avoiding showing the obvious landmarks. Instead we see exteriors of inner-city backstreets and cluttered multi-ethnic markets. It is a London that is distinctive, but one that is rarely focused on. In many respects it feels like the London of Neil Jordan's *Mona Lisa* (1986), a London of the half light, a perpetually moving city serviced by unseen hordes of workers, without whom the whole system would crumble.

Iain Sinclair's piece on *Dirty Pretty Things* sees it as too televisual, in many respects weighed down by its own adherence to plot and by its rather simplistic take on the issues. He stresses that the asylum seekers or 'the lost souls of London, are all too visible' and in many respects this is true – the host community just tend not to acknowledge them. As a great writer on London himself he sees the film as:

'A London of the mind. Where all sexual transactions are hierarchic: inferiors service superiors, in kitchens, in sweatshops, borrowed hotel rooms … Not enough dirty, too much pretty …A workmanlike product, well constructed enough to hide its flaws.'[16]

To an extent this is true, and coupled with some of the stereotypical characterisations – the innocent heroine, the bear-like Russian doorman, the philosophical Chinese hospital worker and the self-effacing African hero – the film at first glance might be seen as a conventional thriller. That said, the film does offer many interesting points about how Britain is viewed through the eyes of the immigrants. This is clear in the few representations of British characters. Juliette, the lovable 'tart with a heart', is the only identifiable British character and she conducts her work here with good humour and with the unspoken agreement of the Baltic's staff. But she is every bit as invisible as the illegal immigrants. The immigration officers point warrant cards in faces, but their only concern is in tracking down Senay. Sneaky's accomplice in the organ trade is faceless, not recognising Okwe as he hands over Sneaky's still warm kidney. The response to this signposts the film's key speech by Okwe which seems to underpin the major political context presented in *Dirty Pretty Things*: 'We are the people that you don't see. We drive your cabs. We clean your rooms. We suck your cocks.'

The film does try to be all things to all viewers and in many respects achieves this – for good or ill. It is, as Jonathan Romney has said, 'a drama of London's underclass, an essay in multiculturalism, a bit of a state of the nation essay. Its story of immigrants scrabbling for any living they can get … ought to make for a pitch-black, hard-boiled drama. So it's surprising what a gently entertaining crowd pleaser it turns out to be'[17]. This is, after all, the London that Tanya in *Last Resort* wants to escape to from the hellhole of Stonehaven. The place is also starkly different to the small-town semi-detached horrors presented in *Ghosts* and the Essex wastelands of *It's a Free World*. With its tightly constructed ending it offers a great deal of hope for the lead characters.

The calling on of favours by Okwe to trick Sneaky shows an alternative sense of community forged amongst the exiles, but it is also interesting to note that the villains of the piece Sneaky and Senay's Asian boss are not British either, which adds a further complex dimension to the narrative. The use of these characters as antagonists could be seen in one major way. It seems to absolve the British hosts of any sense of guilt in the exploitation of the immigrants as the characters that that are the most explicit agents of abuse, are in fact also immigrants to the United Kingdom. Perhaps this is a statement more on the hierarchy of the hotel and also the sweatshop, textile industry, but it is still interesting to note.

The end of the film may at first seem rather trite and easily resolved – the chase to the airport, the frantic phone calls home, protracted and moving goodbyes. On forged passports Senay heads west and Okwe back to Nigeria, giving the closure a melodramatic feel, with its slowly building score, use of close-ups and two-shots. The overall feeling that this ending seems to suggest is that Britain is an unwelcoming and difficult place

for newcomers. The 'escape' at Heathrow airport can actually be viewed as a failure of Britain's multicultural society to integrate someone of Okwe's education and talent and the script conveniently positions Okwe's daughter as the main reason for his return to Africa, but with no sense of what the future holds for him in his native land. Senay seems to have bought into the American dream which promises meritocracy and her flight seems ill-judged and rather naïve. While Frears' direction tugs at the heartstrings by accentuating the feelings between both characters at the departure desk, it ultimately masks important messages about attitudes to immigrants and their treatment in this country.

In many respects *Dirty Pretty Things* is the most mainstream of all the films in this chapter with its thriller-like approach to the subject, because it presents an accessible view of the issues with clearly defined archetypes and plot construction. In turn it is arguable that this very generic method may well present complex questions about immigration for a more mainstream audience in a simpler way than either the more social-realist *Last Resort* or *Ghosts* could manage.

GHOSTS: ON THE BEACH

Aiqin Lin, *Ghosts*

The 'ghosts' of Nick Broomfield's powerful drama-documentary have a two-fold meaning. They firstly refer to the British, who float phantom-like around the periphery of this film never fully in view; most tellingly the second meaning could refer to the 23 Chinese cockle pickers who perished in Morecambe Bay in February 2003, the event that provides the main focus for this film. That this understated, quietly powerful piece of film-making could come from veteran documentary-maker Broomfield, so often an active participant in his own work, might certainly be read as surprising. With his unassuming, often very humourous questioning style, his trademark sound-boom, white T-shirt and puzzled look to camera, Broomfield's persona has often divided both critics and audiences alike. However, his brand of performative documentary has been tremendously influential on a whole raft of film-makers such as Michael Moore, Louis Theroux and Morgan Spurlock. The subjects of his films have ranged from the famous

Hollywood prostitute in *Heidi Fleiss: Hollywood Madam* (1995), the autocratic Afrikaner Party leader Eugene Terre Blanche in *The Leader, The Driver and the Driver's Wife* (1991), doomed rock-star Kurt Cobain in *Kurt and Courtney* (1998) and the murderer Aileen Wournos in *Aileen, Portrait of a Serial Killer* (2002).

Thursday 5 February 2004 was when the first alarms were raised about a number of people stranded on the Red Bank sands at Morecambe Bay. The particular stretch of beach in question was well-known locally for its unpredictable tide patterns and quicksand. It was a popular place for cockle picking, an important local industry. The shellfish have a high export value, however the monotonous and backbreaking work offers scant reward for the pickers. The bay's high-quality cockles fetch around £10 for a 50kg bag for the employer and a picker can usually fill one an hour. There is said to be £8 million of cockles on these beaches (Herbert, 07/02/04)[18]. This work had long been done by locals but in recent years there had been a significant number of Chinese pickers working the sands. There had been some animosity evident in the area with an unnamed source from the local village of Hest Bank commenting, 'Some say the Chinese are earning £150 a day. That's a lot when some people in Morecambe can't get a wage.' There had also been reports that antagonised locals had poured diesel over the pickings and burnt them (Herbert, ibid.).

The other grim reality is that these poor people were forced by Chinese gangmasters to collect cockles in the most perilous of conditions as dusk loomed on a seafront, where they weren't really aware of the dangerous and ever-changing conditions. Many of these were illegally working in the United Kingdom, either asylum seekers or not known to the authorities. The way that the gangmasters operated was outlined by a former Chinese cockle picker in The Guardian. Workers were sent to the north-west in teams of ten or more and met by an associate of the gangmaster. They had to pay a £150 registration fee each before being taken to overcrowded and dangerous accommodation, for which they paid between £20 and £30 a week (Lawrence et al, 07/02/04)[19].

What was also clear was that many of the people who had died had paid large amounts of money to 'snakehead' gangsters who had organised the long and difficult trip, often financed by loans from relatives and neighbours. In the aftermath of these deaths, the debts still exist ranging from £6000 to £20,000 with very little hope of ever paying them back[20]. This gives a much wider framework to the story. In March 2006, a Chinese gangmaster, Lin Liang Ren, was found guilty of the unlawful killing of 21 cockle pickers; although police believe that there were 23 people on the beach, two bodies weren't found. The British firm Liverpool Bay Fishing Company was cleared of breaching immigration law by employing illegal immigrants in connection with the tragedy.

The real-life events on which *Ghosts* is based are only part of the overall narrative of the film. The approach that Broomfield takes here is to flesh out the context of how and why these people were stranded on a gloomy Lancashire beach by focusing his film on the journey and experiences of one young single mother, Ai Qin, from a poor Chinese village in the Fujian province. She travels alone to the United Kingdom hoping to earn enough money to pay for her son's education in China and to clear the debt she has incurred for her trip. We get an indication of her hazardous six-month journey via Kazakhstan, Belgrade and Calais and on arriving in London, she falls into the hands of a rough and ready gangmaster Mr Lin (Zhan Yu). We see her working in a variety of grim jobs, living in an overcrowded semi in Norfolk. She is paid a pittance and her living conditions are appalling. On being forced out of the house, Lin takes the workers northwards to the bleak Irish Sea shoreline where they meet their eventual fate.

Jonathan Romney, in his review, gives a good sense of the purpose of *Ghosts*: 'Ai Qin's story, informed by the research of Broomfield and of journalist Hsiao-Hung Pai, is presented with few stylistic or rhetorical trimmings. The catalogue of horrors is so stark that anti-immigration factions could use *Ghosts* as propaganda to deter anyone from ever coming here again: this island comes across as hostile, heartless, squalidly grubby, quite apart from the lousy weather'[21]. This description is appropriate when analysing the narrative. From the opening shots, there is a sense of desperation that envelops the film. Broomfield, in an uncharacteristically subtle fashion, presents a sense of truth through the eyes of Ai Qin. Instead of being just a blank statistic, she is shown as a fully rounded character, one who both attracts our attention and elicits our sympathy. The Britain that Broomfield presents is closer in spirit, certainly stylistically, to the view portrayed in *Last Resort* and it is an acutely depressing one.

The film opens with a caption that states that 'In the UK there are three million migrant workers who are the backbone of the construction, hospitality and health industries', which clearly sets out the film-maker's intentions. We start at the end of the story with a cramped minibus careering across sand against a grey, ominous looking sky. The action switches to a young woman with a nosebleed raking the sand for shellfish, there is a sense of the light fading quickly, the sound of the wind very apparent. We see the workers on top of the minibus, all caught in close, hand-held shots, their faces full of fear, shouting hopelessly for help. There are final phone calls – the role of the mobile phone is very much to the forefront of this film as opposed to both *Last Resort* and *Dirty Pretty Things*. These calls are desperate, last words to people at home before trying to swim for shore. Ai Qin asks about the moneylender and in a poignant moment sings her son a song.

We flashback to a year previously as we see where Ai Qin has come from. What is interesting and what lends the film an extra sense of authenticity is that the main roles were all taken by non-professional actors, including the lead, played by Aiqin Lin, who had also travelled to this country illegally in 1997 after a five-month journey. She, too, had a succession of low-paid jobs and had applied for asylum quite soon after arriving here. When she originally auditioned for the film in 2006 she still had no legal status and, like Ai Qin, she also has a son back in China. He was born here but she couldn't afford to keep him in England and he returned home to be reared by her parents. We see both him and her parents in her departure scenes – which she flew back home to film. These sequences were understandably very difficult for her to shoot and add another layer of realism to the film. It is interesting that Lin has said that she might not have come to England if she had seen this film first:

'I think if people at home see this, it would make them understand what it's really like in England. I have met a few Chinese people here who've found what they are looking for. A few. But I think that it mostly comes down to luck. And I know others who have had serious mental problems. Two very serious, in fact. One I know died in hospital. Another one is still in hospital.'[22]

In *Ghosts* we see brief snapshots of the horror of the arduous six-month trip here, in cramped, claustrophobic conditions that echo the fate of the 58 illegal Chinese immigrants found suffocated in the back of a truck in Dover in 2000. There is also a sense from Belgrade that there are many other migrants from, for example, the Indian subcontinent, often with children also prepared to run the risks to reach Western Europe. The last leg of the trip from Calais is particularly effective in showing this with our main protagonist put in a small box-like container, the camera placed with her. There is little light and Broomfield creates a real sense of a lack of air. The grim nature of the journey doesn't end on arrival in the promised land. Ai Qin is forced to make a hasty phone call home to release the final payment to the 'snakeheads' and then she is handed over to the gangmaster Mr Lin on a piece of deserted wasteland.

What Broomfield does to excellent effect is to avoid the idea that these migrants are swallowed up in the urban sprawl of London or another big city. Lin drives Ai Qin eastwards to the flatlands of East Anglia, negotiating deals on his mobile phone with women who he has set up in massage parlours – clearly, in reality, the sex trade. The final destination is a nondescript house in an anonymous suburb in Thetford that is painfully overcrowded, five to a room, with mattresses on floors and one bathroom/toilet. For this, Lin informs Ai Qin, she will have to pay £25 a week. It is something that Broomfield himself was relatively unaware of:

'It [*Ghosts*] started off as a film of modern slavery, really, which to my amazement happened in England, which we all think of as a fairly civilized country. There are all these people who are like a non-people living in caravans, 15 to a house in parts of England. Completely under the radar, completely unprotected. Like Dickensian England, it's all here. These people are working for Sainsbury's, Tesco's and ASDA. [They] all pretend they don't know it's going on. And the government pretends it doesn't know it's going on. They've designed everything so that those people can be used to keep the costs of living low.'[23]

We see pretty widespread corruption from the start: Ai Qin pays Lin £250 for a 'work permit', the local employment agency is seen as a place where its workers are routinely bribed by the gangmasters, with cigarettes and money, to assign temporary contracts. Ai

Qin ends up working in a meat factory for Sainsburys, cutting and gutting duck carcasses. Broomfield captures really well the monotony of labour, the sense of the long day underscored by the use of the captions. Ai Qin sings away the hours, the unhappiness, the homesickness. She makes a connection with a young, English worker who remains unnamed. The workers are dropped off late at night, sleepwalking their way through the quiet country town. It is £100 for a 40-hour week, the income tax at 44 per cent £2 for transport. There is no indication of what the agency makes. Ai Qin cries alone in the grimy green of the house's solitary bathroom. 'God, when can I go home?' she wails. 'This is so hard.'

The English 'ghosts' are on the margins of this film and are few and far between. The English landlord Robert (Shalin Gallagher), shaven-headed, wearing a leather-jacket and flashy gold jewellery, sleeping with Lin's erstwhile Chinese girlfriend, is little more than a caricature or a figure of fun. This depiction of Robert, positions the audience with his Chinese tenants, as they insult and joke about him in Mandarin. He is deliberately under-developed as a character, his motivations are purely profit-driven, out for a fast buck. In renting his semi out to Lin and his desperate workers, he is as exploitative as everybody else in this film – only in a much more obvious way than the supermarkets or employment agency. We see a local farmer employing the group to harvest her crop of apples and she comes across as more sympathetic, teaching the migrants about drinking tea with milk. Broomfield chooses to show this work in a rather idyllic fashion, with the use of fades, fast film and beautiful Chinese music, underscoring the process of picking the apples, pulling up and burning the trees.

The use of Chinese music in the film is extremely powerful with its explicit harking back to home for the migrants. It is used in a variety of ways: individual singing of folk songs, group singing and, of course, non-diegetically. It is something that Broomfield felt was extremely important in creating mood and empathy with the characters. The music is also interesting juxtaposed against the bleak, rainy English countryside where much of this film takes place, giving the *mise-en-scène* an exotic, almost otherworldly feel.

The film is full of small ironies, the most explicit being that, when she is shopping at the local supermarket, Ai Qin isn't able to afford the spring onions that she has been picking that morning for minimum wage (if that). The gap between labour and profit, between first and third world, is made with absolute clarity here.

 The group is moved from the overcrowded semi by the police, some are arrested, most run off and return to find 'Fuck Off' graffitied on the broken front-door, urine in the hallway, rubbish on the floor. Broomfield gives a sense of the neighbours' concern with a couple of cutaway shots, behind lace curtains. The group heads northwards to a small, dank terrace house, near the coast. In a rather poetic scene, Ai Qin

and one of her fellow migrants, Xiao Li (Zhe Wei), look westwards and spot a rainbow, where he says her son and her home are. The rainbow is seen as a good start and a good omen. The reality couldn't be further from the truth.

The cockle picking is shown through the use of a variety of tracking shots as the minibus crosses the seemingly endless beach. It is depicted as backbreaking, cold work, as the migrants, in their sand-encrusted cagoules, rake the top surface of the sand searching for the shellfish. There is confrontation with the locals, who swear at them, tip their bags over and attack Lin. In many respects the eventual drownings might be seen to stem from these altercations – they go out when the English 'ghosts' themselves deem it too dangerous.

The increasing lack of light, the sense of uncertainty, the threat of quicksand and mounting confusion are all captured wonderfully by Broomfield's Steadicam. The inevitability of their fates is evident on their faces and in those despairing last phone-calls, some trying to swim, not knowing which way to go. It is a difficult and unsettling scene to watch, even though it is a re-enactment.

Broomfield fades to black and utilises the device of the caption to spell out what we already know: '23 people drowned on 05/02/04. The victims' families are still paying off their debts. The British Government refuses to help them.' However, rather than ending on an absolute note of hopelessness, Broomfield at least shows us Ai Qin returning home, reunited with her parents and son. That said, he tempers this with the sobering legend, 'Most Chinese illegals will never see their families again.' It is a bittersweet ending for a stark, necessary film.

PULLING THESE FILMS TOGETHER

In many respects these films share a great deal more than just looking at the fate of asylum seekers and economic migrants. They depict a bleak Britain, suspicious, exploitative and cruel. Its sympathetic occupants are thin on the ground: Alfie in *Last Resort*, Juliette the prostitute in *Dirty Pretty Things* and a couple of unnamed characters in *Ghosts* are about the sum-total of the *Welcome to Britain* 'welcoming' committee. The exploiters, such as the huge supermarkets who pay a pittance for gutting poultry and pulling vegetables, are anonymous in *Ghosts*; the entire staff of the Baltic in *Dirty Pretty Things* are all exiles and there is no evidence of any British characters working there at any level. Les, the online pornographer in *Last Resort*, on the other hand, is a vividly drawn character, upfront and relatively honest about his intentions towards Tanya. He even turns up at her flat to reimburse her for her 'act' and tries to entice her back. There is an odd sense of sympathy towards him, especially when Alfie attacks him.

In *Last Resort* we are positioned in a bleak, winter seaside venue, which seems to enhance the island siege mentality of the film. The use of the sea is equally as valid in *Ghosts* but unlike in Pawlikowski's film where we see it being used to enable Tanya and Artiom's escape, it seals most of the cockle pickers' fates when they are stranded by the rising tide. The *mise-en-scène* of both films is bleak. Stonehaven is a giant concrete gulag, battered by gales from the Channel, but there is an eerie, tarnished beauty in Lenczewski's framing. Broomfield's film, on the other hand, jumps from the suburban ordinariness of Thetford to the lush green flatlands of the East of England and storm-battered Lancastrian terraces. England is seen in snatches, small-town and generally rural, the new slave economy is vividly portrayed. London, in *Dirty Pretty Things*, is a largely nocturnal experience: the brash interior lights, the neon clock, the transitory nature of the hotel seem an apt representation of the capital. What we see outside the Baltic is a million miles away from the traditional picture postcard view of London as shown in many Working Title films. Backstreet sweatshops, crowded multicultural markets and Senay's small cramped apartment offer a more authentic depiction of metropolitan life.

The airport is seen as a place ultimately of escape and it is this sense of escape that unites these three films. The central characters all leave Britain, in nearly all cases to return home and perhaps this suggests that the film-makers saw this as the easiest solution to resolve each narrative in a rather simplistic and conclusive way. There is no chance of Okwe, Senay, Tanya or Ai Qin staying in Britain and settling down. Okwe and Tanya may in their own way be tied by the demands of parenthood, Okwe with a daughter back in Nigeria and in Tanya's case the ever-present Artiom. Senay is blinded by the attractions of life in New York and Ai Qin, traumatised by her experiences, is reunited with her young son. Their brief time in England is one of struggle and desperation but it is interesting that in both Tanya and Senay's case they do find love with their respective 'saviours', Alfie and Okwe, but neither relationship is fully consummated. These heroes rescue them from situations tainted by sex, and from predatory men such as Les and Sneaky. In Ai Qin's case, she is pursued by Mr Lin, perhaps to sleep with him, but certainly to work in a massage parlour. That said, she rejects his advances and he is aware of her feelings towards him. These women are also attractive and certainly stand out from the crowd, and at first glance appear to be victims. However, Tanya proves to be quite resilient in fighting against her feelings for Alfie and returning home. Certainly Senay stands up to the sexual advances of the sweatshop owner and is a key part of the plan to entrap Sneaky and remove his kidney. Ai Qin's sheer instinct to survive is shown by her subsequent return to China and her escape from the horrors of life in England.

Aspects of authority or state institutions like the police or immigration services have a different impact in each of these films. Pawlikowski's Stonehaven feels and looks like a mini police state, its unwilling occupants hemmed in by the sea, barbed wire and barking dogs. Vouchers and blood are the only currencies, the only views are the endless grey from the brutalist tower blocks. The cheap-suited immigration officers of *Dirty Pretty Things* look out of place as they lurch from one lead to the next in their pursuit of Senay. Certainly in this film and *Last Resort* the whole subject of the bureaucratic minefield surrounding asylum issues seems insurmountable. *Ghosts*, by comparison, has very few skirmishes with the law: barring the raid on the Norfolk semi, the characters live unnoticed in the half-light. They are largely unseen and ignored, as they provide the cheap labour that ensures profits for the gangmasters, employment agencies and the supermarkets.

These films are all worthy attempts to portray the migrant's experience in Britain in the new century and they are all rooted in a social-realist approach to the subject. In many respects they offer quite complex readings of what it is like to come to this country illegally, but crucially they depict the nation as it is seen through an outsider's eyes. The approach is sympathetic, and they can, on occasion rely too much on archetypal representations of the characters: the noble African, the helpless female victim, the kindly ex-criminal or prostitute, and this is especially true of *Dirty Pretty Things*. That said, certainly *Ghosts* and *Last Resort*, while capturing the awful plight of their central protagonists, are also vividly cinematic experiences and are ultimately uplifting in their quite similar conclusions.

REFERENCES

1. Pines, J., 'British Cinema and Black Representation' in The British Cinema Book, Murphy, R. (ed.), London: BFI, 2001

2. Sandbrook, D., White Heat, London: Little Brown, 2006

3. Pines, J., 'British Cinema and Black Representation' in The British Cinema Book, Murphy, R. (ed.), London: BFI, 2001

4. Woodward, W., 'Higher figures for foreign workers undermine ministers claims' in The Guardian, 11/12/2007

5. Travis, A., 'Home Office grants 19000 asylum seekers permission to remain' in The Guardian, 18/12/2007

6. Whitehead T., 'Over 860 migrants flood in every day' in The Daily Express, 13/02/2008

7. www.bbc.co.uk/cinema/features/last_resort.shtml
    Norton-Smith, C., Review of Last Resort

8. Sinclair, I., 'The Cruel Seaside' in Sight and Sound, March 2001

9. Romney, J., 'Welcome to England – A spiritual Siberia' in The Independent on Sunday, 18/03/2001

10. Francke, L., Review of Last Resort in Sight and Sound, March 2001

11. www.netribution.co.uk/features/interviews/2001/Pawel_Pawilkowski/2.html
    Interview with Pawel Pawlikowski

12. Knight, N., 'The Exploited' in The Guardian, 01/11/2002

13. Quinn, A., 'London Kills Me' in The Independent, 13/12/2002

14. Frears, S., in Sweet, M., 'Asylum. With added glamour' in The Independent, 08/12/2002

15. Roddick, N., Review of *Dirty Pretty Things* in Sight and Sound, December 2002

16. Sinclair, I., Heartsnatch Hotel' in Sight and Sound, December 2002

17. Romney, J., 'One goody-goody Samaritan and a fancy French truffle' in The Independent on Sunday, 16/12/02

18. Herbert, M., 'Gangmasters blamed as 19 Chinese cocklers drown in Morecambe Bay' in The Independent, 07/02/2004

19. Lawerence et al, 'Victims of the sands and the snakeheads' in The Guardian, 07/02/2004

20. Watts, J., 'Going Under' in The Guardian, 20/06/2007

21. Romney, J., Review of *Ghosts* in The Independent on Sunday, 14/11/2007

22. Lin, A., in Aitkenhead, D., 'The Stowaway's Story' in The Guardian, 06/01/2007

23. http://rcrdlbl.com/2007/12/11/exclusive_interview_with_ghosts_director_nick_broomfield
    Interview with Nick Broomfield

AUTHORSHIP IN NOUGHTIES BRITISH CINEMA — MICHAEL WINTERBOTTOM AND SHANE MEADOWS

THE AUTEUR IN 21ST CENTURY BRITISH FILM

One of the cornerstones of the auteur theory is to critically assess if a group of films by a particular director show a consistency of style, structure and theme. If this is the case, the period between 1999 and 2009 has been relatively bereft of British entries to the fold. The previous towering presences of Mike Leigh and Ken Loach have each produced films which strengthened their reputations. Leigh's proto-realist *All or Nothing* (2002) brought viewers back to the council estates and disadvantaged London of *Meantime* (1983) and *High Hopes* (1988), while his tale of a 1950s abortionist, *Vera Drake* (2005), was a grim but compelling period piece, enhanced by a strong central performance by Imelda Staunton. Loach, on the other hand, locates his vision in the Celtic hinterlands for the bleak tale of teenage desperation in *Sweet Sixteen* (2002), the disappointing Romeo (Muslim) and Juliet (Catholic) of *Ae Fond Kiss* (2004) and the historical, Palme D'or-winning *The Wind that Shakes the Barley* (2006), based on the Irish War of Independence and the subsequent Civil War.

Leigh and Loach are, of course, established *auteurs*, very much in the tradition of a realist style, their signatures clearly marked in the minds of audiences and critics alike. A new release by either of these directors is a big event, certainly in the review pages of the broadsheets and *Sight and Sound*. Their features are feted at film festivals and — in Loach's case especially — raise controversial issues that give them greater exposure. However, unlike previous periods in British cinema — namely the 1960s, or even the 1980s — there seems to have been a falling away of young (or youngish) British directors producing a body of work that might be considered worthy of gaining the authorship tag.

The 1960s, with directors such as Joseph Losey, Karel Reisz, Tony Richardson and John Schlesinger, and the 1980s, with Alan Clarke, Stephen Frears, Derek Jarman and the aforementioned Leigh and Loach, had clear groups of auteurs whose films were explicitly part of a greater and unified body of work. Promising young directors have often struggled to get beyond two and in some cases one feature — which doesn't help any claims for authorship. It is a point that Nick James places firmly at the feet of film financiers, as he discusses:

'A cynic might suggest that association with someone's second or third film never makes the career of any production executive. Hence everyone is eager for the new discovery, and the list of directors who manage to complete only one feature is very long indeed.'[1]

James goes on to cite Carine Adler, the director of *Under the Skin* (1997), as an example, but this could be further added to. Directors such as Lynne Ramsay, Amma Asante, Jamie Thraves, John Maybury and even established and highly regarded film-makers such as Terence Davies and Nicolas Roeg, have all been very quiet in recent years, in Davies' case, as least, not for want of trying.

As far back as 2002, Vincent Maravel at Wild Bunch (a French production outfit) gave reasons why he backs so few British films: 'We are looking for strong, original movies and England is too much influenced by Hollywood. Most English directors are trying to repeat the Working Title movies or do movies like Guy Ritchie. I think the dream of each English director is to move to Hollywood. They want success in order to work with big actors on a major budget'[2]. If this is the case, then it certainly explains the exodus of directors like Paul Greengrass and Christopher Nolan, both of whom could be classified as auteurs. Apart from his first, low-budget feature *Following* (1999), Nolan has worked exclusively in the United States and Greengrass hasn't made a British film in terms of subject matter (*United 93* was in part funded by Working Title) since the docudrama *Bloody Sunday* (2002).

So who are the key directors in British cinema in this period? Who are the directors who have created a signature, across either similar or a diverse set of films, who have created an explicit sense of an identifiable *mise-en-scène* and have attempted to address common themes in a number of movies? The two names that readily spring to mind are Michael Winterbottom and Shane Meadows.

Both are directors who have primarily made films based in Britain, concentrating on domestic subject matter. They are also both relatively young and have managed to get enough funding for their projects to appear to be pretty prolific. Their careers first started in the late 1990s with well-received features and they have continued to develop ever since. They also offer an interesting contrast in approaches to film-making. Winterbottom is the restless wanderer, using a variety of styles and genres while Meadows is firmly rooted in the working-class environs of the East Midlands, continuing the social-realist tradition of Alan Clarke and Ken Loach. Between them they have been the standard-bearers for often controversial and exciting movies. They have both had unsuccessful projects, but they have been given the chance to rectify these misfires.

MICHAEL WINTERBOTTOM – BEYOND CATEGORIES

Winterbottom's background was in television in both documentary films and fictional texts, the standout being the Roddy Doyle-scripted BBC series *Family* (1994), set on a grim Dublin council estate. He had always wanted to transcend the limitations of the small screen and in 1994 formed his own production company, Revolution; the following year he released his first feature, *Butterfly Kiss*. The sense of consistency that has become evident in his work and especially in his prolific output can be attributed in part to the sense of control afforded by having his own production company. Added to this, he has almost exclusively worked with the producer Andrew Eaton and the writer Frank Cottrell Boyce and these partnerships have been vital to Winterbottom's abundant CV. He has also been aided by collaboration with the editor Trevor Waite, production designer Mark Tildesley and the composer Michael Nyman. In Deborah Allison's article on Winterbottom in *SensesofCinema* this is something that she sees as key to developing an authorship approach to his work:

Michael Winterbottom

> 'The greater than average degree of repeat collaboration makes the case for collectively generated authorial traits especially relevant and yet the stylistic and thematic commonality that exists across films whose contributors have varied confirms that the control exerted by Winterbottom himself underpins their shared structures.'[3]

Much of the discussion around Winterbottom's work, however, has tended to question any claims to authorship at all. This may have something to do with the subject matter and generic content of his work, which at first glance seems to be rather fractured and disparate. Looking at his late-1990s work gives a sense of this: the intense, obsessive, same-sex love story/road movie *Butterfly Kiss*, his adaptation of Thomas Hardy's *Jude the Obscure*, *Jude* (1996), the Bosnia-set war film *Welcome to Sarajevo* (1997) and the thriller *I Want You* (1998). Allison does see links between these films in terms of themes such as spiritual despair, an explicit and open approach to showing sexual acts and the choices available to the characters as a direct consequence of the environment they inhabit. That said, there are many who question Winterbottom's credentials here. Xan Brooks, at the start of his review of *Wonderland* (1999), echoes this view:

> 'If *auteur* status is defined by a director's ability to stamp a film with his or her particular visual or thematic imprimatur, then Michael Winterbottom is no auteur.'[4]

Even Winterbottom has sought to distance himself from this debate, in the films that he has made and in his approach to the whole business of directing:

'Asked in 2000 about the apparent absence of auteurist fingerprints on his films, he said: "I'm sure it irritates people, but so what? I find that attitude ludicrous because film-making is a collaborative process, whatever way you want to describe it. So to have this bourgeois, liberal-romantic idea of the creator seems to me like the ultimate perversion. All auteur theory has become is: if you make the same film over and over again, and you write your own scripts, you're an *auteur*, if you don't, you're not.'"[5]

But this hasn't stopped critics trying to find elements in Winterbottom's work which might be regarded as consistent. Even as far back as 2001, one American commentator who admired his work suggested that Winterbottom might be undervalued in some quarters because he does not have a recognisable 'signature'[6]. Is it valuable, then, to use this as a framework for looking at Winterbottom's work at all? Perhaps a good place to start this debate is his turn-of-the-millennium film, the London-based dreamscape of *Wonderland*.

Wonderland – Real London, Impressionistic London

Winterbottom's tale about the lives of three sisters during a single weekend was one that created a great deal of interest, if not spectacular box-office returns. The film uses London as a key player in constructing meaning. It avoids the clichéd Red

Gina McKee,
Wonderland

Bus/Trafalgar Square shot designed to appeal to American audiences and is a long way from the Working Title view of leafy, cosmopolitan north London. It is a point that Stuart Jeffries picks up on:

'…you become conscious of the press of people, the yellow London brick, the neon. The colours drizzle and glisten wetly, like they do when Scorsese films New York at night, although here the density of the crowds and the buildings, as well as the grainy film stock that Winterbottom uses, give this scene a cherishable London specificity.'[7]

The film cross-cuts between the three sisters, Nadia (Gina McKee), Debbie (Shirley Henderson) and Molly (Molly Parker), voicing their problems with loneliness, family and relationships set against the backdrop of the metropolis. The film is rooted in a social-realist tradition. These are ordinary people leading largely uneventful lives, tied together by familial links. Winterbottom utilises a number of visual techniques that give the film an impressionistic and surreal feel. Slow-motion and time-lapse techniques are employed, which portray the capital as a place of beauty as Nadia strides through late-night Soho after another unsuccessful date. Hand-held cameras give *Wonderland* a documentary feel, picking up on the casual look, the occasional glance, encouraging the viewer to look beyond the often mumbled dialogue to discern the subtle nature of the interactions on show. The low-budget approach gives the film a spontaneity and freshness making the usually familiar London *mise-en-scène* feel oddly unfamiliar.

Xan Brooks described the film as 'Dogme-lite', which is apt; stylistically it is close to some of the central tenets of the Vow of Chastity. Although it is a considerable distance away from Thomas Vinterberg's *Festen* (1997) and Lars Von Trier's *The Idiots* (1998) in terms of controversial subject matter, it does, however, feel like a piece of art-house cinema. There are clear links with Wong Kai-Wai's *Chungking Express* (1994) and *Fallen Angels* (1995), with their dreamy atmosphere and themes of solitude, urban alienation and the search for love. Despite this, *Wonderland* was widely received as yet another grim piece of British social-realism concentrating largely on working-class characters – a charge that Winterbottom was quick to refute in an interview with *IndieWire*:

> 'It's not an essay on the plight of the working class. I don't want these people to be explained so much by economic things; I wanted to go beyond that. The world of the movie is just like the world I live in, in London. Part of the attraction was just to get on film what it's like living there at the moment.'[8]

Wonderland is rooted in revealing the real, with its hand-held 16mm approach and use of documentary techniques. But there is a beauty in some of the sequences (the bingo hall, the back garden fireworks display) that positions the film closer to the work of Lynne Ramsay in the way it makes the ordinary look and feel extraordinary. Its loose, at times impressionistic, narrative structure doesn't offer simplistic solutions to all the characters' woes, although the birth of Molly's baby does afford the sort of familial community lacking in, say, Wong's films. Winterbottom's next project was equally loose in terms of its structure, but very different in its subject matter.

Madchester – So Much to Answer For

After the big-budget trials of *The Claim* (2000), Winterbottom returned to something more modest in the shape of *24 Hour Party People* (2002), the story of Granada local news presenter Tony Wilson and the establishment of Factory Records. The film's epic span, from Wilson's epiphany at the infamous Sex Pistols concert in 1976 through to the end of the record label in the early 1990s, records the changing nature of Manchester's role in the pop world. If the structure of the film reflects Factory Records' roster in any way, it is far from the regimented, controlled, tension-filled sounds of arguably Factory's

Steve Coogan,
*24hr Party
People*

most highly-regarded act, Joy Division and instead is much closer in spirit to the loose, sprawling, rhythmic uncertainty of their last great band, the Happy Mondays. It is a biopic that uses a range of techniques, documentary and fictional footage, historical and mythological representations, narrative and non-narrative impulses (Allison, SensesofCinema) and it employs Steve Coogan as Wilson, directly addressing us, guiding us through the chaos of the Manchester music scene. It is this messiness, this sense of the incomplete, which is the core argument for Winterbottom as an auteur director.

> 'Subject-wise his films have nothing in common. And yet there is a recognisable
> Winterbottom style – a studied messiness, a desire to move between film and video, to
> confuse and explore.'[9]

The film is undercut with a great sense of humour, as Wilson's vision of Manchester and of his own role in the film – 'a minor character in a film about my life' – is both knowing and curiously disarming. The first act of *24 Hour Party People* ends with the suicide of Joy Division's lead singer Ian Curtis and is emblematic of the style of the film in the way that Winterbottom presents us with it. Unlike the stern, linear kitchen-sink approach undertaken by Anton Corbijn in *Control* (2007), Curtis's death is presented with a clear sense of pathos beautifully played out with a very British sense of good humour – something one would not at first associate with Joy Division's music. The combination and juxtaposition of sequences sums up the conflicting emotions almost perfectly. There is a real sense of shock on Wilson's face when told of Curtis's death while interviewing a town-crier for his news programme. His 'tribute' – which we see on-screen – is to have the death announced by the town-crier. A flashback to Wilson's memories of Curtis taking lead vocals in a Christmas party version of 'Louie, Louie' lends a celebratory note to the scene. We next see Wilson arriving at Curtis's funeral, glad-handing journalists, refusing autographs, in short acting out his infuriatingly smug public persona. However, it is when he is alone with Curtis's body that we glimpse a different side of him, as he gently kisses the dead man's forehead. Despite the bluster of Wilson's character and the exuberance of Coogan's performance, it is an extremely moving moment. Maybe it is part of the 'messiness' of Winterbottom's approach that he unexpectedly intercuts this scene with Anton Corbijn's ethereal video for 'Atmosphere' and leaves us with the caption 'Ian Curtis 1956–1980'.

The subject matter of *24 Hour Party People* perhaps lends itself to a mythical reconstruction of the truth of the period and Winterbottom warmly embraces it. Wilson himself saw the film as being very much in this vein:

> "'It's all made up. Which is good! I always quote Howard Hawks – that between legend and truth always choose the legend. Well, that's what's happening with this film. They've gone for the legend. I tried hard to get them to make the film about the two great stories, Curtis and Ryder (of the Happy Mondays), but I gave up when I realised where Coogan was going with it".'(in Morley, 23/02/01)[10]

The second half of the film tells the story of the rise of New Order, the band that Joy Division became. It recounts the rise and fall of the Hacienda nightclub and Factory Records' eventual collapse due to Wilson's legendary poor sense of business acumen and by debt, drug-pushers and violence and his over-indulgence of his acts, namely the Happy Mondays. This mythical reconstruction takes advantage of a variety of different styles and approaches. Winterbottom favours a quick editing style that gives a sustained narrative pace; coupled with wonderful cinematography by the legendary Robby Müller, the film continues to be constantly engaging and wonderfully inventive. For example, the seminal meeting of Shaun Ryder (Danny Cunningham), the shambolic, drug-addled poetic genius lead singer of the Happy Mondays and the future dancer (and iconoclastic figure) Bez (Chris Coghill) is shown as a surreal encounter with a flying saucer over grey Manchester skies. The disastrous opening of the Hacienda nightclub uses space effectively to indicate the lack of a crowd. The criminal drug culture of the late 1980s is shown to good effect with voice-over and montage editing.

The film is grounded in Winterbottom's own experience growing up in Blackburn and the soundtrack is that of his youth and this does feel in many respects like a labour of love, but the film had struggles in gaining funding and audiences. Winterbottom's long-time collaborator, producer Andrew Eaton, makes this clear:

> "'It was hard to get backers to appreciate why anyone would be interested in these characters. They didn't think anyone would know who they were. But it doesn't matter whether you know who these characters are or not. It's such a great story. You couldn't make up stuff that was funnier, or sadder.'" (Quoted in Morley, ibid.)

Winterbottom is aware that his films are not destined for the multiplexes, even a film like this that on the surface is one of the most commercial of all his work:

"'It's a problem that 90 per cent of screens are in multiplexes, which are designed to recreate a bit of suburban America. There's still a 1950s view of cinema, that there's one audience and they all want to see the same thing''.[10]

Another Winterbottom film that was never going to be conventional fodder at the local mainstream cinema chain was the controversial, sexually explicit *9 Songs*.

No Sex, Please – We're British

Margo Stilley,
Kieran O'Brien,
9 Songs

9 Songs (2004) is a love story based on the relationship between two London twenty-somethings Matt (Kieran O'Brien) and Lisa (Margo Stilley), an American student. It is told retrospectively, as Matt reflects on the affair from the Antarctic where he is working as a research geologist. The intensity of the liaison is reflected in the graphic sex scenes, amongst the most revealing in any British film to date. The sexual content led to problems with its original distributor Tartan Films. But the British Board of Film Classification (BBFC) did pass the film uncut saying that the sexual content was 'exceptionally justified by context' but with the warning that the film featured 'frequent strong real sex'[12]. These scenes are very extreme and the film's controversial reputation is rooted in the explicit imagery of ejaculation and cunnilingus in which the labia are clearly in shot. The film is unscripted and the scenes of copulation are punctuated by footage of a number of bands such as Primal Scream, The Super Furry Animals and Franz Ferdinand playing live, providing the nine songs of the title. The film is once again shot on grainy digital video and the accompanying score by Michael Nyman is stark and sad, setting the tone of remorse for a lost time.

So is this more than just a simple piece of art-porn mired in its unflinching 'realness'? It outlines the power of attraction so common in the initial stirrings of a relationship. But crucially it maps out issues about commitment and the mores of modern courtship to great effect, by steadfastly being oblique regarding the central characters' motives aside, of course, from what they get up to in the bedroom. The sex itself is largely deglamourised; shot in sepia-tinted colours, declarations of love are thin on the ground. *9 Songs'* blank *mise-en-scène* also invites self-identification for the discomforting sake of showing sex as utterly, deflatingly common'[13]. The result of this is rather than concentrating on the sexual euphoria of the relationship, it tends to drift towards melancholy; after all, Matt is looking back at this relationship, remembering Lisa as '21, beautiful, egotistical, careless and crazy'. There are indications that Matt has fallen in love with the young American, which in turn prompts Lisa's gradual coolness to the point where she leaves.

The relationship as it stands feels fragmentary, liable to fall apart at any point – and it is this rather than the unsimulated sex scenes that hark back to the uncertainty and urban angst of *Wonderland*. This is picked up by Peter Bradshaw in his review: 'Its very casualness, its unfinishedness and downbeat messiness give the affair the feeling of real life, which by a further paradox makes it more engaging than something more obviously dramatic'[14].

Lisa appears to be in control for much of the film and she ultimately walks out on the relationship. The film, however, is caught in the male gaze, an extended flashback as Matt reflects back from the snowy Antarctic wastes, so they are his memories of Lisa that we are privy to. Linda Ruth Williams found this to be rather clichéd: 'there's still something stereotypical about the way that Lisa's pleasure is conveyed, whether she's pictured dancing for her man or tossing back her head in exquisite ecstasy'[15]. Certainly Lisa lacks the humanity and roundness that Winterbottom gives to his female characters in *Wonderland* – but her very elusiveness makes her a much more self-possessed character than the usual Bridget Jones characterisations of single women. She is in control of her sexuality and her destiny. It is entirely possible that it is this sense of confidence that structure Matt's memories of her. Margo Stilley, in her first film, is clear about the role and the sexual content: 'I wanted to make a film about something that I really believe in, which is to show sex in a very positive light as a very important piece of everyday life and a very important piece of a relationship, whether it is successful or unsuccessful. What I find in films I see is that sex is always a turning point in action, someone's cheating on someone or someone dies'[16]. The honesty with which Winterbottom shows this is revealing but also alienating. We are placed in the position of the voyeur, so we look for signs of power shifts and developments between the two central characters. Since they are so thinly drawn every slight nuance has to drive the narrative on.

The mixture of live concert footage reflects the social side of their relationship and counterpoints the erotic scenes. Winterbottom shoots the band conventionally, largely in long shot from the audience's perspective, which contrasts with the closeness of the scenes with the lovers. The songs reflect the early excitement of the affair; the sheer joy of Primal Scream's 'Movin' on Up' and the dark and bitter break-up song 'Love Burns' by the Black Rebel Motorcycle Club, wonderfully and in a relatively subtle way give markers to the on-going development of this messy relationship.

Winterbottom as Auteur

Winterbottom's other work in the decade has been prolific, ranging from the refugee drama *In This World* (2002) through to his postmodern comedy *A Cock and Bull Story* (2005) and the worthy American film *A World Apart* (2007). It is worth saying that perhaps one of the keys to Winterbottom's signature may well be his very refusal to be drawn into a particular type of film. Like Howard Hawks, his thematic preoccupations are more important. Looking at *Wonderland*, *24 Hour Party People* and *9 Songs*, issues around alienation, relationships, the urban experience and sexuality are drawn on regularly. Certainly the highly mobile camerawork and willingness to move between film and video are stylistic features that can be seen in the films discussed in this chapter, but more importantly there is also the notion of control that he has on his output that marks him out as a strong authorial voice in British cinema. Yes, he has a number of important collaborators, but there is clearly a sense that Winterbottom will only do projects that interest him and it is this that makes the pinning down of his work very difficult, which hasn't done him any favours either critically or commercially. His personal profile still remains relatively low, despite (or because of) the range of his output. As an *auteur* director he does provide a fascinating contrast to the more high-profile Shane Meadows – someone who throughout the decade has returned to the same location and shot low-key stories amongst the working class of the East Midlands.

SHANE MEADOWS – A BREED APART

In a similar way to Michael Winterbottom, Shane Meadows appears rooted in the auteur tradition but there are clearer thematic links between his films. That said it is fair to say that like Winterbottom this would be a label that he would refute. His

Shane Meadows

background is a vital part of understanding his work and his films reflect this.

Born in the early 1970s, Meadows grew up in a working-class family in the Staffordshire town of Uttoxeter. He draws on his own past rooted in the Midlands and fashions highly moral tales of ordinary, recognisable characters often drawn into life-changing situations. His youth was one of drifting into skinhead groups and occasional petty crime, but he always had an interest in drama and art at school. He managed to get himself together to study photography at college and on leaving began making short films, funded by his unemployment benefit. His first major short *Where's the Money Ronnie?* (1995) was an inventive take on the British crime genre. His first feature *Smalltime* (1996), funded by the BFI, was a comedy focusing on petty criminals on a Nottingham estate. Elements of *Smalltime* can be seen in Paul Abbott's Channel 4 television drama *Shameless* (2004–2010), with regard to themes, tone and *mise-en-scène*.

24 7 (1997), his next project, funded by BBC films, was a huge critical success, being selected for the Venice Film Festival. The film, set around a boxing club on the edge of Nottingham, starred Bob Hoskins as Alan Darcy, a local man who sets out to help disadvantaged young men in his neighbourhood. Shot in stark black-and-white, this is a rites of passage film for all the characters and introduces some of the major themes that Meadows would return to again and again. It is a touching and largely optimistic film that focuses on the centrality of community and presents a flawed, problematic patriarchal figure in the shape of Darcy. The alternative father figure was to become a key feature in much of Meadows' subsequent work. His violence against one of his charges, Tim's (Danny Nussbaum) appalling father and, ultimately, his alcoholism, undermines this position as a role model. It is touching how Meadows chooses to show Darcy's funeral, with the members of the now-defunct boxing club showing their respect for their former mentor. This feeling of sentiment is a major feature of his films and the final sequence works beautifully, because it is undercut with humour and never outstays its welcome. Xan Brooks saw *24 7* as being firmly positioned in the tradition of British social-realism:

> 'Despite the contemporary trimmings (the kids all wear Adidas, Tacchini and Kappa labels), this is essentially a social-realist drama with nods to Italian neo-realism and kitchen-sink British tele-plays. Significantly Meadows and co-writer Paul Fraser developed the film organically according to the Mike Leigh method via lengthy improvisations. So despite this being in the vanguard of homegrown cinema, Meadows' influences look determinedly old school.'[17]

Stylistically Meadows mixes the bleak suburban estates and the surrounding countryside to fine effect as well as introducing an underlying sense of humour which was to become a key characteristic of his later work. It is a moving and heartfelt film which announced him as a young film-maker to watch.

Odd couples – *A Room for Romeo Brass*

Meadows' next feature was also funded by BBC Films. *A Room for Romeo Brass* (1999), also set in the East Midlands, continued the theme of unsuitable mentors. The film was based on elements of the director's own childhood and his relationship with his best friend and co-scriptwriter Paul Fraser. The film follows two Nottingham schoolboys, the overweight, dual-heritage, streetwise Romeo (Andrew Shim) and his next-door neighbour Gavin (Ben Marshall), nicknamed Knocks, who has a damaged spine. It centres on their destructive relationship with twenty-something misfit Morrell, played by Meadows' college friend Paddy Considine. This was Considine's first role and the springboard for a career that has encompassed some of the most interesting British films of the decade, *24 Hour Party People, Last Resort, My Summer of Love* and Meadows' own *Dead Man's Shoes* (2004).

The film has a lot of the humour evident in his earlier work, much of it based around Morrell's wooing of Romeo's sister Ladine (Vicky McClure) and the early scenes with the

(l-r) Andrew Shim and Paddy Considine, *A Room for Romeo Brass*

boys. But there is a menace surrounding Morrell and his effect on Romeo, who starts to see him as a father figure, and also on Gavin who he threatens after a wind-up. This splits the boys up during the middle of the narrative. Morrell is different every time we see him, ranging from the delusional, vulnerable loner to the violent, unpredictable stalker driven by rage. As Paddy Considine has remarked about his depiction of Morrell, he is a 'wounded whippet, no father or family, a loner, a bomb waiting to go off'[18].

The film's denouement is predictable, with the boys reunited and Morrell chastened by Romeo's father, but there is a freshness here, much of it linked to the improvised nature of the acting. Meadows has nearly always used first-time or non-professional actors to develop this sense of immediacy. It is something that Meadows says adds to the authenticity of his films, pitched somewhere between film and documentary (ibid.). The naturalistic feel of the camerawork, moving as in *24 7* between semi-detached landscaped exteriors and the subdued beauty of the Midlands countryside, is also present. The interiors feel cramped and claustrophobic — from Morrell's Robin Reliant to Gavin's bedroom.

The soundtrack, another feature of Meadows' work, is inspired, from the opening of The Specials' 'A Message to You Rudy' set against Romeo's journey back from the chip shop to the use of the uplifting 'Mersey Paradise' by the Stone Roses, which closes the film. Certainly after the preceding sequence where Morrell sets about Knocks' father with a hammer, it changes the tone of the film and ensures a feel-good ending. Donavan's 'Colours' is most effectively set against a montage that covers Knocks' slow recovery from the operation on his back and Romeo's burgeoning relationship with Morrell. The dream-like nature of the song captures the slow sense of his convalescence beautifully. The non-diegetic music doesn't feel at any point tacked on, it is an essential part of creating meaning.

Meadows also manages to shift the tone of the film with consummate ease, and this has in turn become a major signature in his work. This is seen a number of times in *A Room for Romeo Brass*, from Morrell's ridiculous dance at the seaside directly followed by his holding a knife at Knocks' throat and threatening to kill his family. We are taken on a rollercoaster ride of conflicting emotions, juxtaposed to encourage us to reflect on and react to what we have just seen. Mark Kermode, a long time supporter of Meadows' work, also picks up on this point:

'[in Morrell's] attempted seduction-cum-rape of Ladine, the juncture between laughter and violence is crossed so subtly that the audience is left genuinely shocked.'[19]

A Room for Romeo Brass sets out the template for Meadows' finest work of the decade in Dead Man's Shoes and This is England (2007). The disturbing balance between humour and darkness, the corrupting patriarchal figure, the realistic violence, bullying and debates surrounding working-class culture are all present here and all key issues to his work.

A revenger's tragedy – *Dead Man's Shoes*

FilmFour's *Once Upon a Time in the Midlands* (2002) is considered by Meadows himself to be his weakest effort. This romantic comedy kept some elements of his earlier films by focusing on working-class characters. It starred Robert Carlyle as Jimmy, Paddy Considine, *Dead Man's Shoes*

who returns to the Midlands to reclaim his ex-girlfriend Shirley (Shirley Henderson) and his estranged daughter. The all-star cast, including Ricky Tomlinson and Rhys Ifans as Shirley's boyfriend Dek, saw a shift away from Meadows' use of unknowns. This is something that Meadows himself said was part of the problem with the film. Working with well-known faces meant that the sense of realism in his previous work was plainly missing here.

There are allusions to the Western, with its use of empty streets and Morricone-style score, but the film seems like an attempt by Meadows to enter the mainstream, and to get a box-office hit. Although the settings, many of the themes, characters and stylistic juxtapositions are familiar to fans of his work, the film lacks cohesion and clarity. Meadows himself had problems with his producer and was not happy on the shoot which is evident in the final cut. The largely negative critical response was a setback for Meadows and heralded a 'back to basics' approach to the style of his earlier films with Dead Man's Shoes.

One of the things that is interesting about *Dead Man's Shoes* is its production context. After his rather mixed work with the film wings of terrestrial television channels, Meadows finally found a home with Warp Films. Warp is a record company, possibly best known for its work with Aphex Twin, which decided to branch into film production in 2003. It is based outside London, with a digital studio in Sheffield and an office in Nottingham. Most of the funding for Warp's films come from the Film Council and FilmFour and also the Regional Screen Agencies, most notably Screen Yorkshire and EM Media. This is a film production company far away from the London-centic industry and much suited to the type of films that Shane Meadows wanted to develop; low-budget, cutting- edge work. There was also a tie-in with the distributor Optimum Releasing, which meant that the films would be released theatrically and could also be heavily promoted on DVD.

Meadows' association with Mark Herbert, producer at Warp, meant that there was no immediate pressure – as there had been on *Once Upon a Time in the Midlands* – for fast returns, and the production of the film was extremely quick:

> '*Dead Man's Shoes* has no outward commercial pressure because it was made for less than £1 million. I met the producer [Mark Herbert] in March last year and on 1 May we were shooting the feature.'[20]

It was shot in six weeks on fast 16mm stock and the guerrilla-style production techniques suit the mood of the film perfectly. The story moves away from the suburban terrain of Meadows' previous work into a small Derbyshire town in the picturesque Peak District. The largely improvised film was made in chronological order which gave a sense of unpredictability to the proceedings. Written with the film's star Paddy Considine, *Dead Man's Shoes* sees ex-army officer Richard (Considine) returning to his hometown to avenge the death of his brother, Anthony (Toby Kebbel), who had special needs. His abusers were a gang of small-time drug dealers and gangsters and their protracted bullying of Anthony is shown in a black-and-white flashback. Meadows however chooses to show Anthony alongside Richard for the majority of the narrative – it is only revealed towards the end of the film that he is actually dead. Anthony is still alive in Richard's mind and his revenge is driven by the guilt he feels for abandoning his vulnerable sibling. The film is a curious mix of horror and comedy, with the killers effectively fleshed out to demonstrate this: Big Al (Seamus O'Neill) and Gypsy John (George Newton) are depicted as drunken middle-aged idiots; Herbie (Stuart Wolfenden), Soz (Neil Bell) and Tuff (Paul Sadot) are the three stooges, tormented by their increasing fear of Richard, careering around the town in their battered, lime-green 2CV in a parody of *Wayne's World*, rocking along to Danger Mouse. Only the leader, Sonny (Gary Stretch), feels dangerous, but even he is made into a figure of fun with his face painted as a clown, while he is sleeping, by the elusive Richard.

They inhabit a closed world, a world of instant and simplistic gratification and their lifestyle reflects this. Peter Bradshaw has acknowledged

> 'their natural and appalling habitat: sprawled on sofas, drenched in arrested-development squalor, getting off their faces on the gear that they're supposed to be

selling and cheerily reading aloud the captions from porn magazines.'[21]

Meadows draws us into their world and encourages our sympathy with their fate. As he has said, 'Even though the characters were pretty dark I wanted to make sure the audience felt something for them when they were killed'[22]. Herbie, Soz and Tuff are established as weak men and no match for the psychopathic Richard. They are not painted as mere villains, but as defenceless against Richard and fearful of the preening, vain Sonny. Sonny is portrayed as the only one that can stand up to Richard, but even at their first meeting he seems scared and uncertain.

There is a beauty and subtlety in the *mise-en-scène*, which is often reminiscent of Ken Loach's *Kes*. Meadows combines an eclectic soundtrack with stunning cinematography capturing the late spring splendour of the Derbyshire Dales. A good example of this is the opening frames where we see Richard and Anthony walking across the sun-drenched English countryside to the strains of Smog's low-fi classic '*Vessel in Vain*'. This is intercut with Super 8 home-movie footage of the brothers as boys offering a powerful and moving exposition. The bearded Richard, complete with his kitbag slung over his shoulder, is a man of few words, and Anthony in Richard's imagination (or even memory) is clearly in awe of him. There is no mention of the rest of their family and as the story develops with Richard despatching each of the gang in different ways it becomes more and more apparent that Richard is driven by guilt as much as by anger and revenge – guilt at abandoning his helpless brother.

The first confrontation with one of Sonny's gang comes with the weakest member, Herbie, in a down-at-heel working men's club. Herbie, all small-town bravado, is clearly stung and frightened by Richard's reaction to his 'what you looking at?' Richard plays with the gang, breaking into their shabby houses, painting their faces, destroying their cheap suits, donning a gasmask and stealing their stash of drugs. Meadows plays this for laughs, the gang's growing frustration and incredulity at Richard's actions contrasting sharply with the murder of Big Al by an axe at Sonny's club, 'One down' written in his blood in the dimly-lit toilet where he is discovered.

It dawns on the gang that Richard is Anthony's brother and that he wants payback. Any power that they had is rendered null and void. The scene where Sonny attempts to shoot Richard turns into farce with him killing Gypsy John. Again the journey to the abandoned farm where Richard is staying is wonderfully observed, the packed 2CV driving along the tight country lanes in the early morning light to Adem's 'Statued'.

Meadows builds the tension, counter-pointing Richard's tender conversations with Anthony with his confrontations with the gang. The set-piece is where Richard spikes the remaining members of the gang with a concoction of drugs and torments them, before killing each one. It is a scene that Meadows is particularly proud of and one that drew on personal experiences:

'With the acid sequence we wanted something that has all the fluctuations of taking the drug where you're off your box and laughing one moment, then suddenly there are fucking spiders in your eye sockets. Herbie's still off his case in that scene, but his instincts are, "I'm going to get killed if I don't straighten up here." I didn't take acid with hippies – I took it with rough lads who would smash you round the head with a hammer when they were off their heads. I came through that hard school of taking drugs and I wanted to get that down.'[23]

He uses a variety of techniques to allow us into the nightmare: jump cuts, fades, reduced lighting and extreme close-ups. He speeds up and slows down the action and uses flashbacks of Anthony and the home-movie footage. The actors were encouraged to forego sleep for a number of days to imitate the effects of the lethal drugs dose. The use of sound here is also very important. The driving beat of the dance music is muffled and distorted as are the characters' voices, much like their minds. 'Are you the devil?' the damned Soz asks Richard, not sure of what he is witnessing. The scene is compelling, as we see not just the murder of each of these characters, but their utter degradation at Richard's hands.

'Certainly there is something demonic about the spectre of a killer who torments his victims by making them dance like puppets before methodically dispatching them with cold calculation.'[24]

There are elements of horror here. Tuff, who had earlier run away, is shown to Herbie, dismembered and presented in a suitcase. 'Do you want me to shut it now?' whispers Richard in the distraught Herbie's ear. Sonny gets killed with military efficiency with a bullet in the head; Soz's neck is broken. Herbie's function is to tell Richard about the whereabouts of the last remaining member of the group that tortured Anthony – Mark. He then stabs him, when we think that he is giving him a hug. Shane Meadows, although establishing some of these characters in a less than negative light, is unrepentant about the messages that are spelt out here:

'I'm not a violent man, but at the end of the day the characters who get killed in *Dead Man's Shoes* are based on people that I want to kill.' (*Sight and Sound*, October 2004)

It is only with Mark that we encounter the full story of Anthony's death. He is different to the rest of the ill-fated gang. He lives in another town, is in a steady relationship living with Marie (Jo Hartley) and he has two young sons. Richard meets the boys and gives them the gasmask and knife that he used to kill Herbie. Once again the director builds up the tension as Mark slowly realises who Richard is. He tells Marie the story of Anthony's death. We have already seen the systematic abuse of Anthony throughout the film and now we see its conclusion. The gang had taken him to an old abandoned zoo where they tortured him by parading him around, hitting him and forcing him to take LSD. They then left him there and it emerges that he hanged himself as a result of this sustained bullying. Mark could have and should have intervened, but didn't. It is only at this stage in the narrative that the audience learn that the 'Anthony' that they have been seeing in conversation with Richard, is in fact a figment of his imagination and crucially that rather than the gang murdering Anthony, they have in fact driven the poor boy to suicide. In Richard's mind however they are Anthony's killers and in many respects Meadows leads the audience to draw the same conclusions.

The end of the film sees Richard sparing Mark, after seeing him as a family man. But there is another twist as he goads Mark successfully to stab him. Richard has avenged his brother's death, and punished Mark by getting him to murder him. The final crane shot and the haunting use of 'De Profundis' give the film a reflective and powerful ending.

Although rooted in a combination of revenge classics from the 1970s such as *Straw Dogs* (Peckinpah, 1970) and *Death Wish* (Winner, 1974) is it just a homage to the vigilante movie or something much more? It resembles most obviously elements of Mike Hodges' *Get Carter* (1971), in that Jack Carter (Michael Caine) returns home to hunt down his brother's killers. At first glance, the aura of widespread corruption that Hodges' film provides the social and contextual backdrop to is seemingly absent here. That said, where Meadows' film is more clearly framed is in the apparently increasing number of murders of young, vulnerable people by gangs in Britain. For example, the savage, drug-crazed murder of Adam Morrell in Loughborough in 2002 by a group of people that he knew springs to mind, alongside more recent cases such the attacks on vulnerable disabled men like Brent Martin, Kevin Davies and Colin Greenwood.

Although the film invites a number of dubious audience pleasures by encouraging us to support Richard's carnage, it also offers a dark view of Britain in the early part of the century that is important. The apparently worthless lives of the gang members, the small-town desperation and Anthony's death seem particularly rooted in real-life, despite the use of the conventions of the slasher film. Sonny's gang don't murder Anthony, but are implicated in his suicide and are punished not by the law but by an ex-Para, hell-bent on retribution. The law has failed and is delivered in a way that will appeal, perhaps, to the baser instincts of an audience. However, like all Meadows' work, this film has a deeply moral tone. The dangers of gang mentality were to be explored even further in his next project, *This Is England*.

Skinhead Moonstomp – *This is England*

This is England is possibly Meadows' most personal film. Set in the early 1980s, it centres on 12-year-old Shaun, played by newcomer Thomas Turgoose, and his induction into a gang of local skinheads led by the affable Woody (Joe Gilgun). Shaun is still reeling from his father's death in the Falklands War. He lives with his mother on a nondescript Midlands' council estate and, like Anthony in *Dead Man's Shoes*, is the victim of bullying, mainly for his unfashionable corduroy flares and wing-collared jacket. Despite his diminutive stature Shaun is unafraid to confront his attackers both physically and verbally.

Thomas Turgoose (seated), *This is England*

Once again there are echoes of *Kes* as Shaun, outside the headteacher's office, waits for a caning. The film acts as a rites of passage for the young boy, as he leaves the paternal Woody for the incendiary, racist ex-con Combo (Stephen Graham).

This is England bears the stamp of the 1980s. It opens with a montage of period footage from the early part of the decade, everything from Roland Rat to Duran Duran, Knight Rider and the royal wedding of Charles and Diana. All this is set to the skanking melody of Toots and the Maytals' '54-39 That's My Number'. It is an era that the director clearly feels at home in:

> 'It was a time of great music, brilliant fashion and a vibrant youth culture that makes today's kids look dull and unimaginative by comparison. It was also a time of massive unrest when British people were still prepared to fight for the stuff they believed in.'[125]

Also included in this footage is Margaret Thatcher, then Conservative Prime Minister. It is the results of her policies and philosophies that loom large in this film, from the aftermath of the Falklands War to the shattering of working-class communities; the erosion of heavy industries and the crushing of the trade unions. Shaun's loss of his father acts as a catalyst for much of his behaviour, searching for a patriarchal figure and making a poor decision by gravitating towards Combo.

The skinhead movement came to prominence in the late 1960s. They were essentially working-class youngsters, who were for the first time encountering West Indians in their communities. Although there was some antipathy, common bonds were forged here with the rude boy culture of the Caribbean and this was largely built on a love of ska, soul and bluebeat music. The youth cult re-emerged in the late 1970s, again driven by music and the 2-Tone record label in Coventry. Suddenly young people were starting to get their hair cut in the distinctive suedehead style and dressing like the skinheads of ten years previously. The clothes were distinctive and not too expensive: Fred Perry T-shirts, drainpipe Levis or sta-press trousers and Harrington jackets were the uniform of the day.

2-Tone prided itself on its multi-racial groups and an adherence to a strong anti-racist agenda. This was important because the late 1970s and early 1980s was a period of high unemployment and social disorder with riots in many of Britain's cities. These riots were a reaction by young Afro-Caribbean to what they saw as heavy-handed and prejudiced policing. The far-right political parties like the National Front blamed the economic difficulties on immigrants and started to grow in popularity. They also began to recruit skinheads to spread their message.

The change in tone, an important feature of Meadows' work, is central to this political background. The early part of the film is a delight. We see the gang dressing up and vandalising empty houses. Shaun is treated well by Woody and his friends. He has his hair cut by Woody's girlfriend, Lol (Vicky McClure), and is given a Ben Sherman shirt by the gang. Set against Toots and the Maytals' cover version of 'Louie, Louie', Shaun is depicted in a wonderful montage swimming, playing football and becoming a regular part of the group. We see, in *Reservoir Dogs*-style slow motion, the gang strutting through the graffiti- and rubbish-strewn estates. The *mise-en-scène* here echoes Mike Leigh's *Meantime* (1982); we get a real feel for the period detail. In a revealing scene Shaun's mother, Cynthia (Jo Hartley), confronts the gang about Shaun's transformation and specifically about his new haircut and they are in turn apologetic and courteous to her. It could be argued that Woody represents the 2-Tone model of the skinhead movement in his attitude and outlook. One of the gang, Milky (played by Meadows' regular Andrew Shim), is from a Jamaican background and there is a clear love of black culture – particularly noticeable in Lol's bedroom, where the walls are adorned with posters celebrating ska music. This appearance contrasts with Combo's introduction, which signals a significant mood swing in the narrative.

Combo, in prison for three years, sets about on his release to regain his old gang from Woody. Jail has radicalised him; schooled in the politics of fear and ignorance he is extremely upfront with his racist ideas. It is clear from clever cutaway shots of Lol and the rest of the gang that Combo's views were always there and prison has only exacerbated them. He blames ethnic minorities for rising unemployment and rhetorically challenges the group – fight or flight:

> '…alpha skinhead Combo, fresh out of prison, perpetually snarling and cracking with hatred. Quickly establishing who's the daddy, this slyly charismatic despot gains most of the gang's allegiance with a divide and rule policy.'[26]

Shaun sides with Combo and rejects Woody as his surrogate father and the innocence of the first part of the narrative is replaced by something much darker; there are clear echoes of Romeo Brass's relationship with Morrell here.

'Two fucking world wars men have laid down their lives and for what? So we can stick our fucking flag in the ground and say this is England, this is England, this is England,' Combo rants, all bulldog features and blood red Harrington jacket. His monologue appeals to the impressionable, still grieving Shaun and this ugly speech divides the gang. The film's tone changes significantly as Combo takes the remaining skinheads on their mission to protect England. We see the stupidity of Combo's plan – the meeting in a battered country pub with members of the National Front on a recruitment and propaganda drive, all well observed, with its backroom politics and lowest common denominator logic. The respectable middle-class appearance of these so-called politicians contrasts with the boot boys in the audience. Combo sees them providing a voice for his beliefs.

The stupidity of Combo's 'fight' is reinforced by his and the gang's actions – racist graffiti, the intimidation of young Bengali boys and threatening an Asian shopkeeper with a machete. It is the latter scene that the BBFC had the most problems with because of the abusive language – but it is a scene that explores two key issues: Shaun's transformation from a cheeky kid sneaking a look at a comic into the unpleasant Crombie-wearing thug ordering the shopkeeper to give him 'fags and booze' and the crystallisation of Combo's violent hatred with language and weaponry; a deeply unsettling experience for an audience.

Meadows has suggested in interviews that Combo's racist ideas and actions are rooted in a lack of identity and uncertainty of what being English actually entails. Jon Savage, in an excellent piece in *Sight and Sound*, makes an additional point that Combo's rejection by Lol also fuels his behaviour:

> 'Combo's unravelling occurs when he tries to rekindle his brief romance with Lol. Alone of all the skins, she stands up to him. Quivering with disgust, her beautiful eyes wide, she derides his rosy memory of their one-night stand: "It was the worst night of my life." Kicked right where it hurts, in his vulnerability, Combo shuts down.'[27]

The final violent attack on Milky is expertly handled by Meadows and provides a great deal more complexity in explaining Combo's actions. There are indications here of a broken family, a lost childhood, a poor father. A mellow, stoned afternoon turns into a vicious unprovoked physical assault. The dialogue initially centres on the common bonds between the white skinheads and black culture, but the tone changes as Milky starts to recount his family experiences, which are close and loving. Combo's reaction, uncertain at first, almost watery-eyed, becomes more and more problematic as he starts to react to Milky. 'What makes a bad dad?' he roars. Milky's response is to smile impassively, which further irks him. The attack is brutal and witnessed by the appalled Shaun who realises that the choice he made to reject the gentle Woody, was the wrong one. The complexity mentioned above comes to the fore after the attack, when Combo's acolytes are also attacked by him, as they question both what he has done and the fact that they wanted a 'piece of the action'. Oddly Combo breaks down, crying, upset at what he has done before enlisting Shaun to help move the bloodied and unconscious Milky to the hospital.

Meadows chooses to use more footage of the victory in the Falklands – the return of the Task Force and in one telling shot the movement of bodies by British soldiers. It is possible that he is making some correlation with the far-right agenda of the National

Front at home and Thatcher's adventures in the south Atlantic, but this is more skilfully pulled off in the final few frames.

The film ends with Shaun's rejection of Combo's world as he tosses the Cross of St George flag, given to him as a gift by Combo, into the sea. It is a highly symbolic moment, the flag as a signifier of both nationalism (in this context) and the ending of that relationship. It is played out to the strains of Clayhill's plaintive cover version of The Smiths' 'Please, Please, Please, Let Me Get What I Want', but it feels as much a swansong for Meadows' own youth and for another era:

> 'As the 1980s ended we had the poll tax riots which turned out to be the end of an era. Afterwards, it was like the nation lost its backbone. People were bought off. They were given a little bit of land, the right to buy their council house and put a satellite dish on the front of it. They became content and their lost they will to rock the boat.' (Meadows writing in The Guardian, 21/04/07)

Parallels with contemporary Britain are clear. The title of the film, based on a song by The Clash, is 'This is England' not 'That was England'. It is as much a statement by Meadows about the present as about the past. The skinhead movement has ebbed over the past twenty years but that doesn't mean that racism has disappeared – far from it. The influx of economic migrants in recent years following the enlargement of the EC has led to an increase in racist attacks; there have been race riots in Bradford and Oldham. And it is clear to see that the backdrop of the Falklands War means that sharp parallels can be drawn with the conflicts in Iraq and Afghanistan. The usual fears regarding youth crime and teenage disaffection remain and are highlighted in the film.

The film is also close in spirit to early 1980s British social-realism, such as Mike Leigh's *Meantime*, with its use of the council estate *mise-en-scène* and the transformation of Tim Roth's character Colin, and there are nods to Alan Clarke's *Made in Britain* (1982), in Roth's portrayal of Trevor, the racist skinhead who Combo clearly echoes.

Meadows as Auteur

Unlike Winterbottom, Meadows' credentials as an auteur are much clearer. His films are rooted in his own background and experiences. His locations are resolutely provincial – focusing on the unfashionable East Midlands, these locations are vitally important in constructing a context for his characters. His thematic preoccupations with patriarchy, male identity, rites of passage, violence and community provide the basis for much of his work. The combination of shocking tragedy and laugh-out-loud comedy, and his ability to switch almost seamlessly between both, is also a key signature.

In his follow-up to *This is England*, Meadows relocates from his usual haunts to the area around the revamped St Pancras Eurostar train station in London. Thomas Turgoose is the lead in *Somers Town* (2008), where he plays a young runaway from Nottingham who meets up with Tomas (Pitor Jagiello), a migrant worker's son. They quickly form a friendship built largely around their mutual infatuation with a French café worker. This rough approximation of *Jules et Jim* (Truffaut, 1962) does hint at deeper themes: street robbery, homelessness and issues around new immigrants, although it is much too short to really develop these fully. Instead, what *Somers Town* delivers is a charming exploration of male adolescent relationships. There are echoes of his earlier features, in particular *Romeo Brass*. Although there have been accusations that Meadows works too much within his comfort zone, unable to leave Nottingham (aside from *Somers Town*, of course), it is apparent that he has grown tremendously as a film-maker, or more importantly that he has been given time to grow. Perhaps greater and more diverse work beckons for the man dubbed the Scorsese of the Midlands.

REFERENCES

1. James, N., 'Greenlit Unpleasant Land' in Sight and Sound, January 2007

2. Macnab, G., 'That Shrinking Feeling' in Sight and Sound, October 2002

3. Allison, D., SensesofCinema.com/contents/directors/05/Winterbottom.html

4. Brooks, X., Review of *Wonderland* in Sight and Sound, December 1999

5. Gilbey, R., 'Open Mike' in Sight and Sound, October 2004

6. Applebaum, S., 'Caution; High speed director coming through' in The Independent, 28/01/2001

7. Jeffries, S., 'The walking wounded of *Wonderland*' in The Guardian, 18/01/2000

8. Kaufman, A., www.indiewire.com/people/int_Winter_Michael_00728.html Michael Winterbottom's *Wonderland*

9. Hattenstone, S., 'The Film Factory' in The Guardian, 29/03/2002

10. Morely, P., 'Shooting The Past' in The Guardian, 23/02/2001

11. Bedell, G., 'A Winterbottom's tale' in The Guardian, 01/02/2004

12. Staff and agencies, 'Censors pass British sex film uncut' in The Guardian, 19/10/2004

13. Hynes, www.indiewire.com/movies/movies_050719nine.html, July 2003

14. Bradshaw, P., Review of *9 Songs* in The Guardian, 11/03/2003

15. Williams, L.R., Review of *9 Songs* in Sight and Sound, April 2005

16. Stilley, M., in Anthony, A., 'Caught in the act' in The Observer, 20/02/2005

17. Brooks, X., Review of *24 7* in Sight and Sound, April 1997

18. South Bank Show on Shane Meadows, ITV1, 29/05/2007

19. Kermode, M., Review of *A Room for Romeo Brass* in Sight and Sound, February 2000

20. Lawrenson, E., 'Getting Personal' in Sight and Sound, October 2004

21. Bradshaw, P., Review of *Dead Man's Shoes* in The Guardian, 01/10/2004

22. Blacklock, M., 'Cruel Justice' in The Daily Telegraph, 01/10/2004

23. Meadows, S., in Lawrenson, E., 'Getting Personal', Sight and Sound, October 2004

24. Kermode, M., Review of *Dead Man's Shoes* in Sight and Sound, October 2004

25. Meadows, S., 'Under my skin' in The Guardian, 21/04/2007

26. Romney, J., Review of *This is England* in The Independent, 29/04/2007

27. Savage, J., 'New boots and rants' in Sight and Sound, April 2007

EXISTING IDENTITIES – REFLECTING BLACK AND ASIAN BRITAIN IN THE NOUGHTIES

INTRODUCTION

Films concentrating on the black and Asian Diaspora were rare between 1999 and 2010 and this could be linked to the reluctance of distributors to show support for films that might be seen to deal with difficult subjects such as race. The dearth of black and Asian film-makers and the paucity of films is something that Karen Alexander sees as directly linked to 'the on-going crisis that Britishness has with itself as it shifts and transforms with each generation' (in Murphy [ed.], 2000, p.113)[1]. This is an issue that will be taken up in the films discussed in this chapter, where Asian protagonists' relationships within their families, communities and the wider white society are central themes. In *Bend It Like Beckham* (Chadha, 2002), *Yasmin* (Glennan, 2005) and *Brick Lane* (Gavron, 2007), the focus is on young women and the films challenge stereotypical types of black or Asian protagonists as 'problems' or 'victims' (Mercer, 1988, p.4)[2].

These films show the diversity of the Asian experience in Britain by looking at the Sikh and Muslim communities: there is a suburban, middle-class view in *Bend it Like Beckham*; the impoverished council estates of east London provide the backdrop for *Brick Lane*; and the Asian ghetto in a Yorkshire mill town is the central location in *Yasmin*. The two films dealing with black issues in this chapter look in particular at young people and crime, but take different routes both stylistically and thematically. *Kidulthood* (Huda, 2006) shows us a group of predominately black youth, the action centred in the west end of London. Its MTV-style techniques and explicit subject matter predates Channel Four's teen drama *Skins* (2007) by a year. *Bullet Boy* (Dibb, 2005) is set on the other side of the metropolis in Hackney and directs our attention to a male character, recently released from a remand centre, and his battle to stay on the straight and narrow. It is rooted in the social-realist tradition of Mike Leigh and Ken Loach and although it is a much more traditional film stylistically than *Kidulthood*, it is nonetheless a powerful tale of modern urban Britain.

As we shall see, all these films both support and challenge stereotypes, but more importantly they place black and Asian characters squarely in the frame and tackle everything from gang culture, youth crime, teenage pregnancy, community obligations and family ties to racism and Islamophobia.

KIDULTHOOD – THE OTHER SIDE OF NOTTING HILL

Menhaj Huda's *Kidulthood* is a difficult film. It is in part a teen film, focusing on a small group of West London 15- and 16-year-olds in the aftermath of a schoolmate's suicide.

Ami Ameen,
Kidulthood

It is also a film that has allusions to the gangster genre, with a tenuous revenge plot, explicit drug use and gun play. Even before it had opened, the film had been the subject of opposition in the tabloid press, which had decried its vision of violence, sex and antisocial activity. *The Sun* famously called for it to be banned, labelling it 'the happy slapping movie'. Noel Clarke, who wrote the screenplay and played Sam, counters claims that the film is just about shock value, and states that the narrative is squarely rooted in reality:

> 'There is nothing in this film that is not based on reality and that isn't happening already. And we will stand by that. What you see in the newspapers every day! It's constant. When I was writing the script I was collecting at least three or four articles a week about teenagers getting up to bad stuff, and I did that for a whole year; it goes on right under our noses … a lot of people might see this film as controversial, but I wanted to make something as true to life as possible.' (Quoted in Sullivan, 03/03/06)[3]

Stylistically, *Kidulthood* is far removed from a standard social-realist, documentary-like approach to its subject matter. This is a film aimed at the MTV generation. Huda favours a fast editing style, split screens, jump cuts and a prominent all-British soundtrack ranging from The Streets and Dizzee Rascal to Roots Manuva. The pace of the film is incredibly fast – the narrative takes place over a couple of days, perhaps trying to reflect the reality of the main protagonists' lives.

The film's production history was fraught, with no help from either FilmFour or the UK Film Council. The director had to re-mortgage his LA apartment to get the film started, and only later was the project picked up by Revolver Entertainment. The film was also shunned by both the Edinburgh and London Film Festivals; Clarke suggests a reason for this – that 'some of the hostility is that a lot of parents don't want to believe that their children might be behaving like this. It makes them really uncomfortable, but this is just one day on three kids' lives – a particularly bad day' (Quoted in Sullivan, ibid.).

Kidulthood opens in the playground of a multicultural comprehensive school, students milling about, teachers absent. The main characters are black, but most of the students speak in affected London patois. The first difficulty for a broader audience is understanding the language here, as a great deal of meaning is implicitly expressed by this in the opening scenes of the film, Huda creates an oppressive and uncomfortable atmosphere, with the slang adding to the initial sense of exclusion as to what is going on. What does clearly emerge despite the London street-speech is that there is bullying going on, as well as boasts of sexual prowess. It quickly emerges that Sam (Noel Clarke) is the chief villain of the piece. He is a stocky, miserable-faced boy surrounded by a group of acolytes. He intimidates blonde Katie (Rebecca Martin) and steals a Gameboy from Jay (Adam Deacon). This is intercut with Trife (Ami Ameen) working a drill in the metalwork department, refashioning a replica gun so that it can fire bullets. This is a school with no boundaries – apart from those set by the students. This echoes two American films, Larry Clark's *Kids* (1995) and Catherine Hardwick's *Thirteen* (2003), where the characters have a different and more extreme moral structure.

Watching these events in a British school is much more disturbing for some audiences. We witness a brutal attack by a gang of girls on Katie. This is foreshadowed in the playground, but nothing prepares the spectator for the ferocity of the punches, kicks and insults. Her injuries are captured on the chief bully's mobile phone for rapid distribution around the school and, perhaps, on YouTube. There are no teachers present and the only one we have seen has been stared out by Sam just prior to this. This is a place of chaos, founded on an atmosphere of jealousy and the potential for violence. No reason is offered for the attack on Katie – apart from the fact that she is different. She is marked out by being tall, blonde and pretty. It may also be linked to her middle-class family. We see her father collect her at the school gates, where he witnesses Sam giving Katie what he thinks is just a peck on the cheek, but which is a disguised form of sexual intimidation.

The class tensions that permeate the film are not really explored by Huda and are only hinted at in Clarke's script. We see one of the white, middle-class characters, Blake (Nicholas Hoult), currying favour with his fellow students by inviting them to his house for a party. Later on, we see that he lives in a huge mansion, which raises a crucial question. Why would a character as well-heeled as Blake actually go to the local substandard comprehensive instead of being privately educated? This question could also be levelled at Katie. These concerns about the class divide have been hinted at in some articles exploring the generally poor nature of inner London's schools and feeding the fears of middle-class parents. This is developed in Alice Thomson's piece for The Independent on *Kidulthood*, strikingly titled 'A film to make every mother shudder':

> 'Many inner-city schools are still dire. At one south London school I visited, the deputy headmaster had recently been threatened with a machete. According to research published by Warwick University, almost half of London schools have coped with knife incidents in the past year. "Drugs are tolerated as long as they're not sold inside school premises," said one teacher at an all-girls comprehensive. "The same goes for graffiti, and we try to keep drinking out of the classroom"." (01/03/06)[4]

We notice that Katie's father is unaware of her problems, even when she dismisses the cuts on her face as being the result of a fall. He is wrapped up in his work, taking a call on the way home, retreating straight to the laptop at home as Katie storms up the stairs. Her suicide seems almost inevitable, although there is some indication that her mother is worried by her behaviour. It is her brother Lenny (Rafe Spall) who finds her hanging from the rafters in her room, a note on her locker citing Sam as one of the main reasons for her suicide.

This gives Huda an opportunity to create two narrative strands. One is a poorly conceived plot for Lenny to avenge his sister by murdering Sam and the other looks at Katie's fellow students' response to her death. Clarke's script eschews massed school assemblies, grief counsellors and online tributes written in text-speak in favour of a more hedonistic approach. The school closes for the day so students can reflect on what has happened. The film now focuses its attention on Trife and his friends Jay and Mooney (Femi Oyeniran). Parallel with this is a story about Trife's girlfriend Alisa (Red Manrell) and Becky (Jaime Winstone).

We have already met Trife making a weapon for his gangster Uncle Curtis (Cornell John). There are no role models offered here for teenagers and it is only Curtis who comes anywhere near a paternalistic figure – but it soon becomes clear that he is a controlling sociopath, alternating freely between charm and downright menace. Trife lives with his mother in a cramped council estate flat off Ladbroke Grove and it is evident early on that he is obsessed with materialism.

Alisa tells Trife that she is pregnant with his baby. His reaction is dismissive and angry. Sam had lied to him about sleeping with Alisa and his reaction at first is to think that the child isn't his, but Sam's. As Jay, Moony and Trife plan a revenge attack on Sam, Becky and Alisa go on a drug-fuelled bender which adds to the shocking nature of the film. Becky sells herself for drugs and money, firstly performing oral sex on a middle-aged, middle-class drug dealer, and secondly having full sex with an arrogant young actor. This might be rooted in reality, but it is a bleak and dispiriting representation. Even Alisa, who acts as the moral centre of the film, masturbates the dealer's friend. The sex is largely public and almost always perfunctory (such as Jay's premature encounter with Sam's girlfriend Claire [Madeleine Fairley]) or something used as an act of control (Sam also with Claire) and in this case it acts as a controlling force on all the young female characters. Miranda Sawyer sees the sex as part of a barter situation, where bodily fluids are exchanged for respect, love or as part of supporting a wider image[5] (The Observer, 26/02/06). All the girls in the film are defined in relation to the male characters and by their sexual history or competence. Katie is taunted for being 'a virgin', Claire doesn't want to be known as being bad in bed, Alisa's recent sexual history is common knowledge and Becky prostitutes herself throughout the narrative. Sawyer interviewed a young teenager, Corrine, who recognised the reality of the situation in the film:

> 'That's normal! I know girls who are like, any boy will do! And in front of other people? I do know people like that. Sex isn't really a big issue, it's nothing no more. That is common, you don't think anything of it.' (Sawyer, ibid.)

Drugs are viewed as a regular part of everyday life. Jay and Trife smoke a joint out of the window of his bedroom; Becky and Alisa smoke and snort their way through various substances while drinking alcopops. Rather than an escape from urban deprivation, drugs are taken for fun. To get wasted is part of the rites of passage, as much as losing one's virginity or beating someone up. The film has been accused of middle-class voyeurism largely fuelled by the media's desire to appear hip, real and authentic with its shock tactics. Kevin Maher was particularly truculent discussing this film alongside *The Lives of Saints* (Rankin, 2007) and *Life and Lyrics* (Laxton, 2007):

> 'The film industry – like the wider media – increasingly displays a fawning, reverential, approach to creative representations of poverty, crime and working-class deprivation … this new value system, [is] built entirely around the crass concept of "keeping it real".'[6]

The issue here is how *Kidulthood* might be read by its intended audience who are likely to be impressionable teenagers. Is this a true representation of the lives of young Londoners or is it, as Maher suggests, 'steeped in genre fiction', taking the form of 'teenage noir', with its clearly delineated characters and simplistic melodramatic resolution. James Bell, on the other hand, argues that the film is very much in the tradition of Alan Clarke's film *Scum* (1979) with its confrontational approach depicting 'real, harsh truths, which happen whether an audience looks away or not'[7]. But Bell also feels that the film too often seems like a checklist of shocking events and it is easy to see the film as simply this, rather than a finely crafted narrative with sympathetic and fully rounded characters.

The lack of adults is also interesting, with many on the periphery, just not there at all, unaware of the lives their children lead or, in the case of Trife's Uncle Curtis, totally unsuitable. An example of this is when Sam turns up to confront Claire at her middle-class home and her open-minded mother urges her daughter through her closed bedroom door to 'use a condom, darling'. He is actually there to beat her up. The point is that parents can't win. If they lay the law down (which they don't in this film, since they are largely absent) they are bullies, or if they are liberal they are weak. A key message is the total inability of parents to understand or relate to their offspring on any level, but hasn't this always been a convention of the teen movie anyway, and isn't *Kidulthood* just developing this in a more extreme fashion?

When the protagonists leave Notting Hill they head for the bright lights of Oxford Street. Designer shops and burger bars are the main venues. Huda shows, in a piece of montage editing, Moony constantly being ignored by black London taxi drivers, very possibly highlighting their perceived racism. However, later, when the boys finally hail one down (with the help of white Claire) they run off without paying, followed by the driver shouting 'black bastards!', reaffirming those negative stereotypes. They are falsely accused of stealing in the Burberry shop by an over-zealous security guard, but it is hinted at that this was their original intention. There are indications that perhaps Trife can actually break out of this cycle, when he attempts to chat up an older attractive woman that he meets in a sportswear shop. Jay's earlier failed attempt to talk to the same woman was shouted in his west London patois across the store, whereas Trife talks gently to her. Although she rejects his advances (and he steals her purse), it suggests that Trife is more intelligent and at least knows how to switch codes. A subsequent violent confrontation with some other youths results in a split between Trife and his friends, which leads him back to the violent and unpredictable Curtis.

In the most shocking scene in the film, Curtis encourages Trife to cut a 'C' into the face of a man who owes him money. This is delineated as a symbolic rite of passage into the criminal fraternity. It is the turning point for Trife, as it makes him realise for the first time, perhaps, that the life that he aspires to is the wrong choice. Other choices, such as education, are not fully explored. Quite suddenly, *Kidulthood* becomes a morality tale, with the climactic reconciliation with Alisa at Blake's party and the subsequent confrontation with Sam, which in turn leads to Trife's death. Even the revenge plot peters out with Lenny unable to shoot Sam. Little is made of the gulf between the Blake's west London mansion, which acts as the venue for those final scenes, and the bleak council estates where Trife and Sam come from. Alisa is left as another single teenage mum clutching Trifle's dying body. The final message is one of despair and hopelessness. On the surface there is a feeling that the film's conclusion seems to be like 'a simplistic melodrama'; but there is a quite different, rather overarching sense that Jay, Moony, Becky and the rest of the characters may somehow recover rather quickly in much the same way as they did after Katie's suicide, in a haze of drugs, alcohol, sex and violence. There might be lessons learnt, but they feel short-lived.

BULLET BOY — HE AIN'T HEAVY, HE'S MY BROTHER

Ashley Walters,
Bullet Boy

Saul Dibb's *Bullet Boy* shares many of the thematic concerns as *Kidulthood*, London setting; macho, violent behaviour; and a melodramatic conclusion. It also shares a largely, non-professional cast. But, crucially, there are also key differences: *Bullet Boy* has altogether more believable characters, it has adults who offer a moral compass for the narrative, there is a much more compassionate feel to the proceedings and as a result the film doesn't sledgehammer the audience with shock tactics. But this is still a shocking film, in the way that the central character is drawn back into a world of revenge and retribution, largely against his will. It is a film, as expressed earlier in this chapter, steeped in a more social-realist tradition than *Kidulthood*, eschewing MTV-style techniques in favour of long takes, super 16 film and natural light. Saul Dibb's background in television documentary is central to the *mise-en-scène* of *Bullet Boy*, his feature debut.

Filmed in Hackney, north-east London, the story rarely leaves the area. Unlike *Kidulthood* it doesn't venture into the glitzy west end, nor are there any parties at mansions or privileged kids slumming it at the local comprehensive. Hackney is a borough with a significant Afro-Caribbean community and has a reputation for gangland feuds and gun crime. It is often referred to as 'murder mile'. Dibb shows the crowded estates and congested streets, but starts the film in the countryside where the main protagonist is incarcerated in a juvenile detention centre. He also contrasts the urban sprawl beautifully with the pastoral feel of the nearby Lea Valley in Hackney to good effect. For a film shot largely using a social-realist set of techniques, Dibb's decision to use anamorphic widescreen gives the sense that the wider environment has as much importance as that of the characters' interactions. The distant green fields are as out of reach as the flashing light at the top of Canary Wharf. Although everything in this film seems hemmed in and constrained, there is a real sense that Dibb wants to go beyond the average depiction of the slum-like estates by hinting at a wider world beyond.

The casting of Ashley Walters in the main role of Ricky is significant. As Asher D he had been a member of the chart-topping rap collective *So Solid Crew* and had also served a prison sentence for possession of a loaded gun. Since his release, Walters has starred in a couple of films, written a biography, released a solo album and appeared on stage at the National Theatre. Not all these ventures have been successful, and it is perhaps his performance in *Bullet Boy* that ranks highest. Walters and Ricky share more than just serving jail time. Ricky leaves the detention centre with the best intentions to go straight, but he is quickly derailed by his reckless friend Wisdom (Leon Black).

> 'I could relate to a lot of things that the character had gone through – jail experience, wanting to change your life around. That was a big part of what went into the film and I'd been through that. I felt sorry for Ricky. When I came out of jail, no one cared, I was ridiculed. I think when you come out of jail you should be left alone and people should leave the past behind.' (Walters quoted in Aftab, 06/04/05)[8]

Ricky's past is not left behind and from the start the film feels like it is hurtling towards a tragic conclusion. It begins with a long, flat country road, a young black man, Wisdom, is driving along, and in a homage to the start of Martin Scorsese's *Goodfellas* (1990) he hears a banging noise from the boot. He opens the boot and far from finding an Italian gangster, he sees that it is a young boy, Curtis (Luke Fraser), dressed in school uniform. It transpires that 12-year-old Curtis is Ricky's brother. He hero-worships his older sibling and looks up to the trappings of the gangster lifestyle that Ricky represents[9]. But much of this is just childish bravado; to Curtis, this lifestyle is the only one that could be achievable. Dibb constructs the relationship between Ricky and Curtis as an altogether complex one – they fight and argue like brothers naturally do, but nothing overly sentimental is offered here.

The opening exchanges between Wisdom and Curtis are well played – he leaves him on a desolate road, but has second thoughts and picks him up again, urging him aggressively into the back seat. All this is intercut with Ricky's release from the detention centre: 'It's been emotional', the releasing officer deadpans in the style of Vinnie Jones. On release Ricky harangues his brother for not being at school, but for Wisdom it seems that things are going to pick up from where they were before his incarceration. It is all spliffs and big plans, but as the car re-enters high-rise north-east London, Ricky reveals his plans to change and get a proper job. 'Stacking shelves,' Wisdom scoffs and it starts to dawn on Ricky that this may well be the sum total of his ambitions.

The major complication is all too believable and seems relatively minor at times. On a tight London street, Wisdom accidentally clips a wing mirror and has an altercation with the car's owner, Godfrey (Clark Lawson), a local hard-nut who demands £60 to replace it. Ricky tries to intervene to defuse the situation. Dibb shoots this from the perspective of Curtis and it is apparent that Hackney is a place where these slights mean something. Godfrey goes around a corner and emerges with a vicious looking bull terrier and Ricky and Wisdom flee quickly. It is something that Saul Dibb had seen at first hand:

> 'Both the co-writer and I used to live next to a road that was like a rat run of cars, and we used to see these massive arguments develop between people that just wouldn't give way, and part of the story grew out of that – what happens between people who argue, and how these arguments can just build up.'[10]

This petty dispute returns to haunt Wisdom soon afterwards, with him being taunted at a local club by people barking at him to imply that he had run off, scared by the threat of Godfrey's bull terrier. His reaction is to confront Godfrey and kill his dog. Thus begins the vendetta that permeates the film and the constant, almost obsessive adherence to a macho culture of attack and counterattack.

Once again there are parallels drawn with *Kidulthood*, but Dibb gives an altogether more sympathetic view of the characters by fleshing out Ricky, and by showing a strong, but increasingly helpless single mother, Beverley (Claire Perkins), and her partner, the caring Leon (Curtis Walker), a former gangster turned evangelical pastor and community leader. These characters try to guide and shape the lives of the young people around them in a positive fashion, a theme more or less absent in Huda's film.

Ricky's failure to turn up at his 'coming home' party organised by Beverley and his subsequent failure to meet with his probation officer exposes cracks in his post-release plans. He envisions a future with his girlfriend Shea (Sharea-mounira Samuels) by trying to escape the neighbourhood and start afresh, having 'a normal life'. We see Shea, Ricky and Curtis at an ice-skating rink, generally fooling about, falling over and discussing escape. But we also see the continuation of the feud. The situation grows ever more hopeless, despite the brief reveries of the ice-rink.

Further complications arise when Ricky hides Wisdom's gun in his sock drawer, unknowingly watched by Curtis. Ricky, dragged back in to what he thought he had left behind, has unwittingly involved his younger brother. Armed police raid the flat looking for the gun, which by this stage has been used unsuccessfully in a further attack on Godfrey by Wisdom. But Curtis has hidden it somewhere else. While playing truant with his friend Rio (Rio Tison) Curtis accidentally shoots him in the shoulder. This is filmed in the nearby rural Lea Valley to tremendous effect. Taken out of their urban hell-hole, Curtis and Rio are just two young lads mucking about; it feels innocent and carefree. But they also have a loaded gun and the whole episode is fraught with tragic inevitability. Interestingly, the police aren't involved in this incident – an anguished apology by Beverley and Curtis to Rio's father just about suffices. Rio is almost like a mini Wisdom. He seems uninterested and disrespectful at school and it is he who encourages Curtis to get the gun in the first place. When a chastened Curtis visits him in hospital he is told that he owes him 'big time' and Rio proudly shows him the bullet scar. You sense that the whole cycle has moved down a generation.

After the abortive attack on Godfrey, Wisdom decides to get out, but never makes it. Ricky finds his corpse at his flat and takes some money to enable his escape. Of course, Ricky doesn't make it either, gunned down by Godfrey: yet another dead son and brother; another young, dead black man.

When Dibb was selling the script to its backers at BBC Films he saw the film as 'Kes with guns'. He says, 'I wanted to get across to them it's a film about a 12-year-old and innocence and it's a film with guns, but not a *City of God* type film' (Plunkett, 20/04/05).[11] Ricky is by no means a saint, but he does try to do the right thing by everyone. There is certainly a close tie to Wisdom and the macho code of the street that overrides everything else. In focusing on the younger brother there is some sense of hope and a light at the end of the tunnel. But Curtis's relationship with Rio may follow that of Wisdom and Ricky: potentially dangerous, possibly fatal, although Dibb sees this differently: 'I didn't want to make something without hope. You can have it really bleak, but I don't really see the world in that way, and I don't see the world represented in the film in that way' (Plunkett, ibid.).

Akin Ojumo, in an excellent article in The Observer, noted that the film was 'well made', but also felt the narrative was 'predictable'. He felt that *Bullet Boy* was much too fatalistic in its outcomes by taking a modern story and superimposing a classic melodramatic tragedy template without really challenging existing preconceptions of the black community:

'It features the kind of issues that are very familiar: being young and stuck in a depressing environment, the struggling single mother, the petty dispute that leads to a shoot-out, As a black middle-class Londoner working in the media, I was struck by how different this film was from my experience. I grew up in south-east London, but I've never met a real life bullet boy. As an adult I visited friends on "murder mile" yet never feared for my safety.'[12]

His article serves up different views of the film from the perspective of the Afro-Caribbean community, from very positive to 'This film could have been made about the same characters but they could have done something else apart from crime.' This film also highlights the depressing statistics to do with young, black British men:

'More than 70 per cent of Afro-Caribbean boys grow up in households with an absent father; they are three times more likely to have been excluded from school than white pupils; 70 per cent of gun crime in London occurs in and around the black community.' (Ojumo, ibid.)

Curtis's final gesture, throwing the gun into the canal, indicates hope, but is this as simplistic an ending as *Kidulthood*? Are these films merely perpetuating stereotypes or portraying a brutally realistic view of London life if you are young and black? In answer to that last question, they fall somewhere in the middle. Of course the increase in gun crime, especially as a result of inner-city gang culture, will have an effect on how these films are received by the wider public. *Kidulthood*, with its upfront shock tactics, packs a punch and stylistically there is much to admire, but it is an empty film in comparison with the much warmer *Bullet Boy*, where the relationships, environment and, sadly, the final scenario are all too familiar. It may take a more expansive narrative to do this subject true justice. The model could be HBO's *The Wire* (2002–8), a superlative serial that over the course of five seasons has explored gang culture amongst Afro-Americans in Baltimore by taking a panoramic viewpoint encompassing the law, education and the media. Maybe this is the only way a less reductive approach to the plight of young working-class black Britons can be fully explored.

FRAMING THE BRITISH ASIAN EXPERIENCE – *BEND IT LIKE BECKHAM*, *YASMIN* AND *BRICK LANE*

The sheer diversity of the Asian experience in Britain is one that the media has yet to fully grasp. Looking at these three films together there is at least some recognition of key differences. *Bend it Like Beckham* and *Yasmin* explore issues of the gap between parental and community ties and wider British society, from the perspective of a young British Sikh woman and British Pakistani woman respectively. *Brick Lane*, an adaptation of Monica Ali's highly regarded novel, focuses on a Bangladeshi woman's experience of living in east London. As noted, these films follow a template set down by *Bhaji on the Beach* and *East is East* in that they explore the Asian experience as one of difference, of having a strong cultural orientation to one's roots and to one's adopted home. All three films frame the Asian experience through their female protagonist's eyes and in doing so they explore not only issues around gender, but also deal with racism and events surrounding 9/11.

Parminder Nagra, Keira Knightley, *Bend it Like Beckham*

Bend it Like Beckham was the most commercially successful of all three films. It had a fine distribution deal in the UK with Redbus that saw it open on 450 cinema screens and go on to gross £11 million at the box office. The film played off its links to the David Beckham name and was sold to audiences, especially female audiences, in this way. But it might also appeal to a male spectator because of the perceived football link. The film's release against the build-up to the 2002 World Cup also boosted its overall success. Given that *Bend it Like Beckham* was made for about £3.5 million it also did extremely well in the United States, making $32 million, possibly due to the feel-good plot and the more established popularity of women's soccer there.

The director, Gurinder Chadha, had had considerable critical success with her first feature *Bhaji on the Beach*, her road movie about a group of Asian women from Birmingham on a day trip to Blackpool. That film acts as a journey of self-discovery for the main characters and *Bend it Like Beckham* follows a similar narrative path. The central character, Jess Bhamra (Parminder Nagra), is a football mad A-level student waiting for her results, living in Hounslow, west London. Her bedroom is covered in posters of her hero, the eponymous Beckham. From the start there is conflict with her parents, and in particular her mother, about her obsession. They are relatively well-off, living in a comfortable semi-detached house which is almost constantly passed over by low-flying jets from nearby

Heathrow Airport where both her father and sister work. Her sibling Pinky (Archie Panjabi) is about to get engaged and this forms the main subplot beside Jess's ambitions to become a footballer. The build-up to the on/off wedding also serves as an insight into the enormous value that such events have within the Sikh community. This is apparent when set against Jess's growing success as a footballer in an all-women's team, a fact she keeps hidden from her parents. Chadha was keen to stress the universal qualities of the film, qualities which see this as more than just a story of a struggle within a British Asian family and this is borne out by the film's overseas success:

> 'People don't see the film in terms of race and culture clash, but as a story of suburban Britain, about what it's like to be young, to have parents who don't understand your dreams, to be suffocating in a suburb with your whole life ahead of you … British audiences identify with characters regardless of their background. Multiculturalism isn't the battleground that it is in the US.'[13]

Criticisms did focus on the rather formulaic, thematic approach taken by Chadha, mirroring box-office successes such as *Billy Elliot* (2000) and *The Full Monty* (1997). As Nicholas Barber noted:

> 'There's racism, sexism and homophobia; there's parental pressure and conflicting responsibilities. It's contemporary Britain in all its multicultural diversity, and as everything turns out as happily as possible, *Bend it Like Beckham* must be the most well-meaning, upbeat, right-on film ever made.'[14]

It is true that on occasion there is a distinct lack of subtlety as the narrative unfurls, but there are some very interesting asides and observations. Pinky's character is carefully drawn. She is driven to look as attractive as possible and for her wedding to be as successful as possible. She drags Jess out shopping onto the packed streets of Southall, where she bitches about her fellow Hindi princesses with their dyed hair and their blue contact lenses. Their language is a particular type of west London Asian patois and the subjects they explore are boys and brands, although more innocently than in *Kidulthood*. So while Pinky is positioned differently to Jess, she is oddly conformist too. She has her independence, a job at the airport, her own car (bought by her ever-accommodating parents) and it is implied that she is already having sex with her fiancé. However, her main ambition, it becomes clear, is to get married and get pregnant as soon as possible.

Jess is also an archetypal Asian character. She is bright and studious and when she receives her A-Level grades her father sees her becoming a top-class solicitor. She hides her involvement with the football team by lying to her parents about a job at HMV, but when the truth emerges she bows to her parents' wishes. Her mother constantly nags Jess about running around half-naked and not being able to cook while her father is more worried about how other Sikhs might read Jess's unconventional behaviour. At one point he wants her to start behaving like a 'proper woman'. But it turns out that he is secretly envious of Jess's involvement with the Hounslow Harriers; it is revealed that he was a promising fast bowler before coming to Britain but racist attitudes prevented him from playing cricket in this country. He tells Joe (Jonathan Rhys Meyers), the team's coach, that he doesn't want to raise her hopes only to see them dashed as his own were. When Jess gives the example of Nassir Hussain, at that time England's cricket captain, her mother retorts that Muslim families are different.

Chadha interweaves this with the different reactions of the parents of her friend and teammate Jules (Keira Knightley), played by Juliet Stevenson and Frank Harper. Jules' father is incredibly supportive of his daughter's interest in football, attending matches and playing kickabout in the back garden. Her mother is more concerned, bemoaning Jules' insistence on sports bras and her perceived lack of interest in her appearance, and later on she misinterprets Jules' and Jess's friendship, by thinking that they are involved in a lesbian relationship. Stevenson's performance is reminiscent of Alison Steadman in Mike Leigh's *Life is Sweet* (1990), full of lower-middle-class pretension. On her first meeting with Jess she asks her to teach Jules a bit about her culture – ironically about respect for one's elders. This perception of Jess as different is well-observed.

Yet within the Sikh community there is a keen sense of distinctiveness, which is seen as vitally important to keeping the old traditions and cultural ties relevant:

> 'Everyone is aware, and people are trying to hold on and protect elements that they think are good in terms of their traditions, but also elements that are good in terms of the world that they're living in.' (Chadha in conversation with Paul Fischer, March 2003)[15]

In the build-up to Pinky's wedding there is a striking example of this in the *mise-en-scène*, with the lit-up, decorated suburban semi shining out alongside the dull ordinariness of this nondescript west London street. The house is full of people, food and music, and Chadha shows cultural difference as something celebratory, which has considerable resilience. Philip French's review points out that 'Difficult questions of race relations and the accommodation of tradition of social change are swept under the carpets on which the cast dance'[16]. At only one point is such a question addressed, when Jess is fouled during a game and called a 'Paki' by her opponent. She pushes her back and is sent off. What we note here is that even with the futile gesture of pushing the racist over, she is standing up for herself, though Chadha is keen to avoid pursuing these issues directly:

> 'I've seen a lot of dross about the Asian community. There's not a lot of people who do what I do, I feel, which is to celebrate in their Indianness and their Englishness.'[17]

The community however does appear to be a pretty closed book. Jess's ambitions to be a footballer are unacceptable for a Sikh girl and her burgeoning relationship with Joe is sharply dismissed by Pinky. 'Do you want to be the one that everyone stares at because you're married to an English bloke?' she asks her sister, to which Jess replies, 'He's Irish.' Pinky retorts, 'in their eyes [the parents] they're all the same.' The issue of cross-cultural relationships is rather glossed over here and accepted as the way that the Sikh community stays distinctive. One of Jess's friends is Tony (Ameet Chana), the only young, male Asian character who isn't chauvinistic and superficial happens to be gay, although he has not yet come out of the closet. What the film doesn't make explicit is whether or not Tony's decision to stay quiet about his sexuality is linked to pressures of the Asian community. In many respects the film raises important issues like this, but fails to adequately explore them in any detail.

The enormous success of *Bend it Like Beckham* it could be said is down to it not being a piece of issue-led, realistic drama exploring issues of isolationism and discrimination within the Southall Sikhs. The narrative denouement however, although predictable, does leave one fascinating question hanging in the air and that is the relationship between Joe and Jess. This has been hinted at throughout the film, but fought off by Joe because of his professional standing as the team's coach. When he is promoted, the possibility of a relationship with Jess becomes a reality, but she initially rejects him because of her parents. At the airport (a constant metaphor in the film), before her departure to California on a professional soccer scholarship, she hints that something could happen between them, and in the credit sequence Joe is playing cricket with her father.

It is perhaps useful to note the very different career trajectories of the two leading actresses in this film. Nagra has made a successful career on television playing a doctor in *ER* (from 2003–9), while Knightley has an established place on the A-List of Hollywood stars, despite playing second fiddle to Nagra in *Beckham*. Perhaps the colour of each actress's skin may well be a major factor here, with Nagra taking a rather stereotyped, television role and Knightley starring in billion dollar franchise movies.

The film is a piece of pure escapism and shows a multicultural Britain which is working pretty well. The clean, wide streets of Southall and Hounslow and the almost endless blue skies and bright sunshine captured by Jong Lin's camera gives the film an overwhelmingly optimistic effect. Kenny Glennan's *Yasmin*, on the other hand, takes a very different approach by looking at a young British-Pakistani woman in an unnamed town in the north of England.

The film was originally shown in a late-night slot on Channel Four in January 2005, and had a limited theatrical release both in the UK and internationally. The screenplay was by Simon Beaufoy, who had written the successful *The Full Monty* and is shot as a decidedly stark piece of social realism, closer in spirit to *Bullet Boy* than *Bend it Like Beckham*. The film explores the dilemmas and reactions to life as a Muslim in post-9/11 Britain and in its central character, Yasmin, it gives voice to key debates about identity, culture and community. We are many miles away from the vibrancy of Chadha's Hounslow, in a grey, northern mill town. We see two men, one older and one younger, going to the local mosque, the young man using a microphone which fills the quiet town with the call to prayers. This is intercut with a young woman stopping her car on a deserted country lane to change her clothes behind a dry stone wall. Her traditional dress is discarded in favour of tight jeans and a low-cut top. Her dark hair is revealed as she drives off in her second-hand Golf convertible, or 'sex on wheels' as she tells her bemused colleague John (Steve Jackson) when she pulls up to start work. Glennan uses further examples of parallel editing to show this alongside the sight of the older man cleaning racist graffiti off the front shutters of his television repair shop, and in doing so a number of themes have been explored in a minimalist fashion in the first few minutes of the film. *Yasmin* gives us a much more conflicted view of Britain's ethnic minorities. The desolate country road that the female character has travelled along separates the mill town from the rest of the world. This motif is used throughout to show the gulf between her life on the 'outside' and that at home.

Yasmin is played by Archie Panjabi from *Bend it Like Beckham*, the older man is her father, Khalid (Renu Setna), and the younger man her brother, Nasir (Syed Ahmed). She is also wife to Faysal (Shahid Ahmed), a goatherd from Pakistan with a very slight grasp of English whom her father had arranged for her to marry, very much against her will. Her view is that she will stay with him until he gets his official papers to stay in Britain and then divorce him. It is a relationship that hasn't been consummated and the simple-minded Faysal seems largely happy to go along with this arrangement with his bed on the floor of the spare room.

The gap between Yasmin's life outside is highlighted wonderfully in those opening sequences. She works with John, helping special-needs children. She is bright, confident, lewd and initially dismissive of her background, even down to her choice of car. Not a Toyota, that John has checked out for her, and which she sees as a TPC – 'typical Paki car' – but a more ostentatious red Golf GTI. The early part of the film sees her carefully trying to balance this dual life. She is shown going home to cook for her family, berating Faysal for building a fire in the backyard and buying a goat. She is surrounded by claustrophobic terraced streets, living in a two-up-two-down opposite her father and having to account for her movements. The ever-watchful community contrasts with the apparent 'freedoms' outside of her home town. We see this in her dress sense, going to pubs and flirting openly with John. This central conflict between tradition and Westernisation is further developed, firstly by showing changes in Yasmin's relationships at work and at home post-9/11; secondly, the narrative is broadened by developing a subplot involving her brother Nassir and his increasing radicalisation. As Stuart Jeffries remarks, 'the film's younger Asian characters are tempted by Western society with all its secular joys and perils but, because of rising Islamophobia, are pushed from that milieu into the comforting world of traditional Islamic society or, frighteningly, fundamentalist terror'[18]. Yasmin's reawakening actually starts when she opens a copy of the Qu'ran after being locked in a prison cell without charge.

Nassir, who is seen early on calling the community to prayers, is also revealed to be leading a dual life. With his Nike sportsgear and gelled hair he deals dope for money and solicits sexual favours from the young girls from the local white underclass. Apart from his religious observance and apparent servility to his father, he is just another working-class kid, all small-town bravado and low-level crime. The catalytic moment of 9/11 changes not only Yasmin as we shall see, but Nassir as well. The conflict between the much more moderate Islam of Khalid and Nassir's increasing disillusionment starts slowly with the son making an off-hand comment about the events in the United States, calling them, rather childishly, 'style', much to the chagrin of his father. However, when radicals outside the mosque start handing out leaflets, Nassir is drawn to their cause. At the end of the film, he leaves for Pakistan for further 'training'. The film here is eerily prophetic, foreshadowing the London bombings of 7 July 2005. Glennan and Beaufoy had done extensive research in the north of England on the Muslim communities' reaction to and treatment after 9/11. The original idea by the director and producer Sally Hibbin was to explore the then-unthinkable notion of a British suicide bomber. 'I've always felt that the way to understand terrorism is to understand the roots of terrorism and to tackle those roots', Hibbin told the BBC[19].

The almost continual presence of helicopters flying over the town, the increased number of police officers on the street and the armed raids on both Yasmin and Khalid's homes shows us a community under siege as post-9/11 paranoia takes hold. Yasmin suffers racism at work — a beard on her photograph, 'Yas Loves Osama' on her locker — although she has no idea who Bin Laden is. She is ostracised by workmates and initially even John doesn't understand her problems, saying that the Muslim community hasn't made it easy for itself by not apologising, to which a drunken Yasmin makes a fool of herself by personally saying 'sorry' to everyone in the pub.

A valid criticism of the film is how the white characters are by and large cast as ignorant, reactionary bigots. Munira Mirza, the co-author of *Living Apart Together: British Muslims and the Paradox of Multiculturalism*, was particularly critical of these stereotypes of 'white people as ignorant xenophobes ... Muslims as hapless victims ready to turn terrorist at the first sight of the Union Jack'[20]. Ironically, when a Muslim woman has eggs thrown at her and is verbally attacked by some white children in a busy shopping precinct, Yasmin

'comforts the distressed woman, but what is particularly lovely about the scene is that an elderly white woman, appalled at the boys' behaviour, rushes up to the two women to apologise. The woman turns out to have been a passing shopper who did not realise that she had stumbled on to a film shoot. "It was such a great unscripted moment, we decided to keep it in," says producer Sally Hibbin.'[21]

Mirza sees this as the only point where there is any kind of solidarity or mutual concern between whites and Asians, which isn't strictly true as John is genuinely worried about Yasmin's welfare and visits her at home. This is when the armed police turn up looking for Faysal, whose phone calls back to Pakistan have uncovered a tenuous link to a Kasmiri liberation movement. John is placed in the middle of this incursion. Perhaps the makers of *Yasmin* put him there to get a wider white audience to empathise more with the plight of Yasmin and her family. The police question John and inform him that they are searching for Faysal, Yasmin's husband. John, of course, is completely unaware that she is even married, such is the dual nature of her life. The police find the innocent Faysal by chance, arrest him and take him to a detention centre.

The point that Hibbin makes about understanding the roots of terrorism are developed bluntly in the shape of Nassir's reaction to having a gun pointed at his head. Plain-clothes officers try to bribe him into giving them information about the young radicals distributing their pamphlets. This climate of fear feeds an isolationist stance. Nassir, told that Allah is a forgiving God, is drawn to the message that he will be forgiven and will die with a smile on his face as he enters paradise. The sense of anger that Nassir has thus far failed to articulate finally finds a voice. Although towards the end of the film he wants Yasmin's blessing to leave and fight, it is clear that he had made his decision earlier on with the metaphorical tossing of his mobile phone into a river, a rejection of Western values.

While the film had its critics, at the heart of *Yasmin* is, as Paul Hoggart notes, 'a moving call for the British to remember who we are, a culture which has learnt from centuries of painful experience to be tolerant, sensible and humane'[22]. Glennan's film articulates a sense of anger and isolation in the Muslim community. What it does rather less effectively is to fully explore how these issues have come to arise and it also simplifies the white response to the events of 9/11. Perhaps this is best seen in the last few minutes of the film when John meets Yasmin by chance, but fails to recognise her in her headscarf. She is off to the mosque, he to the pub. Her farewell, 'see ya', is met by John's honest 'probably not love'. But is Yasmin's rediscovery of her cultural roots to be seen as one of retreat or one which is empowering in the face of hostility?

Sarah Gavron's *Brick Lane* is also the story of a young Muslim woman torn between two opposing forces, in this case a loveless long-term marriage to an ageing husband, and a passionate relationship with a much younger British-Asian man, who in a similar vein to Nassir in *Yasmin* gets caught up, post-9/11, in radical street politics. Gavron takes Monica Ali's sprawling novel, which covers 35 years in the life of the central protagonist

Tannistha
Chatterjee, *Brick
Lane*

Nazneen (Tannistha Chatterjee), and concentrates on dreamy flashbacks, showing an idyllic life left in Bangladesh before her arranged marriage to Chanu (Satish Kaushik) and her subsequent life in London's east end raising two daughters. Early on we see her as the dutiful wife and mother, quiet, withdrawn, waiting for her sister's letters. She is always dreaming of returning. When Chanu resigns from his job, Nazneen starts to work at home as a seamstress. This brings her into contact with Karim (Christopher Simpson), a supplier, and over time they begin an affair. Chanu gets increasingly into debt with a local moneylender and sees returning to Bangladesh as the only way out. He is also aware of rumours surrounding his wife's affair. As Karim becomes more radicalised, he and Nazneen start to drift apart. Nazneen slowly realises that her life is in Britain and that her daughters are unwilling to leave home. She also realises that she wants neither Karim nor Chanu and rejects Karim's offer of marriage. Chanu decides to return to Bangladesh alone. This character arc for Nazneen is a key point that the director saw as central to the narrative:

> 'What I loved was this compassionate portrait of a family set against this shifting cultural landscape of London and this journey of a woman who was finding her voice and her place in the world and realising that a country that had been alien to her is in fact home.'[23]

Nazneen's understated journey of self-discovery and independence is told with the minimum of melodrama. Funded by FilmFour and the UK Film Council, this relatively uncontroversial film was dogged by problems right the way through its production. There was a great deal of opposition to the novel, more so when the film went into production, with a successful campaign to get the location shooting moved. The chair of the Brick Lane Traders Association, Abdus Salique, said, 'Nobody can come with a camera and make a film about that book here. She [Ali] has imagined ideas about us in her head. She is not one of us, she has not lived with us, she knows nothing about us, but she has insulted us'[24]. The film had also been lined up as a 2007 Royal Film Performance, but was pulled amid rumours of further protests which would have embarrassed the guest of honour Prince Charles. Parminder Vir, an advisor on the film, said, 'This plays into the hands of people who want us to live in fear of immigration and Islam. Showing this film would not damage anyone. It is not a film about race but about one woman's struggle in a new country. She just happens to be a Muslim from Bangladesh'[25].

The film itself seems too aware of the potential controversies by skirting quite delicately around a number of issues explored in the novel, such as a riot that serves as the backdrop to Nazneen following her fleeing daughter, which was completely changed. Gavron commented, 'We had the riot in lots of drafts and it didn't quite fit dramatically. If you read the book, you don't think of community politics as dominating it, you think of the story as a woman. An image goes a long way in film – an image of a meeting of men with beards says a lot. The book has dozens of love scenes – we have four'[26].

The focus, as Gavron has constantly articulated, is on Nazneen as central to the film, but she was careful to balance the personal and the political and try not to neglect the obvious cultural contextual framework of events:

'It was obviously set against this social and political background, and this gives a very important texture to the story. And what I thought was interesting here is that, for once we were seeing the world through the eyes of a woman. One thing that's political about this film is that we are giving a marginalised section of the community a voice.'[27]

The cot death of Nazneen and Chanu's son, unlike Ali's lengthy account in the novel, is mentioned but registers little impact, so it was unable to function to illuminate some of the problems in Nazneen's marriage, for example. The sense of Bangladesh as a half-remembered paradise is well observed; the mood of loss and exile is subtly handled in an exchange of correspondence between Nazneen and her seemingly wayward sister Hasina. Ultimately, the film lacks the epic scope of the novel, it feels pared down and the subtlety of Ali's work is often overlooked. Karim's radicalisation is also underplayed. His transformation only really serves to offer Nazneen another poor alternative for a prospective husband after Chanu returns home. The film ends on a hopeful note with the main character choosing to remain in London with her daughters and at long last reconciling herself with her place in British society. For Nazneen, this is a form of independence that gently aligns her with Jess, from *Bend it Like Beckham*, who moves to America, and Yasmin, who decides to return in part to her cultural and religious roots. There is a refreshing lack of consistency in each film's resolution of the narrative journey.

REFERENCES

1. Alexander, K., 'Black British Cinema in the 90s: Going Going Gone' in British Cinema of the 90s, Murphy, R. (ed.), London: BFI, 2000

2. Mercer, K., Recoding Narratives of Race and Nation, in Black Film, Black Cinema, Mercer, K. (ed.), London: ICA Documents/BFI, 1988

3. Sullivan, C., 'Kidulthood: Does it really reflect inner-city life?' in The Independent, 03/03/06

4. Thomson, A., 'A film to make every mother shudder' in The Independent, 01/03/06

5. Sawyer, M., 'The film that speaks to Britain's youth in words they understand' in The Observer, 26/02/2006

6. Maher, K., 'Cinema: It's proper sad, man' in The Times, 15/02/2006

7. Bell, J., Review of *Kidulthood* in Sight and Sound, May 2006

8. Aftab, K., 'Ashley Walters: Shadow of the gun' in The Independent, 06/04/2005

9. Brooke, M., Review of *Bullet Boy* on www.screenonline.org.uk

10. Kalinowska, A., Interview with Saul Dibb on www.phase9.tv

11. Plunkett, D., 'I didn't want to make something without hope' in The Guardian, 20/04/2005

12. Ojumo, A., 'Loaded questions' in The Observer, 20/03/2005

13. Chadha, G., 'Call that a melting pot' in The Guardian, 11/04/2002

14. Barber, N., Review of *Bend it Like Beckham* in The Independent, 14/04/2002

15. Fischer, P., 'Gurinder Chadha — Success at last as Beckham finally hits US' on www.filmmonthly.com

16. French, P., Review of *Bend it Like Beckham* in The Observer, 14/04/2002

17. Brookes, E., 'Laughing all the way to the box office' in The Guardian, 19/07/2004

18. Jeffries, S., 'Coming to a small screen near you' in The Guardian, 13/01/2005

19. Unaccredited, 'British film foreshadowed blasts' on bbc.co.uk, 15/07/2005

20. Mirza, M., quoted on www.culturewars.org.uk, 16/01/2005

21. Jeffries, S., 'Coming to a small screen near you' in The Guardian, 13/01/2005

22. Hoggart, P., 'Last night's TV' from The Times, 14/01/2005

23. Interview with Sarah Gavron on www.femalefirst.co.uk, 29/02/2008

24. Lea, R. and Lewis, P., 'Local protests over *Brick Lane* film' in The Guardian, 17/06/2006

25. Staff and agencies, 'Brick Lane royal gala cancelled amid protest fears' in The Guardian, 25/09/2007

26. Ide, W., '*Brick Lane* brickbats' in The Times, 10/11/2007

27. Interview with Sarah Gavron on www.bbc.co,uk, 15/11/2007

THE NEO-COLONIAL FILM — THE BRITISH IN AFRICA

INTRODUCTION

In the period under consideration there have been a small number of films produced which have chosen Africa as the main location and centred on Western approaches to big, important themes and events concerning the continent. Hollywood has made *Hotel Rwanda* (George, 2004), *The Interpreter* (Pollack, 2005), *Catch a Fire* (Noyce, 2006) and *Blood Diamond* (Zwick, 2006), all focusing on telling African stories to global audiences, and although there have been some excellent recent films by indigenous directors, it is these big productions that have tended to frame the African experience. That said, a century of Western film practice in Africa has, according to Marie-Helene Gutberlet, aroused no substantial film-historical interest, except as a focus for ideological critique (from Bergfelder [ed.] et al, 2002, p238)[1]. This chapter concentrates on films that cover the British experience in Africa, as diplomats and activists in *The Constant Gardener* (Meirelles, 2005), as aid-worker turned despot's doctor in *The Last King of Scotland* (Macdonald, 2006) and as priest and teacher in *Shooting Dogs* (Caton-Jones, 2006).

African films such as *Moolaade* (2004), by one of Africa's key auteurs, Ousmane Sembene, are largely neglected outside of an art-house, cinephile audience. This film takes on the delicate matter of female circumcision, a problem that blights the continent and keeps women subservient. Set entirely within a small village in Burkina Faso it is a compelling, moving and ultimately uplifting piece of work, which manages to tell an enlightening story devoid of Western influences. Mark Cousins sees Sembene as 'not so much a state-of-the-nation film-maker as a state-of-the-continent one, the John Ford of Africa'[2] and Sembene sees the African 'voice' as been fundamental to representing Africa in a clear and honest way:

> 'In my films, I try to talk as much as possible of Africans, because Africans belong to different mixtures of cultures and expressions. But they have acute eyesight and hearing. I think that African cinema must find in this sobriety a new aesthetic quality, a new form of expression which is their own.'[3]

Other African film-makers such as Abderrahmane Sissako and Fanto Regina Nacro have made diverse films which further enrich an understanding of African life. Sissako's beautiful *Waiting for Happiness* (2002), shot in his native Mauritania, is a story of the changes wrought by modernity. It is also a fascinating meditation on the pain and necessity of enforced exile that is central to many young Africans' lives. Nacro's tense, reflective *The Night of Truth* (2004) is set in an unnamed African country and deals with the aftermath of a bitter civil war between two ethnic groups. It is a film referencing the Rwandan genocide in the mid-1990s, but it could equally apply to many African conflicts in Sierra Leone, Sudan or Zaire. In a similar fashion to *Moolaade*, the film is redemptive and ultimately uplifting, where past conflicts are solved, but not without pain. Can films made which have Britons as their main protagonists add anything more to representing Africa?

Britain has, of course, a long and complex history with Africa and what this chapter is fundamentally concerned with is how these three films, *The Constant Gardener*, *The Last King of Scotland* and *Shooting Dogs*, reflect this in different ways. Do they capture the essence of Africa albeit through the eyes of British characters? How do they reflect British attitudes to the continent against the backdrop of post-colonial guilt? Is it also possible for these films to actually develop a reading of the British abroad at a diplomatic/economic/personal and even a spiritual level? Or do these films fall into the trap, as suggested by Dave Calhoun, of just focusing on 'stunning landscapes, a fascinating past, but ultimately a continent whose people and politics are too difficult to get to grips with'[4].

DIGGING FOR THE TRUTH — *THE CONSTANT GARDENER*

Ralph Fiennes,
*The Constant
Gardener*

At first glance the Brazilian director Fernando Meirelles seems an odd choice for this John Le Carre adaptation. He began in his native country as a maker of documentaries but after his hyper-real, electrifying second feature, *City of God* (2002), the explosive tale of a Rio favela, it was assumed that he would end up following the money to make a big film in Hollywood. The film had been nominated for a number of Oscars, including one for Meirelles. However, it was the modestly budgeted British co-production *The Constant Gardener* that ended up as his next project. It was a story that attracted him on a number of levels:

'The chance to take on some of the issues that surround the pharmaceutical industry was one of the elements that made me want to direct *The Constant Gardener*. Another was the chance and choice to shoot in Kenya. It is also a very original love story. A man who marries a younger woman, and it's after she dies that he truly falls in love with her and goes looking for her. It's a beautiful tale with a touch of the existential to it.'[5]

Meirelles' Brazilian background gave him an interesting perspective and sense of objectivity on two levels. Firstly, there was a distinct sense of empathy with the poverty that is shown in the film and some parallels can be drawn between the lawless Rio favela and the Nairobi shantytown of Kibera, the largest slum in sub-Saharan Africa where some of the film was shot. And secondly, there is a sense of distance from the typically British machinations that pepper the narrative with a refreshing outlook lacking in other Le Carre adaptations. This was highlighted by Peter Bradshaw, who commented in his review, 'Meirelles gives us something gutsier and less English. We get rage, restless curiosity, agonised self-reproach and whole landscapes lit up with lightning flashes of paranoia'[6]. Meirelles' lack of comprehension at the subtle workings of the British establishment, the gentlemen's clubs, golf courses and colonial attitudes that still prevail, actually works in his favour. He is as much an outsider as the majority of the audience are and this acute sense of detachment ironically allows the audience to see the truth behind the corruption which stalks the upper echelons of big business and government power in the film.

The Constant Gardener is an interesting template for a more global, outward-looking British film. Although at its core it is a tale of the British in Africa, it raises broader points about the West's behaviour on the continent. A great deal of the finance and distribution budget was American (from Universal), but crucially the film was also a UK Film Council project and could be seen as a model for the sort of prestige project that should be encouraged. Although the budget of £15 million was minuscule by Hollywood standards, the film did respectable business in the United States, was critically acclaimed and won Rachel Weisz a best supporting actress Academy Award.

The film, like City of God, is told in a non-linear fashion, moving between different timeframes and enabling different amounts of information to emerge at crucial moments. The film also shifts between a number of different locations – Kenya, London, Berlin and Southern Sudan – and interweaves a complex plot regarding the testing of Dypraxa, a drug for tuberculosis, with high-level fraudulent dealings between government officials and multinational pharmaceutical companies. At its heart, though, is a love story between mild-mannered British diplomat Justin Quayle (Ralph Fiennes) and his fiery activist wife Tessa (Rachel Weisz).

Meirelles' distinctive visual style is very apparent in the film. He uses saturated colours to symbolise the differences between settings. He also favours a kinetic editing style which reinforces the fragmented sense of the narrative. Although he is often at pains to reiterate the power of the story and the acting in his work, it is clear that the finished look or mise-en-scène is also vitally important.

> 'We [Meirelles and his DP] visited all the locations where we were going to shoot to find the exact places. And then he took photos. He was using the same stock, which he was going to use during the shooting. And those pictures that he took were more or less identical with the frames that we have in the finished film. He went to Brazil, where he had a colourist, the guy that corrects colours. And he worked frame by frame with this guy trying to find the colours for each scene.'[7]

This is possibly best seen in the differences in terms of the *mise-en-scène* between Kibera and London. Kibera is presented as a bright, bustling and colourful place. The sun beats down on this swarming view of humanity, the camera swoops everywhere and takes in everything. There is a real sense of energy in the sequences, which acknowledge the poverty while showing graphically that nothing is hidden. London, by contrast, is shot in a muted, rather sedate way. Greys, greens and darker shades dominate under threatening cloudy skies. There is a distinct lack of people in these scenes, which greatly adds to the feelings of loneliness, grief and mounting paranoia that Justin is experiencing. The metropolis is one full of hidden secrets, CCTV cameras at the airport and station seem to follow Justin's every move, the notion of conspiracy is central to these sequences.

The narrative begins in the present but rather unusually with the death of one of the central characters, Tessa, the obvious catalyst for the rest of the story. Meirelles presents the exposition in flashback; the initial meeting between Justin and Tessa is shown and the mutual attraction between opposites is quickly explored. Justin is the archetypal decent English civil servant, unassuming and dedicated to his job and confident of his place in the world. His hobby is gardening which provides an apt metaphor for what emerges later. His dedication to tending plants and flowers suggests someone outside the conventional 'man of action' role. Fiennes' performance is wonderfully understated and is matched well with Weisz's Tessa – her drive and, as Jonathan Romney calls it, 'sweetly confrontational style' acts as an interesting counterpoint[8]. Even their political views seem at the outset to be at odds but this receives no real attention here. Their relationship is consummated quickly and marriage soon follows. Justin receives news of a posting to Kenya, and Meirelles gives us a sequence where our knowledge of Tessa's pregnancy is intercut with scenes of Justin identifying his dead wife's body.

It is apparent early on that the issue of class is fundamental (and we can draw some interesting comparisions with the other films in this chapter) although this is something that Meirelles chose to try and ignore:

> "'Class is very important in the book," he sighs. "Someone's a grammar-school guy, someone else is an Eton guy. It was a surprise to see how British society works. It's a caste society, just like India. You can imagine for a Brazilian, it's a secret code that only Brits understand. I can't tell if someone's a public schoolboy or if they come from Manchester. John [Le Carre] tried to explain it to me, but it's difficult. So I decided to throw the whole lot out."'[9]

But the middle-class credentials of the main protagonists are plain to see straight away. The subtle differences between educational background would be too difficult to develop here and would leave an international audience relatively nonplussed and as confused as Meirelles. Tessa does, though, represent the concerned liberal, an upper-middle-class character, which is apparent from her well-designed west London townhouse. There is a variation on this archetype that Jenny McCartney picked up on in her review: 'She [Tessa] is a type that crops up every so often in films – the Outspoken Impassioned Campaigner for Third-World justice'[10]. Her social background isn't explored at all; there is no sense, for example, of her working for an aid agency or non-government organisation. We see her in flashback helping the destitute in Kibera, but there are few real indications of what drives her: is it middle-class, post-colonial guilt or a 'natural' quest to help the unfortunate? Justin's role as a diplomat is developed more subtly, in that he is a safe pair of hands. He again is likely to come from a particular sort of class background in order to rise so high in the diplomatic corps, although once again Meirelles leaves this up to the audience to decide. Perhaps this is, as Bradshaw (Guardian 11/11/05) puts it, an attempt to make the film 'less English' and by definition less driven by concerns about social class, which would mean very little to a global audience.

The plot itself takes an investigative slant as Justin tries to discover the reasons behind his wife's death in Kenya's remote outback, where she was on a fact-finding mission with her friend, Dr Arnold Bluhm (Hubert Kounde). Meirelles cleverly weaves an interesting parallel plot involving Sandy Woodrow (Danny Huston), Quayle's High Commission colleague, and as the narrative continues it becomes apparent that there may well have been a relationship between him and Tessa.

Tessa miscarries and while in hospital meets and befriends a young HIV-positive woman who is convinced that she is being slowly murdered via drug testing. It is this off-camera revelation that leads to the start of Tessa's quest to find out who is behind this. The aftermath of her miscarriage is interestingly handled. She is in a local hospital, which horrifies Sandy. The audience see her breast-feeding a black baby flanked by Arnold and Justin on either side of her hospital bed. There have been indications earlier on in the flashback that she may have also had a relationship with Arnold, so this shot wrong-foots the audience somewhat. It is a shot that Jessica Winter sees as particularly distasteful: 'a cut to Tessa nursing a dark-skinned baby that makes Justin look like an embarrassed cuckold when we're actually beholding a tableau of grief'[11]. Sandy's reaction is revealing as he tries to make sense (as we do) of what he is seeing. It is clear that the director used this shot to further emphasise Tessa's inherent goodness, even in the light of her losing her own son. The subsequent conversation with Sandy is telling when she reveals to him what she thinks may be happening regarding the suspicious drug testing. His immediate reaction is to ask her to let it go, suggesting that ultimately it may be damaging to Justin's career if she continues digging for further information. Of course she does continue, writes a damming report and gives it to Sandy who in turn passes it to Sir Bernard Pellegrin (Bill Nighy), his and Justin's superior.

This is a film of betrayals, half-truths and misunderstandings. It becomes apparent that although Tessa and Justin's marriage is, on the surface, a happy one, doubts remain about issues of fidelity based largely on the lack of communication between them. Tessa leads a secret life in Kenya, which both Arnold and Sandy are aware of, but about which Justin remains in the dark until after her death. Any hints of a sexual relationship with Arnold are quashed when it emerges that he is a homosexual; however, it becomes apparent that Sandy was in love with Tessa: there is a key scene in flashback where Tessa wants to read a letter from Pellegrin detailing his response to her report. Sandy is clearly interested in her. This is picked up quickly by Tessa who agrees to sleep with him, if he lets her read the letter. Sandy, blinded by lust, agrees. The letter becomes an important narrative motif.

Tessa leaves the narrative here, but her ghost haunts the rest of the film. She is seen as a strong, determined and bloody-minded person; 'a privileged white woman – she's a Westerner to boot – to highlight the forbearance and hope of a long-suffering African nation' (Winter, ibid.). The fact that there are initial doubts about her actually make her a stronger character and there is a sense that there is no way she would have ever slept with Sandy, as driven as she was to discover the truth. What makes this film take off is Justin's emergence from Tessa's shadow. This quiet, introspective man, whose main passion is for horticulture, becomes a man of action as he goes against his deep-set conservative instincts and tries to pick up where his dead wife left off.

At this point the film moves squarely into conventional thriller territory, with Justin's return to a rain-lashed London for a meeting with Pellegrin. Meirelles captures the wood-panelled archaic nature of dealings at the highest levels of the civil service with a beautifully observed scene at a plush gentleman's club. Pellegrin, with studied nonchalance, subtly and in a very unassuming, typically *English* fashion, warns his junior off. It is a frightening exchange, more for what is left unsaid and for Nighy's old public school confidence.

Although the film flits from London, across Europe via Amsterdam and Berlin and back to Africa again, it never loses sight of Justin's transformation, which seems to have a dual purpose. Firstly, to discover the truth about the illegal testing of drugs on African 'guinea pigs' and secondly, to grow closer to understanding Tessa and what she believed in. Justin doesn't turn into a Jason Bourne archetype, crossing continents, suddenly indestructible. He is very fallible and extremely believable, still reeling from Tessa's murder and slowly dismantling all the apparent certainties in his life. As he says to another superior, Tim Donohue (Donald Sumpter), 'Tessa was my home', and now without a home it seems that he has nothing left to lose. The metaphor of the gardener is particularly apt here:

> 'He is the gardener of the title – he digs deep into a stinking morass of official lies and corporate malfeasance to get to the truth, and it's the recognition of his essentially decent, self-contained nature that makes his plight so moving.'[12]

Europe is seen as unsafe. Justin's passport has been taken away but with the help of Tessa's cousin, Arthur Hammond (Richard McCabe) who happens to be a solicitor, he procures another one in order to travel to the Netherlands. Hammond's son Guido

(Rupert Simonian) unlocks Tessa's emails, revealing what she knew about the drug testing. The film is filled with the possibilities of violence. One of Tessa's contacts in the Dutch capital is nearly run over and Justin is beaten up in his Berlin hotel room. He returns to Africa.

Justin's main ally in Kenya is a young, British-Asian civil servant, Gita Person (Archie Punjabi). She tells him of Arnold's sexuality and reassures him of Tessa's fidelity. She is an outsider, not part of the oldboy network. This is also true of Kenny Curtis (Gerald McSorley), a tough-talking, slightly sinister Irish businessman involved in brokering deals between the testing company Three Bees, the large German-Swiss multinational pharmaceutical KDH and the Kenyan government. Sandy and his wife Gloria (Juliet Aubrey) laugh and joke about his knighthood over dinner. Although Curtis has his uses, he will never really be accepted by the likes of Pellegrin and his acolytes. It is Curtis who is set up as the obvious scapegoat for the British establishment and he warns Justin that he is a marked man. He also shows him a mass grave, where 62 people are buried, the victims of Dypraxa testing.

Justin's return visit sees him confront Sandy. Sandy's agenda is solely to retrieve his love letter to Tessa, but crucially he informs Justin to 'stop batting for Africa and show some loyalty'. The truth becomes clearer: KDH had promised to build a plant in Wales which would provide 1500 jobs if the British High Commission could help to facilitate the testing of their new drug. It also becomes apparent what the British role in Africa actually is, when Justin is told that they are 'not paid to be bleeding hearts'. Justin also subsequently learns of a contact, a Dr Lorbeer (Pete Postlethwaite), from Donohue and this takes him to a camp in Southern Sudan where Lorbeer is working. He poses as a journalist to gain access here. We have glimpsed Lorbeer earlier in the narrative, working in the Kibera hospital where Tessa has lost her baby. His association with the Dypraxa testing provides the necessary information which ties up the rest of the film. This is by far the most explicitly political moment, highlighting both Justin's barely contained anger and the West's hypocrisy and greed. Crucially, though, it also deals graphically with the dispensable nature of African lives.

Lorbeer tells Justin that the pharmaceutical industry is right up there with the arms dealers and that 'this is how the world fucks Africa'. The word that lingers most vividly from this exchange is 'guilt', with Lorbeer accusing the West — including the aid agencies — of being part of the problem. This stint in Sudan is seen as his own personal redemption. However, it is the combination of Justin's revelation of his true identity and a raid on the camp by an armed militia that highlights the apparent cheapness of African lives.

Justin lists the crimes and the business interests of his employers, a tale of drugs, pay-offs, cover-ups and murder. The mercenary soldiers are more explicitly brutal, burning homes, mowing down any resistance, stealing children. This clearly echoes Darfur. The dual horrors visited by war and by the West are twinned perfectly here. As Sandy has said earlier, 'We are not killing people who wouldn't be dead otherwise.' As Justin and

Lorbeer escape the carnage in an aid plane they are forced to leave behind a small girl. The poignant image of the child running alongside the plane sums up what this film seeks to highlight: the exploitation of Africa with the continuation of colonial rule through the combination of political interests and the global market.

The closure is bittersweet. Justin has managed to get Pellegrin's letter to Arthur and it is read at his memorial service. He had been shot, close to where Tessa's corpse had been found, and suicide was given as the official line, but it is clear that he was yet another victim of KDH's cover-up. Arthur's eulogy reinforces the political message and Pellegrin leaves surrounded by paparazzi, yet the over-riding feeling is that no one will be held accountable. It is a brave and honest end to the film.

Although *The Constant Gardener* may be viewed as a straightforward love story/thriller shackled to generic conventions, for a mainstream film it feels like a worthy attempt to tackle a set of complex themes. Dave Calhoun, however, thinks that the film fudges the main issue:

> 'The underhand and deadly behaviour of the pharmaceutical companies is never fully explained; it's as if Meirelles resists putting arguments in the mouths for fear of boring his audience, so we leave the cinema with a stronger memory of breathtaking aerial shots of the beautified desert than with any new insight into the scandal of drugs companies and Africa.' (Calhoun, February 2007)

This is questionable. The film is not the right vehicle to adequately respond to the sins of the West in less than two hours, but it does at least raise questions about the state of the continent today, albeit with white European leads. In terms of its final legacy, *The Constant Gardener* is a classy, thought-provoking piece of film-making by a fine director; it explores the British in Africa with verve and insight and for that alone it should be applauded.

CHASING AMIN – *THE LAST KING OF SCOTLAND*

Forest Whitaker, *The Last King of Scotland*

Kevin Macdonald's film shares many similarities, visually and thematically, with *The Constant Gardener*. The brightness of the Ugandan *mise-en-scène*, the emphasis on African suffering, our white guide through the narrative – this time a young Scottish doctor – all have clear comparisions with Meirelles' film. The film-makers themselves also share a background in documentary. Macdonald won an Academy Award for his first film, the documentary *One Day in September* (1999), and a BAFTA for *Touching the Void* in 2003. *Touching the Void*, based on Joe Simpson's book of the same name, was the true-life story of two young climbers and their nightmare ascent of a Peruvian mountain and featured extensive reconstruction sequences that marked Macdonald out as a director to watch.

The Last King of Scotland had a considerably lower budget than Meirelles' Kenyan epic but like that film had American finance and distribution deals in place and also the support of FilmFour, the UK Film Council and Scottish Screen. But again the film looks considerably more expensive and expansive than its £5 million budget suggests. This is enhanced by Anthony Dod Mantle's high-contrast, saturated cinematography and a theatrical, almost Shakespearian performance by Forest Whitaker as Idi Amin.

The Last King of Scotland was originally a novel by Giles Foden; the screenplay is by Peter Morgan. Set in the 1970s, it recounts a fictional relationship with a recently qualified medic, Nicholas Garrigan, and African dictator Idi Amin. The film, like the novel, encourages the audience to see Amin through Garrigan's eyes, which changes as the narrative progresses from wide-eyed awe to sheer terror, as Amin's mood swings and paranoia increase. James McAvoy plays Garrigan as a naïve but cocksure figure entranced initially by Whitaker's charismatic, Oscar-winning portrayal of the Ugandan leader.

The film was shot in Uganda as part of Macdonald's drive for authenticity. He was allowed to use state buildings, including Amin's swimming pool and the main hospital in Kampala, and was even able to resurrect Amin's own limousine. He also used a considerable number of Ugandan extras who were there to reinforce and perhaps test his drive for realism:

'You are surrounded by people that Forest and James could talk to about the real Amin, about those times, about what it was like. You can't get away with faking it if you are Forest Whitaker and you are standing up on a stage with 4,000 Ugandans.'[13]

Amin was initially installed by the British and was seen as a safe pair of hands who could easily be manipulated by the same sort of diplomats who stalk the British High Commission in *The Constant Gardener*. After taking over in a coup Amin pledges to do more for his country, a former British colony. That said, as he becomes more and more powerful this feeling changes as Amin becomes a delusional monster. This was a view that was firmly established in the British press during this period, with tales of Amin's butchery and cannibalistic tendencies, and Macdonald was keen to present a more sympathetic view of the African leader:

'They (Ugandans) didn't want a two-dimensional image of Amin presented … this semi-mythical figure who was a big star of the media, in a way, in the mid-seventies. He was always seen as the man who ate his archbishop's liver and the man who was a cannibal and the man who tortured and killed so many people. But there was an optimistic side of the man, who is trying to do something good for his country, before he was brought low by his own character flaws and paranoia. So the only concern was to show a rounded human being.' (ibid.)

Joel Kibazo, a Ugandan media consultant who grew up during Amin's regime, had to flee the country after his father was appointed Amin's justice minister, a position that he didn't want to take. He was initially sceptical about *The Last King of Scotland*'s ability to capture the regime's horror and to avoid showing Amin as an outlandish figure of fun:

'For most Africans who lived through the years of brutality and terror as family and friends were murdered, tortured, or simply fed to the crocodiles in the river Nile, there has never been anything amusing about Amin. It is believed that by the end of his reign in 1979, perhaps 500,000 Africans had perished at the hands of his death squads. No one will ever know the true figure.'[14]

Kibazo, however, was won over, stating that while it fails to capture the sheer terror of Uganda in the 1970s, it avoids crudely stereotyping Amin as a 'typical' African dictator. Nonetheless, the film was criticised for adding a sympathetic side to Idi Amin's complex personality. The *New Internationalist* compares Whitaker's portrayal to that of the Joker in *Batman* (1989), 'a grotesque bogey man, as if Africa's turmoil is just down to inherent madness. We learn nothing of the internal tensions of multi-ethnic, multi-faith post-colonial Uganda: nor of Amin running that state. This lets too many others off the hook, not least the British, Israelis and Saudis who got him into power or kept him there'[15].

Vanessa Walters was more virulent in her condemnation. She accuses the film of 'playing to some of the worst stereotypes of corrupt, murderous, incompetent and ridiculous black leaders'[16]. She highlights the fact that the film's real focus is the white character Garrigan and that it is his story that is meant to appeal. She draws parallels with *Cry Freedom* (Attenborough, 1988) and its depiction of the relationship between white South African journalist Donald Woods and the revolutionary martyr Steve Biko. She condemns most reviewers' failure to pick up on wider stereotypes of Africa itself:

'Apart from the scary men running around Uganda with AK-47s, there is a plethora of scantily clad go-go dancers and other exotic, sexually available women to be bedded by Garrigan – including one of Amin's wives. There are flies on sick, starving faces, and the hospitals are filled with filthy swarms of humanity. There is the selfish, corrupt elite in their manicured compounds and the peasants portrayed as helpless children.'

These arguments could be levelled at any of the films in this chapter, but in making sense of Africa could any Western director ever do the location justice? Are *The Last King of Scotland*, *The Constant Gardener* and *Shooting Dogs* any less valid because they haven't been made by an indigenous director? It is a criticism that Macdonald was keen to address:

'One of the criticisms people always make about films about Africa is that they come from a white perspective. I think that's a bogus, very PC kind of criticism. Of course if you are a film-maker from the UK who makes a film about Uganda or Namibia or

Angola as though you were Angolan or Namibian, I don't think you'd get it right. You can only look at the world … through your own eyes, through your own culture. This film isn't about Uganda; it's about the relationship between a Ugandan and a Scot. It's about the coming together of two cultures.' (Interview by Bruce Munro, 11/01/2007)[17]

This is central to the narrative and *The Last King of Scotland* is as much about Garrigan's transformation and rites of passage as it is about Amin's despotic reign. So in a similar vein to *The Constant Gardener* and, as we shall see, *Shooting Dogs*, the African experience is framed by the white character for white audiences. The main protagonist is our eyes and ears to an exotic and distant place. It is interesting then that in *The Last King of Scotland* Garrigan is portrayed as such a callow and superficial character.

After graduating, he wants to escape the dour, provincial Scotland where he is expected to follow his father into general practice. It is apparent that he is a solidly middle-class character, although here it is his Scottish background which is key to his relationship with Amin. His decision to leave home is purely random, his finger stopping by chance on the globe at Uganda. Early on we see him riding on an overcrowded bus where he sees from the window a number of soldiers on a jeep passing by. 'Amin will fight for the people,' comments someone on the bus. He has an early sexual encounter with a native girl which gives the audience a foreshadowing of his eventual downfall and he arrives at his intended destination a day late. He has taken a position in the bush assisting a dedicated English doctor, David Merritt (Adam Kotz), and his pretty wife Sarah (Gillian Anderson). It is apparent that the medical services that Merritt and his wife run are overstretched. Garrigan proves a popular character and slowly draws Sarah out. Merritt says that there are problems in terms of the sheer volume of patients and also the adherence to local customs – the witch doctor being used more than modern medicine. We are 'skimming the surface of an ocean,' he confesses to Garrigan.

The film rests on a number of key exchanges between Garrigan and Amin. The first meeting is pivotal and is totally by chance. Garrigan takes Sarah to a local rally organised by Amin's supporters, in which he gives a rousing speech. It is our first sight of Amin. His impressive uniformed bulk fills the screen, and his oratorical powers are very much to the fore, promising a government of action. He is 'a simple man' and he tells the crowd that 'I am you'. As Philip French remarks in his review, 'His shoulders and neck suggest physical power. Then Macdonald cuts to Amin in full flood, his eyes blazing, his nostrils flaring, his forceful rhetoric igniting the crowd'[18].

Nicholas Garrigan is totally taken in by the speech, applauding and whooping loudly. The experienced Sarah is less impressed, she has seen it all before with Amin's corrupt predecessor Milton Obote. On the journey back to their medical centre they are stopped by Amin's military personnel and when it emerges that Garrigan is a medic, he is ordered to treat Amin who has suffered a minor injury when his jeep hit a cow. While bandaging Amin's hand, Garrigan is unable to concentrate due to the dying animal by the roadside. He takes the leader's gun and kills the stricken beast. It is an act of foolhardy impetuousness which strangely impresses Amin, as does Garrigan's Scotland T-Shirt which Amin swops for his own shirt. It emerges that Amin has a great regard for the Scottish after serving in the British Army with them. It is a scene that shifts on the unpredictable nature of Amin's reactions and this provides the prototype for their subsequent meetings. It also draws parallels between Uganda and Scotland's colonial status, both countries subjugated by the English in the past and this seems to further cement the initial attraction between the two men.

After making an ill-advised pass at Sarah, which she gently knocks back, he leaves the medical compound and heads for the capital Kampala where Amin has invited him. He is asked by Amin to consider becoming his personal physician and also to head up the development of a Ugandan health service, although this is presented as an offer that it would be unwise to refuse. Garrigan is soon easily seduced by the big cars, palatial settings and Amin's unsubtle courtship techniques. After curing Amin's bout of midnight flatulence he willingly accepts the position. In this particular sequence, however, it is clear how Amin's mania about being threatened by enemies is growing; in this case he believes that he has been poisoned when in reality it is a combination of too much beer and aspirin. Garrigan's feckless nature is easily swayed by the extravagant lifestyle of the leader – nightclubs, swimming-pool parties, a spacious penthouse apartment and a brand new Mercedes – and he quickly replicates Amin's delusions of grandeur. He becomes Amin's closest advisor, sitting in for him at important meetings, usurping the power of the Health Minister, Jonah Wasswa (Stephen Rwangyezi), and ultimately being responsible for his murder.

The British High Commission is represented in the film by the shadowy figure of Stone (Simon McBurney) and interesting parallels can be drawn here with *The Constant Gardener*. The film makes clear that the British establishment see Amin as 'a little unpredictable, but a firm hand, the only thing that the African really understands'. Amin is 'a brutal but essentially biddable and pro-British strongman who will function as a bulwark against communism in Africa' (Bradshaw, 12/01/2007)[19]. Stone is eager to entice Garrigan through diplomatic doublespeak to keep an eye on Amin, who it transpires they have helped install as leader. Garrigan resists this, until he has to give in.

The relationship between the two men is further reinforced by Garrigan's help for Amin's son Mackenzie, who suffers from epilepsy, and by him inadvertently saving Amin from an armed attack from Obote's supporters. Amin is seen increasingly as a man who truly believes that he is surrounded by traitors and Macdonald chooses to show this in a succession of bewildering quick cuts. But Garrigan is as much a part of Amin's court of deception by informing him that he saw Wasswa in suspicious conference with a white man in the bar of Kampala's Holiday Inn. When the Health Minister disappears and later turns up dead, the naïve Garrigan is horrified and decides to leave the country.

In a key tension-filled scene with Amin he explains that he wants to return home. Macdonald initially underpins the sequence with humour, as Garrigan nervously addresses Amin, who has his back turned away from him. It quickly transpires that this is one of the body doubles that Amin has chosen to surround himself with for his own protection. When Garrigan finally confronts Amin with his wish, the use of silences and his blank stare position him as a frightened child. 'Are you like all the other British, just here to fuck and to take away?' Amin bellows. There is no answer here and the viewer becomes aware of how big Amin is as he hugs the younger man and berates him as 'a silly boy'.

Perhaps a key flaw in the film and one that differs from Foden's novel is Garrigan's affair with Kay (Kerry Washington), Amin's youngest wife. It seems implausible that the increasingly terrified Garrigan would embark on such a perilous escapade. In many respects it does provide the motivation for the latter part of the narrative where Garrigan, driven by guilt, fear and selfishness, decides to try to poison Amin. In a key exchange with the reptilian Stone, after his British passport has been taken by Amin's henchmen and replaced with a Ugandan one, he pleads for help. Stone plays an important part here by delineating the abuses of power that Garrigan has chosen to ignore, depicted by the use of photographs and a montage of images. He tells Garrigan that Amin has been systematically wiping out the opposition. He says that there is evidence of widespread slaughter outside of Kampala with, in some cases, bodies fed to crocodiles. Garrigan is Amin's 'white monkey', a mere chimp in no position to ask the British for help now, unless he can give them something, in this case Amin's life. James McEvoy is quick to point out that Garrigan's character is rooted in a particular darkness and this is in many ways linked to his position as the more intelligent, but ultimately powerless man in the face of Amin's dominant, albeit sociopathic personality:

'I wouldn't be as arrogant and egotistical and self-serving as Garrigan. He's not an evil guy, but he's all of these things. In that situation, I was playing someone who wasn't humble enough to not follow their dick, at one point their ego, at one point their job. I think for me I always saw Nicholas as the British imperialist, he might have been young and it might have been the 70s and he might have been a bit left wing, but he was still a young imperialist, In that he's selfish, he corrupts and destroys.' (From Munro, 11/01/2007)

In many respects the relationship between the two men echoes that between Britain and its African colonies. Garrigan is at all times both spellbound and appalled by Amin's excesses, and only when he is personally threatened and scared does he start to realise and accept his own morally reprehensible behaviour. 'The Last King of Scotland is a riveting satire of white Europe's fascination with Africa as a Conradian heart of darkness, which is nevertheless ripe for plunder for a sufficiently cocksure adventurer' (Bradshaw, 12/01/2007). That Amin has to constantly ask the young Scotsman for help and advice could also be read as a statement on Africa's lack of confidence in dealing with its many problems, a great deal caused by the post-colonial fallout. In many respects Garrigan's initially slightly patronising attitude towards the supposedly gentle giant figure changes as much as a result of Amin's own increasing madness, as of his own deceptions and sexual transgressions. His affair with Kay ends with her getting pregnant and it is clear that the child is his. She begs him to give her an abortion and in desperation he tries to enlist his colleague, Dr Thomas Junju (David Oyelowo), to perform the procedure at the state hospital. Junju refuses, stressing quite correctly that it would be fraught with danger.

This is all set against the background of Amin's expulsion of Uganda's large Asian population who were given ninety days to leave the country. They had great economic clout. In two telling exchanges Garrigan firstly warns the out-of-control president of the folly of this decision, which would bring the Ugandan economy to its knees. Amin reacts angrily and calls Garrigan 'a nobody' who wants to save his 'fucking Asian tailor'. The next exchange sees the incredulous Amin reeling from the overwhelmingly negative international press reaction to his dismissal of the Ugandan Asians. Like a child he rails against this and turns once again to his 'white monkey', his 'nobody', for advice. Using a succession of jerky camera movements, Macdonald captures this gargantuan man in the full throes of a tantrum. In a telling exchange he accuses Garrigan of not warning him of his mistake in throwing the Asians out. Of course Garrigan has previously done this, but Amin responds with a typical bizarre reaction. '*But you did not persuade me, Nicholas!*' he bellows at the shocked Scotsman. It is a revealing scene that reinforces Amin's growing distance from reason and reality.

Perhaps the most vivid and disturbing image in this film is that of Kay Amin. Her husband has known of her relationship with Garrigan and when Nicholas enters the bowels of the state hospital, he and the audience witness the mangled, barely recognisable corpse of his lover. The sequence is beautifully handled and under-lit with muted blues; the sound of cries builds the tension as Garrigan enters the dull mortuary, moving through crowds of Amin's other victims, vomiting when he sees Kay. This is intercut with Amin, at Garrigan's behest, charming the ranks of the international press corps, jokingly pledging food aid for Britain, which at the time was in the middle of an economic crisis.

One of the strangest passages follows this with Garrigan visiting Amin with the intention of poisoning him; his central motivation is the death of Kay and the Faustian pact (the second pact, if we consider his relationship with Amin himself) that he has made with the British to oust Amin in exchange for his release. With a succession of fades, a strange surreal soundtrack and flashbacks we see Amin surrounded by cronies watching *Deep Throat* and asking Garrigan about female sexual organs. 'The washed out vintage Seventies'-esque cinematography perfectly captures the heat-damaged fear and loathing of Nicholas's and Uganda's nightmare' (Rowin, 25/09/2006)[20].

The hijacking of an Air France plane carrying largely Israeli passengers, which lands at the Ugandan airport at Entebbe, draws the film to a close. Garrigan tries to take advantage of the situation by plying Amin with the poisoned pills, but he is discovered and tortured. It is only the sacrifice of Dr Junju that saves him, enabling him to leave with the non-Jewish passengers whose release has been brokered in part by Amin, trying to gain worldwide goodwill while ignoring the atrocities in his own country.

It is a conflicted ending. Although Garrigan has been the main focus of the narrative, he is hardly a sympathetic figure. It is Junju who emerges here with the most dignity, telling Garrigan that he deserves to die but that he can gain redemption by telling the world about Amin. 'They will believe you, you are a white man', is his final line. Garrigan leaves, changed by his African experience, but it is Junju who pays the ultimate price, gunned down by Amin's bodyguards, another African victim, dead because of Western interlopers. It seems that Garrigan's point earlier in the film holds true. He tells Stone, 'This is Africa, you meet violence with violence. Anything else and you're dead.' This is true certainly if you are trying to better your country like Wasswa and Junju or trying to expose corruption like Justin, Tessa and Arnold. The Sandys, Stones, Pellegrins and Garrigans survive. The demarcations in Shooting Dogs, the British take on the genocide in Rwanda are even more explicit and ultimately more shocking.

WHEN ONE TRIBE GOES TO WAR – SHOOTING DOGS

Between April and June 1994 an estimated 800,000 people in the central African country of Rwanda were killed in the space of one hundred days. The former Belgian colony had a turbulent history and this massacre was the result of a long-simmering feud

Hugh Dancy,
Shooting Dogs

between the two main ethnic groups in the country, the Hutus and the Tutsis. The two groups are very similar, speaking the same language, populating the same regions of the country and following the same traditions. However, the Belgians who had arrived in 1916 considered the minority group, the Tutsis, as superior to their fellow countrymen and installed them in key positions to help run the colony. Resentment turned into violence even before the Belgians relinquished the colony in 1962, with the massacre of 20,000 Tutsis in 1959 with many more fleeing to neighbouring countries. The Hutus took power after the Belgians' departure and over the next few years the Tutsi minority were blamed for any crisis that occurred[21].

The build-up to the events of 1994 was an economic slowdown and the establishment of the Rwandan Patriotic Front (RPF), made up of Tutsis and moderate Hutus, to overthrow the incumbent president, Juvenal Habyarimana. When on April 6 1994 the President's plane was shot down and he was killed, the instant reaction was that members of the RPF were behind the attack, and his death became the catalyst for mindless, uncontrolled violence. The Rwandan Armed Forces (FAR) and Hutu militia groups called the Interahamwe set up roadblocks and went from house to house killing Tutsis and

moderate Hutus. Many thousands of people were murdered on that first day. Some UN camps sheltered the terrified civilians, but the mandate was not to intervene and not to shoot unless attacked. They stood by while people were being slaughtered[22]. Michael Caton-Jones' *Shooting Dogs* covers the events of the first few days of the massacre.

Four films were released around the anniversary of the Rwandan tragedy, all with different perspectives on the events. But what sense could mere films make of the terrible events that happened in that country, while the rest of the world failed to intervene? Terry George's Oscar-nominated *Hotel Rwanda* (2004), based on a true-life story, has a *Schindler's List* (1993) plot device as a Hutu hotel manager saves a number of Tutsis, but the violence is very much underplayed. *Sometimes in April* (2004), directed by Raoul Peck, was far more graphic, based on survivors' testimonies. The documentary *Shake Hands with the Devil* (Raymont, 2005) chose as its focus Romeo Dallaire, the former head of the UN peacekeeping forces during the crisis, and his return to the African state.

The BBC-financed *Shooting Dogs* was based on the experiences of David Belton, who in 1994 was a reporter for the BBC current affairs programme *Newsnight*. It centres on events at a school, the Ecole Technique Officielle (ETO), where 2000-plus Tutsis had congregated, seeking protection with the small Belgian UN peacekeeping force stationed there. The film focuses on two white characters – a young teacher, Joe Connor (Hugh Dancy), who is on a short-term volunteer contract, and a much older man, Father Christopher (John Hurt), who is headmaster at the school and has spent many years in Africa. So, like both *The Constant Gardener* and *The Last King of Scotland* the central characters are white and British; the horror is filtered through their eyes:

"'We're absolutely unapologetic about having two white men at the forefront of the story," says [David] Belton. "I certainly have way too much involvement to do it any other way, and nor would David Wolstencroft, who wrote the screenplay, have dreamed of writing it from any other perspective. And it's a very legitimate place to be in the story, because we all know the white man's role in Rwanda is complicated and appalling"'.[23]

The film was seen as controversial in terms of how it dealt with the truth surrounding the events at the ETO and also regarding the role of the BBC. One of the film's fiercest critics, the writer and expert on Rwanda Linda Melvern, is particularly disparaging regarding the media silence around these brutal events. She maintains that unlike the depiction in the film, there was no BBC film crew at the school or in Rwanda during those first few weeks. The BBC didn't use the word 'genocide' until much later, on 29 April, so a key sequence when the hard-bitten BBC reporter Rachel Watson (Nicola Walker) is trying to draw Captain Delon (Domininque Horwitz), the Belgian commander of the unit, into admitting that this is in fact genocide (at which point he cuts the interview to a grinding halt), is a falsehood. As she has stated:

> 'The first international inquiry into the genocide was to conclude that the Western media's failure to describe the genocide underway in Rwanda had contributed to the crime itself. It was left to the NGOs, notably Oxfam and Amnesty International, to draw attention to the terrible events.'[24]

Although Melvern's arguments about accuracy and the failure of the Western media to alert the world to the quickly unfolding horror may well hold some element of truth, the portrayal of the BBC journalists in the film isn't that sympathetic. Joe sees the media as important in highlighting the plight of the Tutsis at the ETO, but Rachel has seen too much and is only interested in a possible story when it becomes clear that a number of white Europeans have also taken sanctuary at the school: this has potential news value. In a later conversation with Joe, she admits that her previous assignment amongst the killing fields of Bosnia had affected her a great deal more, as the victims were white and could have been somebody that she knew back home. In Rwanda they are 'just dead Africans'. She has become immune to the viciousness surrounding her. We see this when she and her chirpy cockney cameraman zoom in on dead, butchered children. There is a professional distance of course, but as Rachel admits she is a 'selfish piece of work'. The story is all.

The impotent nature of the UN forces is also clear to see. Their mandate has been to oversee peacekeeping, but in the growing chaos and the reported deaths of ten of their colleagues they are unable to do anything. This is reminiscent of the powerlessness felt by British UN troops serving in Bosnia in Peter Kosminsky's 1999 BBC series *Warriors*, although Linda Melvern maintains that the forces in Rwanda were severely undermanned and lacked the appropriate armoury to deal with the Hutus. The UN mandate had stated that if any service personnel were fired on, only then could they fire back. In an interesting exchange, which gives the film its title, Delon informs Father Christopher that he will have to shoot the dogs beyond the school's gates – as they feed on the quickly mounting corpses they are becoming a health hazard – to which the incredulous priest responds, 'Did they shoot at you?'

There is a brief exposition, before the onslaught which sees Joe, posited as the archetypal, young popular teacher. We first encounter him encouraging Marie (Claire-Hope Ashitey), one of his students and a talented athlete who is running in front of the school. He does this by the use of an increasingly over-the-top commentary. There are some parallels here with Garrigan from *The Last King of Scotland*. It is from his perspective that we see the events and certainly at the start of the film he is imbued with a high degree of self-confidence. In a revealing exchange with Rachel he tells her that the Rwandan experience is like 'starring in [his] own Oxfam ad'. But as the slaughter starts he, unlike Garrigan, attempts to confront it, but finds that like the blue-helmeted soldiers he is also completely helpless. But as Geoffrey Macnab highlights in his review of the film, Caton-Jones is too concerned with Joe's reading of the events rather than the whole picture:

> 'There is a very telling scene in which Joe is seen watching powerlessly from the (temporary) safety of the school compound as a mother and her baby are hacked to pieces by the Hutu militia. Caton-Jones doesn't skimp on showing such incidents in their full horror, but what grates is the sense that the film-makers are more interested in the psychic trauma Joe endures than in the suffering of the African victims.'[25]

This is a valid statement and could be levelled at the other films cited in this chapter. The white characters do provide a point of contact for audiences outside of Africa and it is the extreme issues faced by them that make the unbelievable and shocking events that occurred in Rwanda slightly easier to grasp. This was an issue taken up by Duncan Woodside who interestingly counterpoints the views expressed by Melvern:

> 'For largely uninformed Westerners, the choices faced by Hurt's and Dancy's characters – whether to leave with the UN or whether to remain with the condemned refugees – provide a readier point of access to the story than the dilemmas of Rwandan principal characters.'[26]

Unlike *Hotel Rwanda*, which was filmed largely in South Africa, the director had made an early decision to film in Rwanda itself, and although McNab makes a strong point about the Western perspective foisted on the audience by the main protagonists, this decision adds an air of authenticity, much as Macdonald and Meirelles did with their films by shooting in the actual locations. Caton-Jones also used extras and crew members (shown in the end credits) who still had vivid memories of what had happened in 1994.

> 'Talking to survivors (and almost the entire country is a survivor) there was often a complete lack of emotion in their stories, just an unaffected re-telling – the unimaginable terror and suffering, the horrific loss, the emptiness and guilt of their survival all told in an open, unsensational way.'[27]

But the narrative by and large neglects to really tell their stories. The attractive Marie is framed largely in terms of her initial 'crush' on Joe and in her relationship with Father Christopher, who helps her escape. She is one of the very few symbols of hope, in a film largely devoid of any. Marie also ends the story five years later in the film's epilogue, visiting Joe who is now ensconced in the plush surroundings of what appears to be a large public school. When he leaves the ETO with the UN forces he can scarcely bear to look at her face and not a great deal has changed. The theme of guilt re-emerges, as it has many times in these films, yet Marie's stance is one of dignified acceptance.

Other African characters are briefly touched on. Roland (Steve Toussaint), Marie's father, is cast as the leader of the Tutsi refugees in the ETO and begs the fleeing UN captain to shoot them, so that they can be spared the pain of the machete, the favoured weapon of the Interahamwe. He once again fits the dignified African archetype, but he isn't developed a great deal. The identified Hutu characters are shown as having a direct connection with the school. We see François (David Gyasi) earlier in the film working at the ETO, driving Joe about and sharing jokes. It slowly emerges that he believes the propaganda spread about the Tutsi minority and at a roadblock Joe sees him emerge from the bush with a bloodstained weapon. It becomes apparent that he is involved in the murders, though it is his intervention that saves Joe's life here, as he gestures to the militia members that he knows him.

The film subtly implies that the genocide was planned. Father Christopher sees government officials making notes on the Tutsis families in a village he is visiting, some days before the President's plane is shot down. The government is represented in the rather slimy form of Councillor Sibomana (Louis Mahoney), the other identified Hutu in the film. We see him earlier trying to get information on the UN's plans from Father Christopher. This is all we are shown of the Hutu establishment; their motives for the madness that ensues are not developed in any meaningful way.

Hurt's performance as the beleaguered priest is the moral compass on which the whole film hinges. Spirituality is key here and in his portrayal of Christopher, Hurt bestows a particular kind of English Catholic benevolence on the proceedings. The rites and rituals of the mass are central to what he believes will help the doomed Tutsis in the ETO. Although he is as hard-bitten as the journalists and to a lesser extent the UN soldiers, he never appears cynical. Wendy Ide comments of his performance, 'His face, always particularly eloquent when it comes to suffering, has never looked so careworn'[28]. This is certainly apt towards the end of *Shooting Dogs* when Joe is leaving the camp and Christopher refuses to join him in the truck, telling him that God is here and in his heart and soul, and if he departs from the ETO he feels that he will not find God again. Later, when trying to smuggle some of the Tutsi children out, Christopher is shot by a Hutu and becomes a martyr figure. This could be another criticism levelled at the film in that it centralises the white experience and in this instance depicts it as heroic. That said, Father Christopher is portrayed as someone who clearly loves the Rwandan people and the country and this informs his decision as much as his sense of spiritual strength sustains him and the unfortunates trapped at the school. Rather than being shown as a post-colonial archetype, he is as African as the people he is serving; unlike Joe, Garrigan or even Justin and Tessa, he is not just passing through but there for the long haul.

Overall these three films seek to simplify the complexities that surround the political, cultural and social problems that beset Africa by encouraging a Western audience to solely identify with British protagonists against a backdrop of African suffering. Exploitation by drug companies and psychopathic despots is expressed through the former colonist's reactions, as is the ethnic cleansing encountered in *Shooting Dogs*. Although this is clearly an issue highlighted during this chapter, it is encouraging that these serious films dealing with difficult and unsettling issues have emerged from Britain at this time. It gave a sense that films made in this country could look out to the rest of the world and give a typically British perspective. It would be interesting to think for example how differently these films might be viewed if the main characters were American. Justin's and Christopher's stoic Englishness in the face of extreme provocation and Garrigan's relationship with Amin which is due to his Scottishness, are key factors in how meaning is created here. These representations of the British abroad perhaps say as much about the British as they do about the location and this is what makes these films feel so distinctive.

REFERENCES

1. Gutberlet, M., 'In the Wilds of the German Imaginary African Vistas' in The German Cinema Book, Bergfelder, T. et al (eds), London: BFI, 2002

2. Cousins, M., 'Invisible Classics' in Sight and Sound, February 2007

3. Interview with Ousmane Sembene on the DVD of *Moolaade* (2004)

4. Calhoun, D., 'White Guides, Black Pain' in Sight and Sound, February 2007

5. Interview with Fernando Meirelles on www.emanuellevy.com

6. Bradshaw, P., Review of *The Constant Gardener* in The Guardian, 11/11/2005

7. Interview with Fernando Meirelles on http://outnow.ch, 08/09/2005

8. Romney, J., Review of *The Constant Gardener* in The Independent on Sunday, 13/11/2005

9. Gritten, D., 'The British class system – I didn't get it' in The Daily Telegraph, 04/11/2005

10. McCartney J, 'Cinematic hopscotch and witty one-liners' in The Daily Telegraph, 13/11/2005

11. Winter, J., Review of *The Constant Gardner* in Sight and Sound, October 2005

12. Quinn, A., Review of *The Constant Gardner* in The Independent, 11/11/2005

13. Interview with Kevin MacDonald 'Last King Shall Be First' on www.iofilm.co.uk, undated.

14. Kibazo, J., 'A brute, not a buffoon' in The Guardian, 13/01/2007

15. Unaccredited, Review of *The Last King of Scotland* in The New Internationalist, April 2007

16. Walters, V., 'Stereotypes that will sell' in The Guardian, 18/01/2007

17. Munro, B., interview with Kevin Macdonald on www.futuremovies.co.uk, 11/01/2007

18. French, P., Review of *The Last King of Scotland* in The Observer, 14/01/2007

19. Bradshaw, P., Review of *The Last King of Scotland* in The Guardian, 12/01/2007

20. Rowin, M.J., Review of *The Last King of Scotland* on www.indiewire.com, 25/09/2006

21. 'Rwanda: How the genocide happened' on http://newsvote.bbc.co.uk

22. 'Frontline: the triumph of evil: 100 days of slaughter' on www.pbs.org

23. Bradshaw, N., 'Film and the fog of war' in The Daily Telegraph, 29/03/2005

24. Melvern, L., 'History? This film is fiction' in The Observer, 19/03/2006

25. Macnab, G., Review of *Shooting Dogs* in Sight and Sound, April 2006

26. Woodside, D., ' *Shooing Dogs*: Rwanda's genocide through European eyes' on www.opendemocracy.net, 06/04/2006

27. Caton-Jones, M., 'Bringing the horrors of the Rwandan genocide to the big screen' in The Independent, 17/03/2006

28. Ide, W, Review of *Shooting Dogs* in The Times, 29/03/2006

DYSTOPIAN BRITAIN

INTRODUCTION

The re-emergence of the British science-fiction film has been one of the most pleasing aspects of recent British film-making. What is clear, however, is the distinctive worldview that some of these films share and, like most of the great science fiction of the past, there are aspects of these films which reflect the audience's lives as they are lived today. In this chapter we are going to discuss three prime examples of this sort of film and assess their importance in terms of how they reflect key contextual issues surrounding identity and representation, look at their production background and crucially assess their relative importance within

28 Days Later

the genre and recent British film in general. The films are Danny Boyles' *28 Days Later* (2002) and its sequel *28 Weeks Later* (Fresnadillo, 2007), *V for Vendetta* (McTeigue, 2006) and *Children of Men* (2006) directed by Alfonso Cuaron.

PLACING THESE FILMS WITHIN THE GENRE

The literary and cinematic roots of British science fiction have had a long and interesting history. The 1950s and 1960s provided many examples of films such as *The Quatermass Experiment* (1955), which is seen, like its contemporary American counterparts, as reflecting concerns regarding the growing threat of the cold war, atomic weapons and, in British sci-fi's case, the lessening of Britain's worldwide influence around the time of the Suez crisis. Hammer was a major producer of sci-fi mainly making cheap, pulp-style examples of the genre such as *The Earth Dies Screaming* (1964), but what is striking is the number of auteur émigrés drawn to these shores to make specifically sci-fi films: François Truffaut with *Fahrenheit 451* (1966), Joseph Losey with *The Dammed* (1961) and, crucially, Stanley Kubrick with *A Clockwork Orange* (1971) (Hunter, 1999, p3-4)[1]. This certainly bears some comparison with Cuaron and McTeigue's work as film-makers bringing a particular, outsiders' view of Britain.

If there is a cinematic starting point for these films it is Kubrick's controversial adaptation of Anthony Burgess's novel, published in 1962. *A Clockwork Orange* was a chilling vision of the near future, of a Britain torn apart by teenage gangs set against the ultra modernist backdrop of the Thamesmead estate in London. As the late film critic Alexander Walker recounts, the film's release coincided with a radical shift away from the optimism of the 1960s: 'The first IRA bombs were going off on the mainland at the time the film came out. A coal strike was taking place so there were power cuts. People felt that the fabric of the country was falling apart'[2]. The fears of youth cults such as skinheads and the growth in violence at football matches were also current and in many respects the film was suggesting that the future was bleak indeed – that society threatened by the violent anarchy of the young could only be controlled by behavioural manipulation, which in turn would result in repression and the destruction of humanity (Chapman, 1999, p134)[3].

If there is a characteristic strain in British sci-fi, it is this notion of a chaotic, uncertain future characterised by a dictatorial government controlling the freedom of this country's inhabitants. These fictional views of the future or near future can take two forms depending on the writer or director's relationship with the socio-political issues in the present. An optimistic outlook suggests a utopian position, a society that is perfectible, possibly attainable. More common, however, is a pessimistic outlook resulting in a dystopian vision, which projects current fears in a semi-fictional situation. These fears were probably best explored in the greatest example of dystopian fiction, George Orwell's *1984* (1949). Written against the backdrop of fascist and communist dictatorships, Orwell's novel brilliantly captures the angst of the early Cold War period and tellingly predicts a world where freedom is curtailed and where relentless false propaganda keeps the population in its place. The most recent film version, Michael Radford's *Nineteen Eighty Four* (1984), certainly captures the claustrophobia and desperation of the book's hero Winston Smith as he struggles with his fear of 'Big Brother' and his feelings for his lover, Julia. This film and Terry Gilliam's *Brazil* (1985) both reflect the directors' feelings about a changing Britain, dominated by the monetarist and the increasing right-wing agenda of Margaret Thatcher's Conservative government.

Viewing these texts today it is telling how some of the issues highlighted and predicted certainly remain valid. The huge number of surveillance cameras in the UK (4.2 million, one for every 14 people) echoes the central mantra of *1984*: 'Big Brother is watching you'. The UK has 20 per cent of the world's allocation of cameras (Brooks, The Guardian, 01/11/07). Other key issues surround the continuing erosion of civil liberties, the numbing mindlessness of work (best envisaged in *Brazil*) and the rise of celebrity culture. This final notion echoes Orwell's use of the tabloid press to nullify the proletariat from revolting against the oppressive regime of Big Brother. It is perhaps rather ironic that the reality TV show, also tellingly called *Big Brother*, where participants are constantly watched by cameras and the television audience vote to evict them, may well have the same nullifying effect on today's audience as Orwell suggested back in the 1940s.

This brings us to the latest additions to the sub-genre of dystopian films made in Britain. These films feel and look radically different from each other, but share certain characteristics that both root them in the present and connect them. They also have very different production contexts, and by looking at aspects of budgetary constraints we will see how the directors' visions have been realised.

A DIFFERENT SORT OF ZOMBIE FILM — 28 DAYS LATER

Danny Boyle was a director best known for his high octane, low-budget films of the 1990s — his twisting, sinister, immoral neo-noir *Shallow Grave* (1994) and his iconic adaptation of Irvine Welsh's tale of Edinburgh's heroin addicts, *Trainspotting* (1996). Critics felt that he became somewhat unstuck with his subsequent, bigger budget, more internationally flavoured films, *A Life Less Ordinary* (1998) and a version of Alex Garland's bestselling novel *The Beach* (2000). But it was the relationship that he forged with Garland on *The Beach* that led to the creation of *28 Days Later*.

Boyle's film, scripted by Garland, is very much in the tradition of the zombie films of George A. Romero, but it also has a range of cultural influences much closer to home. The spirit of the great British dystopian writer J. G. Ballard is evident, especially his 1973 novel *Concrete Island,* and there are allusions to the post-apocalyptic television series *Survivors* (1975–7) and *Threads* (1984)[4].

The film itself has a simple plot and in terms of genre is very conventional. Unlike most other dystopian texts this is actually set in the present. As the narrative progresses it becomes clear that what appears familiar and rooted in the here and now is actually completely dismantled and expectations are quickly undermined.

Animal rights activists raid a Cambridge laboratory and release chimpanzees that have been infected with the 'rage' virus. This deadly virus is the result of experimentation where the chimps are forced to watch scenes of violent actions and rioting on a bank of television screens. The virus is passed on by attack, but also by contact with the blood of the infected. Infected humans in turn lose all rationality and will attack anyone who is uninfected in order to feed. The central protagonist of the film is Jim (Cillian Murphy), a young bicycle courier, who as a result of a collision with a car has been in a coma for 28 days. He awakes in an empty hospital, in a deserted London, not knowing what has happened.

After encountering a group of the infected in a church, he is saved by fellow survivors Selena (Naomie Harris) and Mark (Noah Huntley) and learns about the plague that hasn't just wiped out most of London, but the entire country. Jim wants to learn the fate of his parents and, accompanied by his new allies, he goes to his house in Deptford where he discovers his parents' corpses, after an apparent suicide pact. While there Mark is infected and Selena is forced to kill him.

They make contact with two other survivors, affable cabbie Frank (Brendan Gleeson) and his daughter Hannah (Megan Burns). Frank has heard a looped radio message, entreating any survivors to head towards Manchester where there is an 'answer' for infection. Heading northwards, Frank is infected at a roadblock and shot by the soldiers who had transmitted the message. Jim, Selena and Hannah are taken to a remote, heavily barricaded hideout, where the small battalion led by Major Henry West (Chris Eccleston) firstly take care of but then abuse their new charges. It soon becomes clear that West's idea is that the women be used for reproductive purposes – this is the 'answer' suggested in the broadcast.

Jim, viewed as surplus to these plans, is sentenced to be killed. He escapes, however, and returns to allow the infected to breach the battalion's defences and destroy the small group of soldiers. This enables him to rescue Hannah and Selena and at the film's end we see them signalling to a search plane.

The plot is a generic chase film, but is elevated above the norm by its *mise-en-scène* and the conditions surrounding its filming, the two being related. *28 Days Later* was produced by FilmFour and aided with money from the UK Film Council, East London Film Fund and the European Regional Development fund. It was distributed by Fox and sold as a sci-fi/horror movie set in modern-day Britain. The film was produced on a small budget of $10 million with no major star names and was shot on digital video rather than film. This use of digital video was vital in creating a sense of menace, but also in keeping costs down. As Boyle explains, the rationale behind this sort of filming was a necessity rather than a choice:

> 'Normally making a sci-fi movie requires a huge budget, but we wanted to keep the budget down to about £6 million, and we did that because we didn't want any stars in it. We just wanted ordinary people. Not having the money can be a problem or it can be a kind of freedom, and for us it was a freedom. We couldn't do deserted cars, there'd be bodies everywhere, and we could only get permission to stop the traffic for just a couple of minutes at a time. And we didn't have the time or the money to dress the London streets.'[5]

One of the most startling and memorable sequences in the film, and arguably in the whole of recent British cinema, is Jim's emergence from the hospital into a quietened and deserted London devoid of its usual constant noise and populace. Boyle, in an introduction that he filmed before the FilmFour television screening, talked about multiple camera set-ups that captured the same moment at the same time without the need for extensive camera crews. This meant that the early morning London streets only had to be shut for a very short period of time to enable Boyle and his Director of Photography, the renowned Anthony Dod Mantle, to get what they needed.

Mantle's previous work with the Dogme director Thomas Vinterburg on *Festen* (1998) is clearly referenced throughout *28 Days Later*, with its jerky camera movements, documentary-like *mise-en-scène* and occasionally grainy DV footage. Jim's lonely walk through London is eerie and distinctly unnerving. His journey through the desolate, rubbish-strewn streets with their abandoned cars and overturned red buses, his green hospital scrubs against the grey, silent background, make us even more aware of his isolation and his ignorance about what has happened. Mantle's camera acts as a distant shadow, observing Jim's futile cries of 'hello' as he looks for a fellow traveller. The commuter-less Westminster Bridge and the typical London touristic background of Big Ben and the Houses of Parliament take on a completely new meaning in this empty post-virus London. This notion of the cameras surviving to watch the silent city, as CCTV cameras might, was something very much in Boyle's mind when planning the film, with the director encouraging his crew in some role play:

> 'At one point we were going to have Jim pick up a camera and look back at what someone had recorded. In a funny way, as a crew we could imagine that we were survivors as well, working with minimal equipment.'[6]

What is shocking to both Jim and the audience is the realisation that things could have deteriorated as fast as they have, in less than a month. From *Evening Standard* headlines it soon becomes apparent that Britain has been evacuated. The island isolation from mainland Europe that has for so many years been both a strength and a hindrance to integration has now become so much more. Ballard's *Concrete Island* resonates here.

There is a telling scene when Jim tries to comprehend what has happened and Mark explains: 'No government. No police. No army. No TV. No radio. No electricity.' The certainties of everyday life have been stripped away. Being infected means a living death, the instantaneous effects of the virus mean there can be no preparation for the rabid horror that follows.

Mark's death makes it clear that Selena's priority is to survive and the film avoids for as long as possible the obvious love between her and Jim, although at the end of the film there are hints of a family unit forming with Hannah (who isn't much younger than her surrogate parents) rather than the clichéd romantic entanglement we might have expected.

The small cast keep the film tightly focused. Frank's role initially is that of leader, but it is clear that he and his teenage daughter need Selena and Jim more than the other way around. The use of the traditional London black cab for the journey north is also interesting, again subverting the Richard Curtis view of London – this time the taxi is used as a means of survival, rather than a glamorous icon of the capital. Frank's death is also quite moving – he realises straightaway that he has been infected and pleads for his co-survivors to kill him.

Major West is a complex character, protective of his troops and at first friendly to Jim, Selena and Hannah. His ideas about restarting the human race are flawed and reveal him to be unstable, forcing us to question this representation of the cool, logical man of authority.

Shooting started on 1 September 2001, but it was events ten days later that would give the release of the film an added dimension with the attacks on the World Trade Center and Pentagon by Islamist terrorists. This created what Boyle refers to as 'a sense of paranoia and vulnerability', which *28 Days Later* unwittingly tapped into.

An obvious reference point is when Jim, on his walk through an empty London, encounters messages and photographs of lost family members, friends and lovers at Eros in Piccadilly Circus. This was based on the aftermath of the earthquake in Kobe, Japan some years before. However, in retrospect, it is now reminiscent of the days following the attacks in New York and this scene has now taken on a completely new meaning for audiences.

The film climaxes with a violent bloodbath: 'funhouse-druggy, Grand Guignol, morally dizzying'[7]. The subsequent ending, redemptive and reflective, confirms all the generic expectations after the almost unrelenting onslaught of horror in the previous one hundred minutes.

28 Days Later did show that a low-budget British film with Film Council support and a good distribution deal could do respectable business at the US box office. It also spawned a bigger-budget, but less successful sequel in *28 Weeks Later*, produced by Danny Boyle with considerable backing by Fox. But ultimately this film led the way for others such as the pot-holing horror *The Descent* (Marshall, 2005) and the zombie rom-com *Shaun of the Dead* (Wright, 2004).

TIME MARCHES ON – 28 WEEKS LATER

The Spanish director Juan Carlos Fresnadillo took over the helm of the second film as both Boyle and Garland were busy with their sci-fi film *Sunshine* (2007) and although the dystopian feel of the first film remains largely intact, the sequel lacks the visceral impact of *28 Days Later*, despite an incredible opening sequence.

The film picks up the story slightly later. We find ourselves in an old farmhouse with some remaining survivors including Don (Robert Carlyle) and Alice Harris (Catherine McCormack), who had packed their children off to Europe on holiday a few days before the outbreak of the rage virus. Fresnadillo introduces the relatively serene exposition of a fraught meal and then proceeds to destroy it with a sustained attack by the infected, with shades of Sam Peckinpah's *Straw Dogs* (1970). The fast editing, panning and crane shots introduce that sense of fear and dread familiar from the first film. Naturally the survivors are killed but Don escapes and abandons his wife, which provides the main narrative strand.

As hinted at in the first film the only way to defeat the infected is to starve them, by denying them fresh meat – human flesh. 28 weeks later, the infected seem to have all died and Britain has become a 'protected' state under US military rule. It is curious that rather than the UN, it is the Americans who are there to provide the basis for reconstruction. The east of London is the quarantine base and the remaining survivors, including Don, are resettled amongst the modernist glass towers of the Isle of Dogs. There are echoes here of Ballard's novel *High Rise* (1975), in which the occupants of a luxury block slowly descend into animalistic warfare and chaos. The American occupying force invites comparisons with Iraq – the Canary Wharf area is called the 'green zone' and there is an emphasis on 'rehabilitation'. The Americans are wary and bored – a point picked up in the review in The Guardian:

'The Americans themselves are guarded and suspicious of their new-found contaminated peoples. Here the film speaks eloquently of America's post 7/7 suspicion and profound lack of sympathy for Britain and the dangerous spores and germs being incubated on our island.'[8]

Our first view of the occupying force is that they are efficient and in control, yet keeping their distance from the beleaguered survivors. That, however, changes as the narrative develops.

The action picks up when Don is reunited with his children. However, the story of his abandonment comes to light when the children return to their post-virus home and Alice is revealed to be still alive – although contaminated with the virus. The film develops the theme of Don's guilt and weakness. He knows that after the discovery of his wife his credibility with his children will be destroyed by his deception. He gains entry to the holding cell where his wife is held and he kisses her. Now he too is infected and from him the virus quickly spreads within the compound. This is matched by a brutal shoot-to-kill order by the Americans and the green zone descends into a war zone.

The heroes of the film are both American service personnel – army scientist Scarlet (Rose Byrne) who is searching for a vaccine and Doyle (Jeremy Renner) who is appalled at the carnage caused by his own soldiers. But there is a glimmer of hope that Don's son Andy (Mackintosh Muggleton) may provide the key for an antidote and the latter part of the film focuses on the two American protagonists trying to get him and his sister Tammy (Imogen Poots) to safety in a journey that takes them across London from Regents Park to an overgrown Wembley Stadium.

Given the sacrificial intentions of both Scarlet and Doyle to save the Harris children, the story loses some of the ragged, almost guerrilla feel of the first film and develops into a rather conventional action-horror yarn. Still, there are moments that do have an impact – the dark descent into the tunnels of the London Underground, as Scarlet and the Harris kids step over rotting corpses, is particularly powerful. But the chances to develop a more solid and low-key familial drama based upon Don's lies and anguish are lost here. Also points regarding Don's ability to recall memories as an infected human are never fully explored, nor are the Americans' true motives for taking over the country even hinted at. The film ends with a caption '28 days later' and a group of infected people running through a Parisian subway, perhaps pointing the way to another sequel.

REMEMBER, REMEMBER THE FIFTH OF NOVEMBER – *V FOR VENDETTA*

The production background to *V for Vendetta* couldn't be more different to that of *28 Days Later*. It was a mid-budget ($54 million), Warner Brothers' adaptation of Alan Moore's 1988 graphic novel and was largely shot in Berlin.

Hugo Weaving, *V for Vendetta*

Scripted by the Wachowski Brothers, who had previously directed *The Matrix* trilogy (1999–2003), it was directed by a debut director, the Australian James McTeigue (Assistant Director of *The Matrix* films). Although it has a predominately British cast of fine character actors, the leading part, in common with most other major American co-productions, was taken by a big Hollywood star, Natalie Portman. *V for Vendetta* did relatively well worldwide with $130 million in box-office takings (imdb.com), some of this possibly attributable to Portman's presence as the lead.

Although the film received some poor reviews – Peter Bradshaw labelled it 'V for valueless gibberish'[9] – the film does have an interesting premise, especially when compared with *28 Days Later* and *Children of Men*.

The film stays close to the original source material, although Moore chose to remove his name from the credits. It is set in London in the near future and follows Evey Hammond (Portman) who works for the state-controlled television service, British Television Network (BTN). When she breaks curfew on the fourth of November in order to meet her friend, TV presenter Gordon Dietrich (Stephen Fry), she is set upon by members of the secret police known as the Fingermen and is about to be raped, we infer, when V (Hugo Weaving), a vigilante dressed and masked as Guy Fawkes, kills them. (We have already encountered the trial and execution of the original Fawkes in a prologue before the main titles.)

In a spectacular sequence, just before midnight, V allows Evey to watch him blow up the Old Bailey as a protest against the dictator running Britain, High Chancellor Adam Sutler (John Hurt). He also announces that on the same date next year he will destroy the Houses of Parliament. Sutler orders the chief Fingermen Creedy (Tim Piggot-Smith) and Scotland Yard's Inspector Finch (Stephen Rea) to bring him in.

Evey, who has become a suspect, is traced by Finch to the television station and he arrives just as V is killing Lewis Prothero (Roger Allam), chief propagandist on BTN, who was once a commandant at Larkhill Resettlement Camp. V enables Evey to escape, taking her to his hideout. While holding her captive he persuades her to pose as a pre-pubescent prostitute in order to get close to and murder the corrupt paedophile Bishop Lilliman (John Standing), who had also previously worked at Larkhill. Evey has a change of heart, confessing to Lilliman, but V intervenes and kills him.

Evey escapes to her friend Dietrich's house, whom she discovers to be a closeted homosexual (illegal in born-again Sutler's Britain) and a collector of banned literature. However, Dietrich decides to run a sketch satirising Sutler, which results in his arrest and execution for possessing a copy of the Qu'ran. Evey is captured, her head is shaved and she is tortured to get her to reveal V's whereabouts. She refuses and is prepared to die. She is kept sane by notes that she finds in her cell that have been left by a lesbian actress called Valerie, written following the rise of Sutler's fascist-like regime (called Norsefire) that resulted in purges inflicted on sexual and racial minorities.

Evey is released and it becomes clear that V has been testing her resolve. Evey is angry, but influenced by Valerie's testimony, real or not, realises that there is now nothing that the regime can do to hurt her.

Meanwhile Finch discovers V's origins. Britain had collapsed years before in the wake of a nuclear conflict. Norsefire came to power on the strength of its attacks on 'enemies of the state' which meant any ethnic, sexual or religious minority. With the country deeply divided, Norsefire staged a bio-terrorist attack that killed 80,000 people. The virus used in the attack had been created at Larkhill where V had been a prisoner subjected to horrific experimentation. Curiously, but conveniently, he had gained superhuman powers. He escaped the centre and destroyed it, unfortunately becoming disfigured in the process (hence the mask). His mission now is to bring revenge on this totalitarian state.

As the anniversary of the original gunpowder plot grows nearer, the public are starting to identify and support V more and more. V has also done a deal with Creedy in order to topple Sutler, via various double-crossings of Finch. Creedy agrees to deliver Sutler in return for V's surrender. V kills Sutler, but also kills Creedy and his men and is critically wounded in so doing. Evey has been entrusted to start an underground train loaded with explosives which will detonate under the Houses of Parliament at midnight. However, V returns to her and she places his body on the tube for the journey to destroy the seat of government. The film ends with thousands of Londoners, wearing identical masks to V, marching to Westminster to witness the event and the end of Norsefire's oppression.

It is clear by looking at the narrative of *V for Vendetta* that it is much more rooted in science fiction, with a super-hero at the centre of the film, than *28 Days Later* or, as we shall see, *Children of Men*. The complexities of the plot, though, reveal issues about fear of the future.

The London visualised apes Moore's comic-strip brilliantly, recalling a post-Second World War city with its shadows, decaying brick walls and back-alleys. If anything the atmosphere is closer to Radford's *Nineteen Eighty Four* than anything else and in an interesting intertextual twist, John Hurt, who played Winston Smith in that film, is now the fearsome dictator in this.

Sutler's visage peers out, Big Brother-like, from posters and Fox News-style broadcasts; his voice and image are inescapable. His character is driven by his born-again Christian convictions and his hatred of Muslims and homosexuals. There is more than a nod here to the rise in influence of the religious right in the United States.

The Norsefire regime is founded on lies and corruption: secret tribunals, denial of civil liberties, media manipulation of truth and a close relationship between politics and big business. Sutler's police state ensures compliance and curtails free speech and suppresses any criticism of the government. In many respects this could be viewed as a fantastical, yet not entirely exotic reading of British and American politics.

McTeigue's film, as stated previously, stays close to Moore's original graphic novel and therefore the circumstance in which that was created provides a further context. *V for Vendetta* was written because of Moore's disgust at the Thatcher government, and the heavy hand that the Conservative Party had over the British political landscape in the 1980s is reflected in the brutality of Norsefire. For example, the repressive attitude in the film to the different sexual orientation of Valerie and Dietrich has its roots in Thatcher's Section 28 of her 1988 Local Government Bill. This effectively banned the 'promotion' of gay relationships in schools and led to huge, if ineffectual, protests. The Westland helicopter scandal also highlighted the unhealthy relationship between government and business, and the use of a common national issue, in Thatcher's case the 1982 Falklands War, to unite the whole country (much like the bio-terrorist attack in the film), has parallels with *V for Vendetta*.

An anarchist terrorist, V as a hero-figure was controversial back then, but in the light of 9/11 and the Islamist attacks in Madrid (in March 2004) and London (in July 2005) is even more so today. To actually ask an audience to empathise with this faceless character is brave, although the way that Sutler's brutal regime is portrayed makes this relatively easy. There were rumours that the original release date of 5 November 2005 had been postponed in the wake of the attacks on London's underground transport network on 7 July 2005 and that the film had been re-edited as a result. This was denied by one of the film's producers, Joel Silver, who stated, 'It's a controversial film and it's a controversial time. It's going to make people think' (Kermode, 12/03/06)[10]. The fairly low-key release in March 2006 seemed to underline this. As Mark Kermode suggests, the closeness of the subject matter to its audience is difficult to gauge:

'The question of how movies reflect real events which remain raw in the public consciousness is complex. The general rule is that films about disaster and destruction do best in times of comparative peace, some audiences experiencing horror first hand don't want to have to endure it at the cinema.' (ibid.)

Perhaps the rather over-the-top fantasy-led nature of the narrative distances the viewer enough to avoid the problem, while still retaining that sense of the familiar that is so important to dystopian cinema. Perhaps this distance is enhanced by, as Philip French notes, the sense of kitsch that prevails in the text, making it more of a 'dystope-opera'[11]. This is a good point. Owen Patterson's elaborate and at times beautiful set design is a world away from the harshness of 28 Days Later. The cinematography by Adrian Biddle is impressive, especially in the way that shadows and close-ups are used. His framing of V, in particular, gives that character as much personality as a permanently masked man could conceivably have.

Although the precise nature of how V attained his considerable physical and intellectual powers is unclear, the film never lapses into standard super-hero mode. This is largely due the emphasis on Evey's character as V's more human face. It is her fears and vulnerability that we relate to, especially in the prison segment of the film, in which she is 'tested' by V. Her head shorn, she looks exhausted and emaciated. With her Jewish background, allusions to the imagery of the concentration camps are strong.

The ending is a bit heavy-handed, portentous even. The gunpowder plot has been successfully re-enacted, the masked crowd confronting the riot police. As the masks come off, we see key characters who we know to be dead, for example Valerie and Dietrich, reveal themselves to witness the downfall of Norsefire's regime. Despite the sentimental and uplifting resolution, no easy solutions are offered here. It is unclear how the country will progress now the potential leader V is dead. Perhaps the main hope lies in Evey.

A WORLD RUNNING OUT OF TIME – *CHILDREN OF MEN*

Clive Owen,
Julianne Moore,
Children of Men

Like *V for Vendetta*, *Children of Men*, released in the autumn of 2006, is a mid-budget American co-production made by Universal. Costing in the region of $76 million (imdb.com), the film had a primarily British cast and the acclaimed Mexican film-maker Alfonso Cuaron directed. Cuaron had scored a sizable art-house hit with *Y tu Mama Tambein* (2001). He had brought a dark edge to events at Hogwarts in *Harry Potter and the Prisoner of Azkaban* (2004). He was an interesting choice to direct and write this adaptation of P. D. James' 1992 novel. His eye and ear for the eccentricities of British life and culture are beautifully observed. *Children of Men* also paints a nightmarish and highly recognisable vision of the very near future, which asks the audience to think about their own current fears and dilemmas.

Set in 2027, the film opens in London. It concentrates on Theo Farron (Clive Owen), a disillusioned, hard-drinking former political activist now working as a civil servant. We see television reports on the murder of 'Baby Diego', the youngest person left on the planet and the last child known to have been born. Although no specific reason is offered for the apparent worldwide infertility, it seems that a combination of pollution, genetic experimentation and uncontrollable pandemics are the likely culprits[12]. This has left the world a sad and miserable place, where human beings are becoming extinct.

Theo seems completely unmoved by all this and as he leaves a coffee bar, it blows up, the authorities later blaming a terrorist group called the 'Fishes'. This group's political agenda is based on more human rights for immigrants. Britain, in a similar, if less cartoonish way to the nation shown in *V for Vendetta*, is now run by a right-wing dictatorship, which has tried to close the country to outsiders. Britain, with its tough, harsh administration has become a police state, rounding up refugees and either killing or deporting them to the apparent indifference of the indigenous population.

Theo, upset by the attack, leaves the capital and visits his old friend Jasper Palmer (Michael Caine), a former satirical cartoonist who now spends his time smoking cannabis and looking after his wife who has been previously tortured by the government. On his return to the capital, Theo is kidnapped by the Fishes, led by his estranged wife Julian (Julianne Moore). We later learn that their son Dylan had died as the result of a flu virus contracted in a pandemic in 2009. She offers Theo money to influence his cousin Nigel (Danny Huston), a leading member of the government, into obtaining a travel permit for a young black girl, Kee (Claire-Hope Ashitey). Theo manages to get the appropriate papers, but they stipulate that he must travel with Kee.

A member of the Fishes, Luke (Chiwetel Ejiofor), drives Theo, Kee, Julian and Miriam (Pam Ferris), but they are ambushed on the way and Julian is killed. They make their escape to a safe house and Luke becomes leader. Here, Kee makes clear to Theo the reason for her journey – she is pregnant. She is to be taken to an organisation called the Human Project based in the Azores. Its main purpose is in finding a cure for the barren, childless world. Theo is unconvinced of its existence. It transpires, however, that Luke wants to use Kee's baby for his own political purposes, that he planned Julian's assassination and now plans to murder Theo.

Theo makes his escape with Kee and Miriam and they hide out at Jasper's house. Miriam makes it clear that there is a meeting arranged with a Human Project ship, off the coast from the Bexhill-on-Sea refugee camp. Jasper makes arrangements with a psychopathic, corrupt police officer, Syd (Peter Mullan), to smuggle them in to the camp. Luke and his accomplices track down the fugitives. Theo and the others make their escape, but Jasper is murdered by the Fishes. They meet Syd, and as a cover agree to be his prisoners and are subsequently loaded onto a refugee bus. Kee goes into premature labour; Miriam fakes a spell of religious mania in order to distract the suspicious guards and is taken off the bus.

On arrival at Bexhill-on-Sea, Theo and Kee meet Marichka (Oana Pellea), a contact of Syd's, who gives them shelter. Kee gives birth to a baby girl. Meanwhile, the Fishes break into the camp to try to seize the child. The camp is in complete chaos and the army is sent in to quell the uprising. Syd reappears and betrays Theo and Kee, but with Marichka's help they kill Syd and escape. They are recaptured by the Fishes, but before they can murder Theo and Marichka a battle with the military ensues. Theo finds Kee and the baby with Luke in a besieged apartment block and releases them. He is injured by Luke, who subsequently dies when the building is hit by a shell. The baby's cries instantly stop all the fighting as the protagonists look on in awe at the by now totally unfamiliar sight of mother and child walking through the devastated streets.

Theo, Kee and the baby make their way to a small boat and row out to a buoy that is the rendezvous point. Jets pass over and Bexhill-on-Sea is bombed, the uprising suppressed. Kee tells the injured Theo that she has decided to call the baby Dylan, after his and Julian's dead son, as the Human Project ship (Tomorrow) emerges from the fog.

The film is deeply pessimistic, but does offer some hope for the future; a central theme seems to be that humanity will prevail. The film seems incredibly familiar – the London streets, the clothes, the transport are only slightly different from those of the present day. The *mise-en-scène* is endlessly fascinating, especially the early London scenes. Peter Bradshaw review astutely picks up on this point:

> '…despite the stylisations and grandiloquent drama, there is something just so grimly and grittily plausible about the awful world conjured up here.'[13]

Theo's workplace at the Ministry of Energy has direct links to the bureaucratic nightmare served up in *Brazil* and *Nineteen Eighty Four*. The workstations with their news of Diego's very untimely demise are reminiscent of the growing influence of the broadcast media through computer networks. It is also, perhaps, telling that Diego's death is the result of his spitting in the face of a fan who asked him for an autograph. The retribution for this is a comment on the ever-growing impact of celebrity culture. Diego's death is met by a hysterical outpouring of grief which can only remind us of the death of Diana, Princess of Wales, in 1997.

The *mise-en-scène*, created by production designers Jim Clay and Geoffrey Kirkland, is enhanced by Emmanuel Lubezki's wonderfully bleak cinematography; for example, note the early sequence as Theo travels to Jasper's secret country den – the amount of secondary information embedded in this journey warrants a second or even a third viewing. The street where Theo gets his coffee looks remarkably like Oxford Street now, but the huge advertising screens and motorised rickshaws add that slight, crucial difference that positions the film in the future. When Theo turns up at work after escaping the bomb attack there are posters in the foyer of the grey Ministry of Energy where he works, with the messages 'Jobs for the Brits' and 'Save Water to save lives', which gives us a pretty good idea of what Cuaron's view of the future might be like. Unlike the Fox/Sky-like presentation of *V for Vendetta*'s British Television Network, here there is a recognisable version of BBC News 24 reporting the death of Diego. We also get a sense of the world in a state of utter pandemonium. Seattle has been under siege for a thousand days, the British Muslim community is demanding an end to the Army's occupation of mosques, the Homeland Security bill has been ratified meaning that Britain's borders are to remain closed and the deportation of illegal immigrants will continue. The fact that the news presentation seems so 'real' and familiar makes what we are watching so chilling.

The train journey to Jasper's also throws up fascinating detail to further add to the political and social context. The train, which is heavily fortified with wire mesh, is pelted with bricks and rubble as it passes through what appears to be a desolate, post-industrial landscape. It is uncertain who the stone throwers are – the unemployed, the dispossessed. Perhaps they are refugees, it is never explained. Inside the train there are large screens showing explicit propaganda messages, utilising the iconography of the Union Jack and Big Ben, emphasising that even though the world has collapsed, 'Britain soldiers on'. Sheltering illegal immigrants is a crime, which intensifies the climate of fear that prevails in these opening minutes. This is made even more emphatic when Theo alights at the station.

Here he is met by guards, dressed in black and brandishing guns. Cages with refugees, many old and infirm and speaking German, familiar from footage of the Holocaust and, more recently, Bosnia and Guantánamo Bay, tap into current fears regarding issues about immigration and asylum. We see how these fears can result in barbarism if they become a

mandate for action by political parties in search of scapegoats.

Cuaron himself has recognised the importance of making the film believable, changing many details from the novel and the original script. He was resistant to tackle the middle-class issues in the book and didn't want to make a straight science-fiction film:

'We did a little stuff on how the world may look a generation from now, but the goal was still trying to keep that sense of reality. The biggest challenge was making sure that the scenario we're creating now is congruent with the premise that the story is taking place twenty years from now. But, at the same time, whatever we did should not alienate you from the sense of today. The core of the film is about today. And that's a conversation that I had with the art department. I said "I don't want imagination, I want references and to know why that reference reflects today's human perception of reality."'[14]

Cuaron's style of film-making can be seen to good effect in *Children of Men*. He has talked about avoiding close-ups in order to give the characters the same weight as the social environment. He is interested in achieving a looseness by trying to minimise editing and montage, thus giving a sense of the camera just being there to record a moment of truthfulness. His long-take style might seem inappropriate to this type of film (compare it to either *28 Days Later* or *V for Vendetta*), but it seems to fit in with what he is trying to achieve, even in the high-octane moments such as the death of Julian and the gun-battles at Bexhill-on-Sea.

Theo, a reluctant hero figure, lacking the survival impulse of *28 Days Later*'s Jim or the sheer eccentricity of the eponymous V, is double-crossed by the Fishes, whose initial position as a force for good is soon exposed as false by their murder of Julian, their desire to exploit Kee and her child and their willingness to kill Theo. Jasper, the father figure for Theo, seems representative of an older, more liberal British outlook. With his book-filled lair, copious amounts of dope, beard and long hair, he is a man wildly out of step with the new totalitarian brutality and hence one of the film's most sympathetic characters.

As Andrew Osmond comments in his review, 'The nativity imagery is blatant when [Kee] stands semi-nude amid lowing cattle in a barn while [Theo] incredulously breathes "Jesus Christ". Later, we learn that the conception was hardly immaculate'[15]. The hope offered by the birth of the child counter-balances the despondency reflected in the rest of the film.

The Bexhill scenes are probably the best at showing this despondency. As Theo and Kee reach the shanty town-like slum on the Kent coast, we see the full impact of Homeland Security's policies. The muted grey and green palette suggests that Lubezki has shot the almost impossibly long takes through filters. The *mise-en-scène* is full of darkness, rubble-strewn streets, bombed out buses as permanent shelters. Burning bodies, weeping widows and barking dogs invest the sequence with an almost biblical, apocalyptic texture. The *cinéma-vérité* approach of the battle scenes recalls Greengrass's *Bloody Sunday* (2002) and Steven Spielberg's *Saving Private Ryan* (1998). There is a sense of 'intifada' here – the green banners festooned with Arabic inscriptions, the chanting and the sheer amount of weaponry. This could be Beirut or the Gaza Strip rather than Bexhill-On-Sea. Hand-held, blood-splattered cameras follow Theo through this maze of death and destruction. A jaw-dropping long take follows the capture of Kee by Luke and his renegades and Theo's pursuit. The uncanny nature of the baby's cries stops the carnage (but only momentarily) and allows mother and child to make their escape. Again the religious connotations are emphasised.

It is a film that hints at a hopeful conclusion, with Kee and the child's rescue by The Human Project. But our central protagonist dies for the greater good, so Cuaron avoids the clichéd resolution of the hero reaching the end of the journey – a denouement that spoiled Spielberg's *War of the Worlds* (2005).

PULLING THESE FILMS TOGETHER

While these films certainly share enough attributes to suggest they are like-minded, they also throw up useful differences.

- There is a sense of a deep-rooted fear of the future in these texts.

- The future is going to be one of all-out anarchy (*28 Days Later*) or despotic regimes (*V for Vendetta* and *Children of Men*). Democracy seems to be at a premium, something that belongs in the past.

- Pockets of resistance are small – whether it is the survivors in *28 Days Later*, V or the Fishes. No mass movements are hinted at, apart from at the end of *V for Vendetta*.

- There have been technological strides, but within a believable framework. *28 Days Later*, unlike the other two films, is set in the present day. There is nothing fantastical about weaponry or transport, it is all completely recognisable.

- They share a contextual basis with a number of other recent media texts that deal with dystopian themes; the lavish, multi-layered narrative of *Lost* (2004–10), the refurbished *Doctor Who* (2005–present), which often hints at a fraught and dangerous future, the American small-town, post-apocalyptic angst of *Jericho* (2006) and Cormac McCarthy's novel *The Road* (2006), about a father and son's journey across a nuclear wasteland. These texts, like the films discussed in this chapter, expose our fears of the post-9/11 fallout; the 'war on terror' in Iraq and Afghanistan have made the world seem much more dangerous and the films reflect these fears. Terrorism on the home front also understandably feeds into these concerns, something which, again, these films explore.

- An anxiety about scientific developments is also reflected with the unforeseen effects of bio-technology and genetic experimentation underpinning all three films. The 'rage virus' unleashed in *28 Days Later* leads to the total breakdown of society. It is interesting that it is directly the result of an action by an animal liberation group that causes this – essentially a terrorist group. The motivation for V is the treatment that he suffered at Larkhill. There is also Norsefire's release of a deadly virus that kills thousands, which leads to their rise to power. Of course, in *Children of Men* there is the unexplained condition that has rendered humankind infertile. This again taps into issues around recent health scares such as Swine influenza ('swine flu') and superbugs such as MRSA, which resonate with contemporary audiences.

- Climate change is also a link. In *28 Days Later*, Frank laments that there hasn't been any rain in London for a month. *Children of Men* sees a smog-like gloom permeate many scenes.

- The films do all look very different, from the grainy, hyper-kinetic, jumpy camerawork of Boyle's film to the cartoon-like, visually sumptuous nature of McTeigue's *V for Vendetta*, to the long takes and documentary-like framing of *Children of Men*. Within the actual *mise-en-scène*, there are comparisons to be made between the look of certain characters. The shaven-headed, bewildered Evey, the frightened, uncertain, wide-eyed Jim and the drawn, resigned Theo all share the look of people just about hanging on, merely surviving.

- Although *28 Days Later* and *Children of Men* have a quality of realism that can be linked to earlier British sci-fi films such as *The Quatermass Experiment*, there are also some quite surreal moments in these films (Hutchings, 1997, p150)[16]. For example, the joy of raiding the empty supermarket and the sight of rats running away from the infected in *28 Days Later* to the young deer ambling through the redundant school in *Children of Men*. These moments provide a quirky contrast to the otherwise grim proceedings.

- Distinctions can be drawn from the films' views of London. The empty streets and supermarkets of *28 Days Later* contrast greatly with the noir-like atmosphere of *V for Vendetta*, though both films employ familiar landmarks to anchor the viewer. *Children of Men* focuses on a London grounded in a recognisable reality, but subtly different. Theo's battered, worn fleece with the 2012 London Olympics logo (much better than the actual one chosen) is also particularly well-judged, showing how a world 'event' can quickly be reduced to a tacky, dated cash-in.

However, the main issues, I believe, can be centred on two aspects of representation: gender and of ethnicity, or what can be called 'the fear of others'.

GENDER, SEX AND SEXUALITY IN DYSTOPIAN BRITAIN

The major female characters depicted in these films are uniformly strong. Selena (*28 Days Later*), Evey (*V for Vendetta*) and Julian, Miriam and Kee (*Children of Men*) all show to what extent the gender imbalance has been bridged. They are in the main decisive, active women, unafraid to make important, instant decisions and they initially don't appear to conform to the usual female stereotypes propagated by Hollywood action movies.

But if we look closer at the characters it becomes apparent that they are possibly more conventional than at first glance. The black, British Selena is a young, attractive woman and although there is no hint in the narrative that she and Mark were lovers, it is very possible that they may have been. Her relationship with Jim is trickier. At one point she says, rather matter of factly to him, 'Do you want to find a cure and save the world or just fall in love and fuck?' to which Jim has no reply. Certainly the film posits her as a love interest for Jim, although given the circumstances this takes some time to develop. Despite Selena's obvious survivor skills and her ability to despatch the infected, these effectively all count for nothing in the eyes of Major West, who sees in her reproductive capabilities the cure for the virus. She and Hannah are now merely to be used by his squadron as sex slaves and baby factories in West's mad and misguided attempt to repopulate Britain. After the women are rescued, Jim at last asserts the patriarchal role. There have been a number of obstacles to this, throughout the narrative as he is emasculated early on by the powerful Selena, sidelined in the escape from the city by Frank and towards the end of the film eclipsed by the edgy figure of West. Jim dispatches the remaining soldiers and we see in the closing moments between Selena, Hannah and himself a reconstituted family unit, confirmed by a 'normalised' Selena and Jim as hero or, at least, 'head of the household'.

Evey is similar to Selena in this respect. She is a post-feminist heroine on the surface, yet in thrall to V, bowled over by the mystery surrounding his past and impressed by his apparent sophistication. But it is worth looking at how the hero actually (ab)uses her. Firstly, he sexualises her by creating a fantasy-figure, that of a young girl, to entrap the paedophile Bishop Lilliman. Secondly, he fakes Evey's imprisonment and then de-sexualises her by shearing her hair and dressing her in a smock. He also tortures and brainwashes her with the use of Valerie's letter to ensure utter compliance with his actions. It almost seems that V has taken on the role of the dominant (abusive?) father/husband character by using these rather extreme methods to ensure Evey's loyalty to the cause. It does leave a rather bitter taste in the mouth.

The women in *Children of Men* all help Theo's quest to find self-validation. Julian, his ex-wife, draws him into the Fishes' plan and is quickly killed by her own people. Miriam plays the earth mother and, like Julian, is sacrificed to make sure that the journey to

The Human Project continues. Kee isn't just a receptacle for her unborn child – she is opinionated and determined to do what is best for her baby. But she is ultimately a figure to be helped. What might have been a more radical scenario is Kee attempting to make the journey alone. She survives at the end of the film, while Theo lays slumped in the boat, and one can't help but feel that the film is ultimately 'about' Theo's motivations and his striving for some kind of redemption.

Obviously this taps into some of Laura Mulvey's work on the perception of women in film. The spectator's look, and that of the camera, are both mediated by the ways in which male characters look at them. The male star acts as the point of identification for the audience rather than an object of desire (Ellis, 1992, p97)[17]. This is true to some extent in both *28 Days Later* and *V for Vendetta*. *Children of Men* completely avoids the clichés of the conventional romantic subplot, with only Julian and Theo's past marriage worth mentioning.

For modern films, these are incredibly chaste. Perhaps in the wake of AIDS and the increase in other sexually transmitted diseases there is an implicit message to read into this. Sexual congress is seen in purely violent terms: there is the threat of attack as a means to 'cure' the virus by predatory males affecting Selena and Hannah and, in the case of Evey, possible rape at the hands of both the Fingermen and a Bishop.

THE FEAR OF OTHERS IN DYSTOPIAN BRITAIN

As previously mentioned, *28 Days Later* was in production at the time of 9/11 and its immediate aftermath, and its very impressive US box-office takings of $45 million for a low-budget British film could arguably be due to it tapping into American anxieties. It is very much a genre exercise, a new take on the zombie movie, but with some of its imagery echoing Manhattan in the aftermath of the destruction of the World Trade Center; the infected could be representative of the Islamist perpetrators.

In the new, post-virus Britain, the Army – seemingly the last intact institution – is represented by a delusional sociopath (West) hell-bent on combating the virus with kidnap and rape. The army doesn't offer comfort, nor is it the cavalry coming to rescue the survivors. Its eventual destruction by Jim and from within does show that the old certainties don't hold anymore. This taps into some of the events surrounding the war in Iraq, especially the publicity surrounding the treatment of some of the prisoners by American service personnel at Abu Ghraib Gaol.

V for Vendetta is explicit in identifying groups who are persecuted by the Norsefire regime. The born-again High Chancellor Sutler is a homophobe, and homosexuality appears to be Dietrich's major 'crime'. The flashback of Valerie's life confirms this. This 'fear of others' is also apparent in the treatment of Muslims, with the Qur'an on the banned books list and the country following what appears to be a Christian fundamentalist ideology. This is also echoed in *Children of Men*, with its military occupation of Mosques and the pogrom at Bexhill-on-Sea, which explores Britain's isolationist attitude and treatment of refugees, taking some of the ideas dealt with in Pawel Pawlikowski's *Last Resort* (2000) and extending them into the near future, twenty years from now. The bleak, oppressive open prison that is Stonehaven in Pawlikowski's film has become the violent, alien Bexhill. The tarnished beauty of *Last Resort* has been replaced by civil disorder on a grand scale. All this, Cuaron suggests, is in front of us if we are not careful.

Ultimately, although these films show that the emergence of power from the far right is a distinct possibility, hope is offered in all three texts. Seemingly impossible obstacles can be overcome. The rescue of Jim, Selena and Hannah ends what has been a difficult viewing experience on a positive note. The popular uprising at the end of *V for Vendetta* is less conclusive and in a perhaps controversial twist shows the potential value of a so-called terrorist's actions in overthrowing a corrupt and repressive regime. Such a course of action could be liberally applied in a variety of situations in the present, notably and perhaps controversially, Iraq and Afghanistan.

The air-strikes on Bexhill imply that the political situation in *Children of Men* is unlikely to change and the possible death of Theo gives the narrative a downbeat feel, while Kee and the baby offer a sliver of hope that things are going to be alright. The key theme in all three films, I believe, is survival against the odds, but the director of *Children of Men* has chosen to leave any conclusions to the viewer:

'My intention was to take the viewer on a road trip through the state of things and then once you go through this journey for you to try to come up with your own conclusions about the possibility of hope in a world like this ... So if you are a hopeful person you'll see a lot of hope, and if you are a bleak person you'll see a complete hopelessness at the end.' (Cuaron quoted in *Filmmaker magazine*, Fall 2006)

SUMMARY

Approaching these films in terms of their social and political contextual value is a useful way in. With respect to genre, the sense of pessimism that permeates them is vital in understanding their place in the great tradition of British dystopian texts. These films, in their very different ways, raise questions about current fears and events. Crucially, they place Britain in the centre of a frame usually occupied by America which is in itself extremely refreshing.

Of all the films here, *Children of Men* is the most inventive and it is constantly fascinating, gaining a great deal with repeat viewings. Although it was not a conspicuous hit theatrically, on its DVD release positive word of mouth sparked interest. Time will tell whether it will enter the canon of great British cinema, and just how grimly prophetic it is.

REFERENCES

1. Hunter, I.Q., 'The Strange World of the British science-fiction film' in Hunter, I.Q. (ed.), British Science Fiction Cinema, London: Routledge, 1999

2. Walker, A., quoted in Dalton, S., 'Symphony for the Devil' in *Uncut* magazine, April 2000

3. Chapman, J., 'A bit of the old ultra-violence' in Hunter, I.Q. (ed.), British Science Fiction Cinema, London: Routledge, 1999

4. Kermode, M., Review of *28 Days Later* in Sight and Sound, October 2002

5. Boyle, D. quoted in Newman, K., 'The Diseased World' in Filmmaker magazine.com, Summer 2003

6. Boyle, D. quoted in Lim, D., 'Unchained Malady' in Village Voice, June 2003

7. Edelstein, D., 'Zombies Ate My Neighbour' in Slate, June 2003

8. Bradshaw, P., Review of *28 Weeks Later* in The Guardian 11/05/07

9. Bradshaw, P., Review of *V for Vendetta* in The Guardian, 17/03/06

10. Kermode, M., 'You call it a disaster, Hollywood calls it a vehicle' in The Guardian, 12/03/06

11. French, P., Review of *V for Vendetta* in The Observer, 19/03/06

12. French, P., Review of *Children of Men* in The Observer, 24/09/06

13. Bradshaw, P., Review of *Children of Men* in The Guardian, 22/09/06

14. Cuaron, A., quoted in Guerrasio, J., 'A New Humanity' in *Filmmaker Magazine*, Winter 2006

15. Osmond, A., Review of *Children of Men* in Sight and Sound, December 2006

16. Hutchings, P., 'Beyond the New Wave: Realism in British Cinema' in Murphy, R. (ed.) The British Cinema Book, London: BFI, 1997

17. Ellis, J., Visible Fictions, London: Routledge, 1992

THE REVIVAL OF THE BRITISH HORROR FILM

INTRODUCTION

The long and illustrious reputation of the British horror film has had a real shot in the arm in the opening years of the new century with the emergence of a number of films that have further enhanced that reputation. Forty years ago studios like

Shaun of the Dead

Hammer, Amicus and Tyburn were producing a considerable volume of films for a willing market. In the case of Hammer these films did well abroad and have, retrospectively, gained real cult appeal. But the legacy that these older films have left has also haunted British horror with their velvet jackets, frilly shirts and the 1970s soft-porn asides. Even the Hammer brand has been revived and the company has started to churn out horror films once again, starting with *Beyond the Rave* (2008), which was released on the internet.

The 1990s was a grim time for the horror genre and although the number of films produced has increased it could hardly be called a glut. The emergence of directors like Christopher Smith has been encouraging. His first feature, *Creep* (2004), was a virtual remake of the 1970s classic *Deathline* (Sherman, 1973). *Creep* focused on a German woman, Kate (Franka Potente), trapped in the London Underground and pursued by a flesh-eating creature that lives in the tunnels adjacent to Charing Cross tube station. Kate's transformation from a confident, attractive woman to one who is mistaken for a vagrant is worth a look. She has been terrorised but not just by the film's monster. Near the beginning of the film, a work colleague tries to rape her on an abandoned tube train. She is helped by a homeless character and a sewer worker, reflecting a London ignored by the thousands of commuters that use the station every day. Smith's next film, *Severance* (2007), found itself in much more comic territory. A sales division for a large multinational company head off for a team-building weekend in a remote rural locale in Hungary where they are terrorised by some nasty locals. It plays off the tensions between the group, which includes a Cockney stoner played by Danny Dyer and the officious manager Richard (Tim McInnerny). Although it straddles both comedy and horror – *The Office* meets *Deliverance* – it never manages to fully convince in either genre, although some of Smith's ideas are interesting.

Towards the end of the decade, horror took on a more exploitative nature with films such as Paul Andrew Williams' follow-up to his acclaimed *London to Brighton* (2006), the gore-fest *The Cottage* (2008). *Mum and Dad* (Sheil, 2008) is even more explicit, with distinct echoes of the Fred and Rosemary West case from the mid-1990s through its themes of kidnapping, sexual sadism, ritual torture and murder. It also references – with its main victim/heroine, the Polish migrant Lena (Olga Fedori) – the new European guest workers. It is decidedly unsubtle, but its blood-soaked ending and its commentary on underclass values are extremely engrossing. Tom Shankland's *The Children* (2008), written by Paul Andrew Williams, has a middle-class focus, as a mystery infection changes the youngsters of the title into killers hell-bent on attacking the adults. With its inference to the furore over MMR jabs and its careful deconstruction of liberal parenting values, *The Children* does convince. These films are tremendously interesting as modern British horror movies, and try to emulate elements of some recent European horror-thrillers such as Dominik Moll's *Lemming* (2005) and the films of Michael Haneke, in particular *Caché* (*Hidden*, 2005). Although these continental films are not strictly horror they show a sophisticated, intelligent way to question existing values. In *Hidden*, the visceral, unexpected suicide could be straight from a horror film and it uses shock value to raise fundamental issues about Georges, the main protagonist.

David Pirie's point that the cultural origins of horror are not that important to audiences is one worth examining:

> 'It seems to me, even at its most successful, the British horror film never was marketed as being British. The crowds who flocked to the early Hammer movies were entirely uninterested in the fact that they were British, they just knew that they were thrilling which is exactly how it should be. National success at a genre is generally, with a very few exceptions, an intuitive, unconscious process, not an overt one.' (2008, p212)[1]

The Noughties saw a general growth in horror films from the American mainstream and beyond, and it is conceivable that the success and re-emergence of the British horror movie caught the coat tails of this. The fact that these films are British may be no less vital to audiences than the Saw series (2004–present) being American or *[Rec]* (Plaza and Balaguero, 2007) being Spanish. Although their unique cultural specificity could be seen to add to British horror's appeal, the conventional, universal themes of the genre have also been central to their relative success. This chapter will concentrate on both of these elements by looking at the most successful horror film of the decade, *Shaun of the Dead* (Wright, 2004). Then we will discuss the work of Neil Marshall, who has become the most highly feted of the recent group of British horror director/writers. The focus here will be his debut feature *Dog Soldiers* (2002) and the follow-up *The Descent* (2005). The chapter will end with one of the most interesting horror films of recent years, James Watkins' *Eden Lake* (2008), which strays into the territory explored by Michael Haneke in his films in a much more unsubtle fashion, by deconstructing middle-class fears of a feral underclass.

HORROR HYBRID — LAUGHTER AND GORE IN *SHAUN OF THE DEAD*

Shaun of the Dead tapped into the unlikely comedic potential offered by horror. Edgar Wright's film positioned itself as a rom-com-zombie movie, utilising elements from a relatively broad range of genres. What the film does is to show that the line between laughs and

Dylan Moran, Kate Ashfield, Simon Pegg, Lucy Davis, *Shaun of the Dead*

genuine shock can be effectively blurred and be exploited to maximum effect.

The creators of *Shaun of the Dead* had their roots in the cult Channel 4 sitcom *Spaced*, where slacker twenty-somethings stumbled around a flatshare in Crouch End, north London. It was full of intertextual references to horror, science fiction and old television shows, but also employed inventive use of sound, zooms and camera angles to make it a truly innovative piece of comedy. Wright teamed up once again with the co-writer and lead actor of *Spaced*, Simon Pegg, and one of its other stars, Nick Frost, to further extend some of the cinematic ideas first tried out in the sitcom. There are interesting parallels between *Spaced* and *Shaun of the Dead*, in that both Pegg and Frost reprise their archetypal roles as overgrown children, whose stunted development provides many of the initial gags. Wright chooses to employ a lengthy exposition to show Shaun's life of underachievement on all levels. The initial complication is when his girlfriend of three years, Liz (Kate Ashfield), dumps him. Their limited social life revolves around Shaun's local pub, the down-at-heel Winchester Arms, and Liz, exasperated by Shaun's lack of imagination, wants more excitement in their relationship. The amount of time Shaun spends with his drug-dealing friend, waster Ed (Nick Frost), and his straight-laced flat-mate Pete (Peter Serafinowicz) is also a problem. Theirs is a life of too much Playstation, of beery nights, thrown-together flatmates and wallowing in the ever-increasing gap between being a teenager and a responsible adult. This is the world of the kidult and it is absolutely recognisable to its target audience. Shaun's job as a junior manager at a local electrical goods store is portrayed as totally uninspiring, as he wastes time lecturing his adolescent workers in the ethics of teamwork.

Wright also establishes a real sense of drone-like behaviour around Shaun even before the zombie invasion gets fully into its stride. The monotonous actions of the supermarket checkout, a bored queue at a bus stop all glaring at their mobile phones in unison and finally a group of hooded youths walking robotically. The mundane, highly routine nature of modern British life is captured here with real simplicity. This is further strengthened by

Shaun's own behaviour from his daily trip to the corner shop to purchase a newspaper and can of Coke to the mind-numbing bus ride to work. Self-absorbed, he fails to see what is actually going on around him – the growing, random attacks reported on the televisions he is trying to sell, explicit tabloid headlines testifying to the increasingly strange behaviour of people on the street. He is, of course, as oblivious to the feelings of Liz, Pete and his mother Barbara (Penelope Wilton). There is a particularly tetchy early meeting with Shaun's stepfather Phillip (Bill Nighy) who orders him to be more considerate of Barbara, but you sense that Shaun isn't really listening to what Phillip is trying to say. Instead, he acts like a surly teenager. Shaun lives in a bubble of his own making, a world where he is as much a zombie as the creatures that he encounters later in the story. This is captured well by writer Matthew Sweet discussing what he sees as the most shocking scene in the film – Shaun's final trip to the convenience store for his daily shot of cola:

> 'This time, however, the details are a little different. The pavements are scattered with rubbish and dead bodies. The glass door of the corner shop's refrigerated drinks cabinet is spattered with blood. The proprietor is thrashing around at the back of the premises, slaked with gore. The animated cadavers of his neighbours are roaming the streets in search of fresh human flesh. There are no newspapers on the counter. And it is only the last of these that Shaun registers. Although he remains untouched by the mysterious radiation that has reduced most of London to a state of vicious imbecility, he too is one of the walking dead. Civilisation as we know it has just ended, and he's too glazed to notice.'[2]

Although less visually sophisticated than the other big British zombie film of the era, *28 Days Later*, this actually feels more realistic. Danny Boyle's incredible shots of an empty central London are impressive, but the nondescript suburban neighbourhood that the walking dead are stalking in Wright's film is more recognisable. Ed and Shaun's first confrontation with a zombie takes place in their scruffy back garden and thus captures this sense of the casual. A young woman is aimlessly strolling about and the lads assume that she is drunk. When she falls on Shaun and tries to bite him, Ed just laughs, but as Shaun pushes her off she becomes impaled on an old piece of garden furniture. Their shock is quickly replaced by anguish as she lifts herself off the spike, the hole going right through her midriff. Finally the penny drops that something very serious is going on and, following advice from *Sky News*, they destroy both the woman and another male intruder with a shovel and cricket bat by bashing their brains in. They then retire to the sofa, completely covered in blood, to scoff ice-cream. Events in the garden are as unrealistic as the computer games that take up much of their lives. This combination of extreme violence and goof-ball comedy is the major hallmark of *Shaun of the Dead*.

The film doesn't offer some of the more serious themes of consumerism, urban alienation and scientific experimentation that we see in the films of zombie auteur George A. Romero or in Danny Boyle's film. Instead, it opts for a rites of passage approach as Shaun transforms from a lazy, unambitious slacker into a reluctant hero. This was something that was central to co-writer Pegg's intentions:

'*Shaun of the Dead* is about having to take responsibility in your early thirties. It's about realising you can't be young and frivolous forever. The zombies are a metaphor for the inexorable tide of responsibilities that engulfs you as you grow older. You can't keep ignoring the issues of buying a house or having children. The skeletal idea of the film is that this guy gets his life sorted through a crisis. Anything could have got him motivated to get on with his life … It just happens to be a zombie invasion.'[3]

The film follows this acceptance of responsibility based upon Shaun's newly decisive frame of mind. He and Ed commandeer Pete's car and head to his mother's house, their overall intention to rescue Barbara, then Liz and to finally decamp at the Winchester Arms to sit out the crisis. Here the film's pace greatly increases. It is interesting that although the zombie attacks are pretty brutal, they are easy to avoid with Shaun simply dispatching zombies with his cricket bat as if he was in the training nets. Kim Newman saw this as being one of the most obvious ways of parodying the genre: 'for the most part the dead here are generic bloody-mouthed fumblers and the laughs come from the binds their presence puts the living characters into'[4]. This is particularly true when Di (Lucy Davis), Liz's flatmate and a drama teacher, instructs the group in how to act like zombies in order to safely navigate their way past them and into the pub. What adds a degree of sensitivity to the proceedings are the reactions when one of the group is bitten. This leads to some of the most moving scenes in the film: for example, the dying Philip's revelation that he always believed in and loved Shaun. What supersedes this is the emotional impact of Barbara's death in the Winchester, also carefully handled as Shaun takes responsibility to kill her, once she has become one of the living dead. The build-up to this is well handled, as the odious David (Dylan Moran), Di's partner and another flatmate of Liz's, is about to shoot Barbara, when he is prevented by the distraught Shaun. Although it is revealed that David has long harboured romantic designs on Liz, this doesn't detract from the central conceit surrounding Shaun's growth as a hero, having to dispatch his mother to protect his friends.

The romantic element is relatively underplayed, and although part of Shaun's main motivation to win Liz back is an integral part of his enforced heroism, the central relationship is between him and Ed. The film can also be read as a buddy movie, as Ed at turns both exasperates and entertains Shaun, although the rest of the characters, Barbara excepted, can't quite see the attraction. Ed is an unreconstructed moron, texting as Shaun is trying to see off a middle-aged zombie by using some children's garden toys. This level of utter detachment from reality reaches its peak when, under siege in the doorway of the Winchester Arms, Ed takes a phone call about supplying some drugs to a friend. When Shaun slaps the phone from Ed's hand, he remains incredulous until Shaun informs him that he has been sticking up for him all his life. It is also telling that earlier in the film Pete informs Shaun that the only reason that he is still friends with Ed is that he actually

makes him look like less of a loser. Shaun has no response to this. When the final climactic battle occurs, it is shown in a series of quick reaction shots, demonstrating how Shaun is torn between his love for Liz and his obvious affection for his friend. The main question seems to be not whether they survive the attack, but if Shaun can retain some elements of his life with Ed and convince Liz that he is worth another go. Wright's ending allows both of these possibilities.

Ed is bitten and infected, intriguingly enough by his nemesis, the naked Pete, who has re-emerged in the pub battle. After using burning alcohol to partially subdue the hordes of zombies who have by now invaded the bar, Liz, Shaun and the badly injured Ed make it to the cellar. It is decided that Ed will remain as the couple make their escape on a hydraulic lift, which will get them outside. Even here as they part for perhaps the last time, Ed still manages to break wind and make Shaun laugh. The themes loosely explored here in this friendship have parallels with a range of classic British sitcoms, where male relationships are central and where any hint of female intervention is frowned upon. The most obvious reference points are *Whatever Happened to the Likely Lads* (1973–4) and *Men Behaving Badly* (1992–9), where the male protagonists' stunted development is in clear defiance of what is expected of them by their female counterparts. The development of this 'buddy' motif was further extended, using the same actors, in Wright's next project, the spoof police procedural *Hot Fuzz* (2006).

Outside, Shaun and Liz find that the army has arrived and the film moves into an epilogue six months later. It is clear from the snippets of television we see that some of the zombies still exist and they have been put to work in repetitive, boring jobs such as collecting shopping trolleys or, in an ironic twist, being participants in tedious reality game shows. Ultimately, though, *Shaun of the Dead* offers an ideologically sound resolution. Liz and Shaun are now happily living together in his old house, tastefully decorated and without the male clutter of empty beer cans, loaded ashtrays and empty pizza boxes that had previously surrounded Ed's marathon video-game sessions. They seem contented, planning out their leisurely Sunday as any aspirational middle-class couple might. The final shots, however, show that although there has been a change in Shaun's lifestyle, he still has a foot in the past. The shed at the bottom of the garden contains the zombiefied Ed, chained up and playing a seemingly endless *Playstation* game. Wright's rather touching ending to the strains of Queen's '*You're My Best Friend*' shows that although Shaun has come a long way in the film, his heart is still with his mate, forever on the settee laughing at fart gags.

The film, made by Working Title, although a long way from the company's usual output, did very respectable business both in the UK and abroad. It showed that even though it had quite specific British cultural references, it transcended these with universal themes.

As a horror movie, it is a film about fear, but it is more about fear of growing up, of commitment, of loss, of being trapped in a life the characters don't want. The zombie invasion exposes these fears to good effect, all the while managing to be funny, moving and surprisingly thoughtful.

THE DISTURBING WORLD OF NEIL MARSHALL

Dog Soldiers

Neil Marshall has established himself as the pre-eminent director of British horror of the era with two films, *Dog Soldiers* and *The Descent*. Both films exploit the fear of entrapment: in the case of *Dog Soldiers* a remote Scottish forest and in *The Descent* a cave in

Dog Soldiers

the Appalachian Mountains. The first film has elements of black comedy embedded within a plot concerning a family of werewolves terrorising a small battalion of soldiers. *The Descent* has few laughs; instead we see a group of young women on a potholing expedition who are attacked by grotesque subterranean creatures. What is key in both films is the different way that Marshall builds up the group dynamics and there is a clear variation in gender reactions to the threats posed by the unearthly creatures.

Dog Soldiers' exposition quickly establishes the central confrontation within the film. The first shots of a young couple camping in a secluded Highlands forest, attacked in their tent by unseen foes, quickly delineates the werewolf theme, with the howling, full moon and a gift of a silver knife that remains unused. Marshall uses captions to move the action to two hours earlier to show the start of the main conflict between the martinet Captain Ryan (Liam Cunningham) and Private Cooper (Kevin McKidd). It transpires that this is a training exercise for Cooper's entry into Cunningham's elite special unit, which he passes quite easily. But by refusing to kill a dog, he fails to enter the squad. The two men will meet up later on.

The film then jumps to four weeks later and once again we are back in the wild Scottish countryside, its desolation shown in a series of panning shots of lakes and seemingly endless forests. A helicopter lands and soldiers emerge in full battle dress. The leader, known as Sarge (Sean Pertwee), is the older man, well-respected within the squad. Cooper is Sarge's right-hand man. The rest of the unit are Spooney (Darren Morfitt),

Terry (Leslie Simpson), Bruce (Thomas Lockyer) and Joe (Chris Robson). In true horror convention, we are in no doubt that some of these characters will be dispatched rather nastily. Joe's main preoccupation is with an England-Germany football fixture, taking place that evening; his constant moaning at having to partake in this war-game exercise is an attempt to lighten the tone.

What is interesting here is that although the men have only been 'armed' with blanks they are prepared for most eventualities. They are highly trained, professional soldiers, but as the Scottish dusk gathers and stories are told of missing hikers in the area, even the massed whistling of The Piranha's 'Tom Hark' seems strangely out of kilter with the prevailing mood. With the oncoming night, Sarge's character is developed through a hellish tale from the first Gulf War. A mutilated Aberdeen Angus, which literally falls onto the men, further exacerbates the increasingly oppressive atmosphere. Parallel editing using night vision techniques shows an attack on Ryan's squadron – there are brief glimpses of a fast-running creature. Later on the next day, Sarge's unit find Ryan, terrified, with evidence of human remains scattered about. There are also nets, tranquiliser darts and live ammunition, which suggest some covert action on the part of Ryan and his team. His mantra, 'there was only supposed to be one', makes no sense to Sarge, but it quickly becomes clear to the audience that rather than just one werewolf, there is a formidable number of the beasts. It is also obvious that the war game was no more than just a cover up for something more sinister.

Once more a full moon is seen as the film moves into a protracted chase sequence. The howling starts and the men, including Ryan, start to run away whilst shooting aimlessly at shadows. A panicked Bruce finds himself impaled on a branch before being taken away by a creature. Sarge is attacked in a vain attempt to save the hapless Bruce. Sarge, the alpha male, has his stomach practically ripped out and is in a terrible way. Rather than leaving him to his fate, Cooper and the rest of the team help him to his feet and make a dash for it, closely pursued by the werewolves. They are picked up, in a jeep, by a young woman, Megan (Emma Cleasby). She takes them to an isolated farmhouse, which seems to have been only recently abandoned, with a fire set and dinner cooking on the hob. The house's sole occupant is a dog hidden in a cupboard. Megan tells them that the nearest town, Fort William, is a four-hour drive away, which re-emphasises their sense of desperation.

The film then becomes reminiscent of siege-based narratives like *Assault on Precinct 13* (Carpenter, 1978) or, as Spooney draws parallels to Roark's Drift, seeing the soldiers as 'British steel' up against the 'wolfmen', *Zulu* (Enfield, 1964). The macho posturing continues as the werewolves surround the house but the men find that their firepower is no use against the beasts. Sarge has his stomach super-glued and Cooper becomes the leader, but slowly the men are killed off one by one, starting with Terry. With no electricity and only flimsy wooden barriers against creatures that are more intelligent than one would have hoped, the situation becomes increasingly desperate.

Megan is a zoologist who has been researching the werewolves for two years and she knows Ryan, who has previously been sent to capture one of the beasts – perhaps to harness its power as a potential weapon. It also becomes clear that Sarge and his team were used as bait for the werewolves, but that this plot had backfired. Ryan changes into a werewolf and escapes the besieged house and the film enters its final act. Sarge has made a miraculous recovery but it is evident that he, too, will soon change into a werewolf. The final twist is that the family that own the farmhouse are indeed the werewolves and Megan, as part of the family, has lured the unit there. In a final confrontation Cooper escapes to the cellar and Sarge, just before his transformation, manages to blow the building up with all the werewolves in it. Only a final battle with Cooper and Ryan remains, with Cooper finding the silver knife that was spotted at the start of the film, using it to stab the transformed Ryan in the heart. The film ends with a spoof tabloid headline leading with England's 5-1 victory over Germany. The second story is on the werewolf attack, portrayed in a mocking fashion.

There is plenty of gore and the fast-paced narrative is extremely assured. There is some sense of class antagonism between the 'toffee-nosed' Ryan and Cooper, but this is never really fully developed. The main thrust of the story is this 'band of brothers' pitted against a seemingly unbeatable enemy, the unifying bond is their reliance on each other and a pronounced sense of a slightly humourous male camaraderie. Megan is an interloper. When Cooper is asked early on what he fears most he mentions spiders and, tellingly, women. There is a cursory attempt to develop a relationship between Megan and Cooper, but doubts are constantly voiced about her back-story and when it is revealed that she has dragged the men to the werewolves' lair, Cooper's point about his greatest fear is reinforced. This is a very male film and its appeal may well primarily lie with an audience of teenage boys. There is little complexity beyond the initial tensions between Ryan and Cooper. The film might be read retrospectively as a foretaste of the subsequent invasions of Iraq and Afghanistan with their considerable casualty list. Marshall's next film, however, was to be a step up in terms of narrative development and character establishment.

The Descent

'Looking back at *Dog Soldiers* I thought it wasn't particularly scary. It came out as a black comedy more than anything else. I still had this fundamental need in me to make a horror film that genuinely terrified people. In the same way that I was genuinely terrified by *Deliverance* or *Alien* or *The Shining*, all those films from the 70s that I grew up with and that have haunted me ever since. There was also a need to make a horror film that took itself seriously, that played it straight. So the story emerged from that desire really.'[5]

Shauna McDonald, *The Descent*

There were a number of similarities and differences between Marshall's debut film and *The Descent*. Like *Dog Soldiers*, his second film is about a group of able, highly motivated individuals trapped in a remote location, surrounded by otherworldly monsters that they struggle to defeat. However, the women in this film don't share the solidarity of Sarge's team. Their relationships are strained and there is little real sense of organisation, which becomes clear once they enter the caves gorged deep into the Appalachian Mountains. *The Descent's* wonderfully downbeat ending, which firstly tricks the audience into imagining a straightforward resolution and then takes that away with a return underground, lacks the inevitability of Cooper's survival in *Dog Soldiers*, and makes it a more rewarding movie. It is a film that feeds off the fear of entrapment and being buried alive, but it also offers interesting post-feminist representations of its lead characters. These are by and large strong, assertive women whose gender isn't central to their actions; the squadron in *Dog Soldiers* would have also struggled to cope in the dank and forbidding atmosphere of the cave.

Like in his first film, Marshall presents a short prologue set in the Scottish Highlands to establish relationships and narrative tensions. We see three young women white-water rafting. They are watched by a man and a young girl from the shoreline. Very quickly potential conflict is developed when the women get off the raft. It is strange that Paul (Oliver Milburn) attends to Juno (Natalie Mendoza), rather than his wife Sarah (Shauna McDonald), who rushes straight to their daughter Jessica (Molly Kayll). There is an interesting reaction shot of the third woman, English teacher Beth (Alex Reid), which acknowledges the relationship between Juno and the married Paul. On the way back Paul and Jessica are killed after the car that they are travelling in has a direct collision with a van, which results in some loose scaffolding going through the windscreen. This first shock is a real jolt to the nervous system as the metal pole enters Paul's head. It is a horrific beginning and sets up the themes of death and fate which run through the rest of the narrative. Sarah wakes up in hospital and unhooks herself from the machines. The realisation that her daughter may be dead slowly starts to dawn on her. We see this in a dream sequence, with Sarah running down an empty hospital corridor as the lights start one by one to go out. There is also a recurring image of Jessica in the dark, blowing out the candles on a birthday cake, which is reprised a number of times in the film when Sarah is under stress. She wakes up and is comforted by Beth.

The Descent then moves on by a year and the location changes to the desolate mountains of North Carolina, established by an aerial tracking shot of a car on a lonely road surrounded by forest. The car contains Beth and Sarah on their way to another extreme sport experience, potholing, run by Juno. Once again conventional indicators of the horror ahead are given in these establishing shots: bullet-holes adorn the sign for Chatooga National Park, there are skulls on the post of the cabin in which the women are staying and later on the group find some mutilated deer in the woods. Like Marshall's earlier film, there are six main characters – Beth, Sarah, Juno, her prodigy Holly (Nora Jane Noone) and sisters Rebecca (Saskia Mulder) and trainee doctor Sam (Myanna Buring). Once again character archetypes are soon established with Juno clearly presented as the alpha-female. She has planned the excursion and she takes command of the proceedings. Holly is the impetuous youngest member of the group who sees the proposed expedition as boring and designed primarily for tourists. The sisters seem the most expendable, as they have been relatively undeveloped alongside the other characters. Sarah is still in mourning and the pragmatic Beth is her closest friend in the group. We see the women drunkenly bonding. The camera peers in through the windows, suggesting some unseen force watching on. It is interesting that all these twenty-something women are driven less by female companionship and more by finding their next potential high and this is particularly true of both Juno and Holly. On one hand, it is refreshing to see these women unencumbered by their links to men, but it also feels as though they are running away from something in their own lives. Obviously this is the case with Sarah, and the subtle build-up of the tensions exploits this more fully as the narrative progresses.

The trip to the cave reiterates the totally remote nature of the area. The mouth of the cave is huge and Marshall fully exploits the spectacle of the surroundings as each woman lowers themselves in and they glimpse their last view of daylight. Before this, there is a close-up of Juno deliberately leaving the guide book to the caves in the back of her jeep. This is exposed later on in the narrative, as is the fact that these caves are completely uncharted and not the ones that the group had originally intended to visit. Once again this is a ruse engineered by Juno in search of the ultimate adventure. The sense of potential threat is once again developed, even before the group has gone properly underground, when Sarah sees scratch marks on one of the rocks.

The Descent enters into possibly its most interesting phase as a psychological thriller feeding off the audience's fear of entombment. Minimal lighting is used and the all-encompassing darkness is constantly reinforced. Rebecca, before entering the cavern, ticked off the various conditions associated with being trapped underground

– dehydration, paranoia, breathing difficulties, panic attacks and hallucinations. These spring to mind as the women work their way through the dark, winding, narrow passages with Marshall's camera wonderfully capturing the claustrophobia of their journey. This is the second act of the film, and it is probably closest to James Watkins' *Eden Lake* in the way that the horror of what unfolds is recognisable and very realistic. Here are six women who, despite having a background in adventure-led activities, have put themselves in a potentially perilous situation. It is also, according to David Pirie, by far the most interesting part of the narrative:

> 'Not only was the film technically highly impressive, Marshall also tried hard to make something more interesting out of his team of threatened pot-holers. He was partly successful; indeed, the film's first half, which has no monsters at all, was unexpectedly almost more interesting and more exciting than its second.' (p228, 2008)

This second act is bathed in the blood-red light of the torches and flares, which gives the *mise-en-scène* a hellish quality. The tension increases when Sarah is trapped in a cramped tunnel, suffers a panic attack and then a considerable rockfall follows, blocking their way back. The revelation that Juno has led the women into an unknown passage only further splinters the group. The feeling of hopelessness amplifies with each minute. A dangerous, seemingly bottomless crevasse is navigated, with Rebecca struggling with a gashed hand. There is evidence of others who have been here before. There are also crude cave-drawings that suggest another exit. It is at this point the first sight of the creatures occurs – a full 45 minutes into the film. This is where the pace of *The Descent* accelerates. Holly's foolhardy nature is soon exposed when she follows what she believes to be a light source but which turns out to be a phosphorescent rock. She falls heavily down a hole, breaking her leg. The camera lingers on the shattered bone poking through the skin as trainee medic Sam tries to reset it. It is a gut-wrenching sequence, as Holly twists, screams and swears.

The Descent now moves into its third and final act, with the introduction of the subterranean creatures or the 'crawlers' as Marshall has dubbed them. It is much more solidly generic and it becomes more closely associated with his debut feature. The very real horror of entrapment and desperation is replaced with a protracted chase and battle with grotesque beasts which, although exciting, lacks the realism of the first part of the film. Sound is used effectively to signal the arrival of the crawlers, with their clicking, cricket-like hum. The creatures are pale-skinned and blind, and their sole motivation, it seems, is to feed off their human prey, resembling a mixture of Nosferatu, Gollum and the zombies from *28 Days Later*. They seem to be the result of a repulsive nightmare and the visual fear factor is considerably higher than the werewolves in Marshall's earlier film. They move at tremendous speed and are able to crawl up the rock walls with minimal effort. The infra-red light of the hand-held DV camera and the orange flares expose a myriad of bones, stripped bare of all flesh. They also reveal the crawlers. With their first attack on the injured Holly, they show a small degree of intelligence by killing the weakest first.

The group splinters with the sisters, Rebecca and Sam, going their own way. Juno, the strongest of the team, fights and successfully kills one of the crawlers trying to claim Holly's corpse. But the elation of her 'victory' is inadvertently shattered when she accidentally sticks a pick in Beth's throat. Of course, this also exposes the tension that has been building from the start regarding Beth's knowledge of Juno's affair with Paul. Beth grabs a pendant, which Paul had given to her, from Juno's neck. Juno leaves her and soon meets up with the sisters. Sarah remains alone.

The development of Sarah's character is fundamental here. This hellish trip is initially presented as a cathartic experience for this young woman who was the victim of a terrible loss. Strangely, this is what the film fully becomes: she turns into a Lara Croft character, evading and killing the crawlers with relative ease. There are a number of intertextual references to other films – Sarah's emergence from a blood filled pool calls to mind *Apocalypse Now* (Coppola, 1980) but also has links to another classic piece of American cinema according to Sam Davies's review: 'Sarah is even baptised in a lake of gore, emerging as aggressor rather than victim … The visual echo of Sissy Spacek drenched in blood in *Carrie* is unmistakable'[6]. Sarah's growth as a stronger character is reinforced when she finds the dying Beth, who tells her about her late husband's affair with her friend. Her final meeting with Juno is then set up as the climactic sequence where, despite the threat of the crawlers, old scores are to be settled.

Both Rebecca and Sam are killed, and once again Juno escapes and predictably is reunited with Sarah. They fight off a group of crawlers and Sarah in particular shows incredible violence by killing one of the creatures by gouging out its eye sockets. Juno is equally vicious when dispatching the enemy. The aftermath of the confrontation, with Juno and Sarah still standing, has none of the sacrificial theme concerning Sarge in *Dog Soldiers*. Instead of this, Sarah intentionally wounds Juno in the leg so that she will struggle to evade the next swarm of creatures. Any sense of sisterhood has evaporated as the untrustworthy, self-serving Juno is left to her fate. Marshall then takes a big chance with a false ending. Sarah slips, loses consciousness and wakes to a shard of light which she follows. This is shown in a beautiful shot as the camera pans away, and against a pitch black background Sarah follows the light source, clambering up a ladder of bones. She reaches the surface and takes in a great gulp of air and runs away from the subterranean slaughterhouse. She finds the jeep and drives away but when the ghost of Juno appears behind, she wakes and finds herself still two miles underground. The recurring image of her dead daughter and the birthday cake is her last vision as once again the camera pans away to reveal the reality of her entombment. It is, as Mark Kermode has remarked, 'a splendidly downbeat finale'[7], which is perhaps what Sarah wanted all along, to be with her daughter in the afterlife.

The film, released in the wake of the London bombings on 7 July 2005, captures the uncertainty and fear of the time. With its hidden underground assailants standing in for the largely British-born Islamist terrorists, *The Descent* struck a chord with British audiences. Tim Robey, in his review in The Daily Telegraph on the day after the attacks, said, 'On a day like today, it feels odd to recommend such a disturbing film'[8], but Marshall's movie, with its strong defiant female leads and bleak ending, somehow felt like a film in the right place, at the right time. It also increased the profile of its director, which was subsequently enhanced by his dystopian film *Doomsday* (2008). In summary, *The Descent* is an intelligent, taut and cleverly shot addition to the British horror canon, which could have done without the workman-like sequel (2009).

EDEN LAKE — MODERN BRITISH NIGHTMARES

Kelly Reilly,
Eden Lake

James Watkins' *Eden Lake* is no conventional horror film with monsters standing in for real fears. Instead, the film opts for an unsubtle but incredibly effective approach regarding the perceived threat felt by the middle classes from young working-class youth in modern-day Britain, by pitching a young couple, schoolteacher Jenny (Kelly Reilly) and her boyfriend Steve (Michael Fassbender), in a semi-isolated location near a flooded quarry. They soon encounter a group of local teenagers who terrorise them and this ultimately results in torture, violence and death.

Eden Lake certainly echoes a number of other films. The spirit of the controversial *Straw Dogs* (Peckinpah, 1970) lurks here. The initially passive academic David Sumner (Dustin Hoffman) moves to a rural English village and is steadily humiliated and taunted by the locals. When his wife is brutally raped and his house is besieged, Sumner turns on his attackers with a murderous rage. The film has been often criticised as a simplistic and, in places, deeply problematic piece that celebrates violence without offering any real context for it. However, when placed against, as David Weddle puts it, 'The hidden rage [that] seemed to be racing up through the fissures of the American landscape and spewing out everywhere: the Manson family, Charles Whitman ... My Lai ... Kent State shootings ... Black Panthers ... multiple bomb scares', the anger in *Straw Dogs* does seem to make sense (1996, p395)[9]. The closed, protective community of *The Wicker Man* (Hardy, 1973) and the pack mentality in Shane Meadows' *Dead Man's Shoes* (2004) are also clear reference points for *Eden Lake*. However, what differentiates *Eden Lake* is that the villains are young people with little or no moral compass. Their actions are barbaric and delivered with no real remorse or understanding of their long-term consequences. Like the violent context that, according to Weddle, was in part responsible for *Straw Dogs*, moral panics regarding teenage behaviour have been a seasonal feature of tabloid outrage and also government policy, and the response has been the introduction of a raft of measures regarding anti-social behaviour, predominantly aimed at the young.

The question of intervention is most pertinent here. The case of Gary Newlove is important in relation to the film. Newlove was beaten to death on his own doorstep in Warrington, Cheshire, in the summer of 2007 after a confrontation with some teenage vandals. This outrage, coupled with an increase in the murder of teenagers by other teenagers and a rise in gang-related violence, has all the hallmarks of a moral panic. A fear of young people who are often commonly known as 'hoodies', because of the adoption of hooded sweatshirts to hide their faces, has been exploited in the media, and it is this fear that *Eden Lake* feeds off. Libby Brooks takes this point up to good effect: '[the film] suggests that what we most fear today is not the supernatural or the alien, but children – specifically working-class children – and their boozy, indiscriminately shagging, incompetent parents. And the reason for that lingering aftertaste is that it's true'[10].

The film starts in what appears to be a leafy London suburb where we meet Jenny. She is finishing the day with a small class of very young pupils and contrasts are made here between her later experiences in the film, where the highly structured, regulated world of the school is replaced with the chaos of dangerous adolescence. Her occupation also tellingly signifies her as middle class and also perhaps archetypally as someone who might well be considered reasonably liberal in terms of her attitude towards disenfranchised groups. Part of the strength of *Eden Lake* is Jenny's transformation from a gentle, maternal figure to a killer herself and this change seems more dramatic than that offered in *The Descent*. Steve picks her up for a weekend in the country, driving a borrowed off-road vehicle, and although his occupation is not revealed it is apparent that he is educated and may well share similar values to Jenny, who he intends to propose to on their trip. Their destination is a beauty spot in the north Midlands, where they want to camp.

There is a feeling of unease created as they near the lake; they decide to stay at a nearby pub for the night. What is interesting here is the sense of Steve and Jenny as outsiders. When Steve tries to attract the barman he is completely ignored and it is the pretty Jenny who is served instead. The beer garden is full of drunken parents and very young children. There is a great deal of swearing and one child is harshly slapped across the face for some slight misdemeanour. As Steve and Jenny look on horrified, their stare is returned by the unrepentant mother. This is another world, one which the young couple may be aware of but one which is outside their everyday experiences. As they lie in bed, they listen to the cursing, shouting and drunken threats outside with a somewhat bemused indifference. This is a visit to another country and they are just travellers, passing through. This slow build-up isn't that familiar in a more conventional horror film and there is little sense that the potential threat will be closer to hand than say the creatures in Neil Marshall's films. Barry Langford's point about psychological horror is pertinent here:

> 'Modern horror films are much more likely to centre on threats originating from inside both the individual psyche (psychopathic killers) and – because even isolated individuals live in a necessary relationship of some kind to a larger human community – our own social institutions (above all the family), that are pathological rather than supernatural.' (p168, 2005)[11]

In many respects *Eden Lake* can be compared to the Australian horror *Wolf Creek* (Mclean, 2005), where three young backpackers become stranded in the bush, only to discover that their saviour, a middle-aged rancher, is actually a sociopathic mass murderer. The sense of being in an alien environment, surrounded by an extreme macho culture in *Wolf Creek*, is replicated in the pub beer garden and further enforced when Jenny and Steve encounter the teenage gang. They have ventured into a culture that is as remote to them as the Australian outback.

The next morning they go to the woods which lead down to the flooded quarry. The impression of seclusion is intensified by the woods being fenced in, the area earmarked for the development of a luxury, gated community called Eden Lake. Jenny wonders aloud about whom they are trying to keep out; it quickly becomes all too apparent. As Richard Morrison remarks, 'the yuppie couple start by pouring fashionable liberal scorn on a plan to turn the beauty spot into a "gated community" of executive homes, but then find out exactly what it means to have no protection from the vicious youths of the area and their equally sociopathic parents'[12].

Steve, undeterred by the barrier, finds an opening. They park their 4X4 and walk through the woods to get to the lake and indeed it is a peaceful idyll. In the early summer sun they start to enjoy their surroundings. The grim foreshadowing at the inn from hell and the fact that the area has now been cordoned off is reinforced when a group of teenagers appear at the lakeside, complete with an aggressive Rottweiler and a boom box blaring out music. The group members, in their early- to mid-teens, are led by the bullying, menacing figure of Brett (Jack O'Connell). The music is loud and Steve gets increasingly wound-up. These might be kids who simply need to be confronted with reason, but this is not to be and what makes the first altercation so impressive is how these youngsters don't look like average stage school students. With the exception of Thomas Turgoose from *This is England* (Meadows, 2007), who plays the more sympathetic Cooper, the gang members are all relative unknowns and in their dress and looks there is a strong sense of authenticity. The female of the group, the hard-faced Paige (Finn

Atkins), accuses Steve of looking at her breasts. He retreats, temporarily chastened. At this point the opportunity to call it a day and leave the lakeside beach is an option, but Steve convinces a worried Jenny that they have as much right to be there as the youths further up the shore. So they remain, Steve scuba-diving and Jenny increasingly anxious about the barking Rottweiler. The gang members leave but not without a number of lewd remarks.

Watkins avoids the obvious and conventional. The couple are camping out that night and it would be too easy for the teenagers to start to terrorise Jenny and Steve in the dark. Watkins avoids this, as he was only too aware of the balance between producing a horror film and a film that raised interesting points about contemporary British society:

'I didn't have any direct experience of being beaten up or anything like that. I think that I thought there was something in the ether, this powder keg of this sense of disconnect between adults and kids and youth and this sense of fear and sense of a threat and do they ever match up. I just thought those were interesting issues but at the same time I wanted to write a hard muscular genre horror thriller and glance at them – it's not a social realist Ken Loach film. I'm trying to walk a line and make a film that works as a genre film but also something that has a little more resonance.'[13]

The catalytic moment happens the next morning when, on discovering that their food has been infested by maggots, Steve and Jenny decide to go into the local town for breakfast, only to find that the tyres on their jeep have been slashed. Steve is clearly annoyed and this carries over when they get to a café. He asks the waitress about the local kids and she becomes defensive. The lack of awareness of what these young people are up to is profound; their behaviour is simply dismissed as childish, part of their natural development. The waitress, perhaps one of the gang's mothers, can't believe that a grown-up like Steve could be terrorised by a group of children. This sense of denial is further built upon at the film's conclusion when the community comes together to cover up the atrocities in the woods and also their own failure as responsible adult role models. The accusation that this film is 'a study of the effects of bad parenting'[14] is particularly apt. This is further emphasised when the couple pull up outside Brett's house where Steve recognises the gang's BMX bikes strewn across the lawn. Steve enters the unlocked house to speak to the parents and finds it empty. As Peter Bradshaw remarks in his review, it is 'a teeth-gnawingly tense moment, because by swaggering and then sneaking around the empty house, Steve has suddenly put himself in the wrong'[15]. What is more troublesome is the return of Jon (Shaun Dooley) who, it later transpires, is Brett's dad. Complete with carrier bags from the off-licence, Jon stomps around the house angrily bellowing at his son who he supposes is somewhere inside. Steve is suddenly spooked and genuinely frightened and he makes his escape via a window, across a rooftop, returning to his vehicle clearly shaken. The aggressive Jon, although only briefly glimpsed at this point, does offer some perspective on the extreme behaviour of the gang's leader Brett.

However, in the tradition of the horror film, the potential victims return to the site where they are most vulnerable. This could be down to Steve's inability to back down in the face of obvious provocation, or even a sense of middle-class arrogance in assuming that everything will be resolved. Jenny tries earlier on to stop Steve from confronting the gang by saying that 'It's not worth it', to which he replies that 'If everybody said that, where would we be?' This, of course, raises the question of intervention: surely, given the previous events, it would have been more prudent to walk away, regardless of the damage to Steve's self-esteem. But bound by the conventions of the genre, the return to the lake is doomed. Their car is stolen by the gang but the film really gathers pace when Steve finds them. Brett, wearing Steve's Rayban sunglasses, surrounded by his acolytes, is supremely self-confident, taunting the older man. The meeting soon develops into a violent altercation and knives are drawn and Steve accidentally kills Brett's Rottweiler. Events spiral out of control and the film moves into a chase narrative. An unsuccessful escape attempt in the car ends in a crash and Steve is captured by the gang, tied to a tree and cut by each member. This scene is particularly gruesome, exploiting the pack mentality and the power of Brett in forcing each gang member to stab Steve in order to spread any blame. Each attack is recorded on Paige's mobile phone, but Watkins avoids showing this in its digital form. Instead, the audience witnesses the torture sequence from Jenny's perspective, which makes it all the more horrifying. The director also has two of the gang members lamely disputing Brett's orders, allowing limited sympathy for the teenagers, but they still cut Steve with relative impunity.

A succession of escapes, injuries and chases through the forest eventually culminates in Steve's death from a knife wound. The occasional use of aerial shots further emphasise this sense of the hunt. Watkins was keen to give the *mise-en-scène* a '1970s Hollywood' feel close to the spirit of John Boorman's *Deliverance* (1972): '[the film] starts very sunlit and glamorous, then degrades into colder, bleaker, grainier stock into wider, more paranoid lens choices. Once in the forest I also wanted to frame out the sky, to make the trees look like prison bars – to max out the claustrophobic sense of the location'[16]. Steve's body is burnt, but once again Jenny escapes. There is also the burning alive of a young boy called Adam (James Gandhi), who is used as bait to lure Jenny, which further serves to highlight the increasingly psychopathic nature of Brett's actions. The fact that Adam is Asian is completely uncommented on and there are no real indications that the murder is racist. Watkins' representation of the gang allows for very little discussion outside of the taunting of their victims, the apportioning of a shared sense of blame and Brett's bullying leadership. Although there are some challenges to his authority, there is no wider information offered about motivation, other than the death of his dog.

Jenny does eventually get away, but only by killing Cooper with a shard of glass and running over Paige in a van commandeered from one of the gang's brothers who has come in search of them. The final twist is that she ends up at a drunken party given at Brett's father's house. The adults of the town are lolling about, there is a bouncy castle in the garden and they seem blissfully unaware of where their children are. The initial concern shown for Jenny soon turns to distrust and then outright hatred as Brett's arrival, with his subsequent retelling of the 'events', position Jenny as a child-murderer. The film ends with her being led away to be dealt with by the men at the party, while Brett poses in Steve's sunglasses in front of a mirror.

The film is incredibly bleak and disturbing and it unflinchingly reveals the capacity for mindless youth violence, but does it stigmatise the protagonists to a point where any sense of context is lost? There is, for example, only a very limited back-story regarding Brett – that he is the end product of a violent father. His feral nature and total lack of remorse for his actions are never fully examined. He is as much a monster as Freddy from *A Nightmare on Elm Street* (1984), and even less explicable. The more sympathetic members of the gang are similarly under-explored, in particular Cooper.

Richard Morrison sees the film as further demonising the young working classes and argues that it does nothing to address the rift between the classes that has grown over the past couple of decades. The film has no basis in reality, he maintains, but instead is founded on a lie: 'the myth that Britain is a more dangerous, anarchic society than ever before is now so generally accepted as "the truth" that films such as *Eden Lake* are regarded more as realistic snapshots of society than as what they are: exploitative and grotesquely gory fantasies'[17]. While there is some validity in his claims, *Eden Lake* is after all a piece of genre cinema, playing to long-established emotional responses in the audience. Perhaps what is so unsettling is that the film forces a spectator reaction that may well tap into his or her own consciousness, whether shaped by a *Daily Mail* banner headline or an unpleasant encounter with an angry stranger. In many respects, *Eden Lake* says as much about class as any piece of social realism, but does so within the realm of the horror-thriller. The malevolent, amoral world that Steve and Jenny stray into is certainly recognisable, even though many of the events depicted are thankfully not. And it is this short stay in that world that makes the film so terrifying and despairing.

REFERENCES

1. Pirie, D., A New Heritage of Horror, London: IB Tauris, 2008

2. Sweet, M., ' Dead and kicking' in The Independent, 21/03/2004

3. Rampton, J., 'Simon Pegg: A grave new world' in The Independent, 26/03/2004

4. Newman, K., Review of Shaun of The Dead in Sight and Sound, May 2004

5. Marshall, N., interview on http://theeveningclass.blogspot.com, 22/07/2006

6. Davies, S., Review of The Descent in Sight and Sound, September 2005

7. Kermode, M., Review of The Descent in The Observer, 10/07/2005

8. Robey, T., Review of The Descent in The Daily Telegraph, 08/07/2005

9. Weddle, D., "If They Move Kill Them", London: Faber & Faber, 1996

10. Brooks, L., 'Forget Zombie Dawn. Now it's the day of the Feral Youth' in The Guardian, 18/09/2008

11. Langford, B., Film Genre — Hollywood and Beyond, Edinburgh: EUP, 2005

12. Morrison, R., 'Eden Lake: just a gory fantasy' in The Times, 17/09/2008

13. Watkins, J., in interview on http://marksalisbury.blogspot.com, 12/09/2008

14. Davies, R., Review of Eden Lake in Sight and Sound, Sept 2008

15. Bradshaw, P., Review of Eden Lake in The Guardian, 12/09/2008

16. Watkins, J., in interview on www.bloodydisgusting.com, no date given

17. Morrison, R., 'Eden Lake: just a gory fantasy' in The Times, 17/09/2008

INDEX

STILLS INFORMATION

The publisher has attempted to correctly identify the primary copyright holders of the images reproduced herein and believes the following copyright information to be correct at the time of going to print. We apologise for any omissions or errors and will be delighted to rectify and errors brought to our attention in future editions.

Wallace and Gromit: Curse of the Were-Rabbit and *Flushed Away* © DreamWorks and Aardman Animation; *Harry Potter and the Chamber of Secrets* © Warner Bros. and Heyday Films; *About a Boy, Love Actually* and *Atonement* © Working Title; *Closer* © Sony-Columbia Pictures; *Breaking and Entering* © Miramax Films and Mirage Enterprises; *The Queen* © Pathé Pictures and Granada Films; *Notes on a Scandal* © Fox Searchlight and DNA Productions; *Red Road* © BBC Films and Scottish Screen; *Gypo* © BBC Films; *Ratcatcher* © Pathé Pictures and BBC Films; *Morvern Callar* © Alliance Atlantis, BBC Films and UK Film Council; *A Way of Life* © AWOL Films and Tantrum Films; *Last Resort* and *Dirty Pretty Things* © BBC Films; *Ghosts* © FilmFour; *Wonderland* © Revolution Films and BBC Films; *24 Hour Party People* © Revolution Films and The Film Consortium; *9 Songs* © Revolution Films; *A Room for Romeo Brass* © BBC Films; *Dead Man's Shoes* © FilmFour; *This is England* © FilmFour and Optimum Releasing; *Kidulthood* © Stealth Films and Cipher Films; *Bullet Boy* © BBC Films and UK Film Council; *Bend it Like Beckham* © Kintop Pictures and UK Film Council; *Yasmin* © Parallax Independent; *Brick Lane* © FilmFour and UK Film Council; *The Constant Gardener* © Universal Pictures and UK Film Council; *The Last King of Scotland* © Fox Searchlight, DNA Films and FilmFour; *Shooting Dogs* © BBC Films; *28 Days Later* © DNA Films and UK Film Council; *V for Vendetta* © Warner Bros.; *Children of Men* © Universal Pictures; *Shaun of the Dead* © Universal Pictures; *Dog Soldiers* © Kismet Entertainment; *The Descent* © Celador Films and Pathé Pictures; *Eden Lake* © Rollercoaster Films. DVD framegrabs are taken from the respective Region 2 DVDs of the films mentioned.

Beyond Hammer

British Horror Cinema Since 1970

James Rose

Studying British Cinema: The 1990s

Eddie Dyja

auteur

Studying British Cinema: The 1960s

Danny Powell